FOODLORE & FLAVO

INSIDE
THE
SOUTHEAST ASIAN KITCHEN

Foodlore and Flavors - Inside the Southeast Asian Kitchen
ArtPostAsia Pte Ltd © 2007

Editor: Tan Su-Lyn
Photographer: Neal Oshima © 2007
Food Stylist: Christopher Tan

Country Contributors:

Brunei Darussalam
Reda Jasmine Abdul Rahman Taib

Cambodia
Her Royal Highness Princess Marie Ranariddh Norodom

Indonesia
Sri Owen (© 2007 chapter introduction and recipes)

Lao PDR
Somsanouk Mixay

Malaysia
Julie Wong
Redzuawan "Chef Wan" Ismail

Myanmar
Ma Thanegi

Philippines
Michaela Fenix

Singapore
Christopher Tan

Thailand
Cora Cunanan Sukhyanga
Mali Pimnart

Viet Nam
Cathy Hong-Praslick
Trieu Thi Koppe (© 2007 chapter recipes)

Design Development: Florentina Colayco
Designer: Aman Santos
Copyeditor: Arnold Moss
Project Manager: Melody Gocheco
Repro and Print Production: John Phang

Produced and Designed by:
ArtPostAsia Pte Ltd
Email: publications@artpostasia.com
www.artpostasia.com

Printed in Malaysia
First Edition 2007

ISBN 978-971-93170-5-0

PAGE 2 to 3 (clockwise from top left) Rice wrapped in lotus leaves, Viet Nam; a wrapped dish, Thailand; Mawk kai (Chicken steamed in banana leaf), Lao PDR.

THIS PAGE Desserts sold at street-side stalls, Myanmar.

PAGE 6 Clay pot chicken rice, Lee Huat Eating House, Geylang, Singapore.

PAGE 8 Suman, a sweet glutinous (sticky) rice dessert or snack, Philippines.

PAGE 9 A woman making rice paper, Viet Nam.

FOODLORE & FLAVORS

INSIDE
THE
SOUTHEAST ASIAN KITCHEN

Editor
Tan Su-Lyn

Photographer
Neal Oshima

Food Stylist
Christopher Tan

Country Contributors

Reda Jasmine Abdul Rahman Taib *(Brunei Darussalam)*
Her Royal Highness Princess Marie
Ranariddh Norodom *(Cambodia)*
Sri Owen *(Indonesia)*
Somsanouk Mixay *(Lao PDR)*
Julie Wong *(Malaysia)*
Redzuawan "Chef Wan" Ismail *(Malaysia)*
Ma Thanegi *(Myanmar)*
Michaela Fenix *(Philippines)*
Christopher Tan *(Singapore)*
Cora Cunanan Sukhyanga *(Thailand)*
Mali Pimnart *(Thailand)*
Cathy Hong-Praslick *(Viet Nam)*
Trieu Thi Koppe *(Viet Nam)*

CONTENTS

Foreword   12

Introduction   14

The Southeast Asian Kitchen

    Brunei Darussalam   22

    Cambodia   42

    Indonesia   60

    Lao PDR   84

    Malaysia   106

    Myanmar   128

    Philippines   154

    Singapore   178

    Thailand   208

    Viet Nam   234

About the Country Contributors   258

Glossary   260

Weights and Measures   263

Index   266

Acknowledgments   272

RECIPES

Brunei Darussalam

32 Daging dinding (Spicy braised beef curry)
34 Kalia hati (Kalia beef liver)
35 Lemak pucuk labu (Pumpkin leaf shoots cooked in coconut cream)
36 Ikan masak ampap (Grilled or boiled spicy fish)
38 Kelupis (Steamed glutinous rice parcels)
39 Nasi minyak (Saffron rice)
40 Penyaram (Palm sugar pancakes)
41 Bingka dadak (Baked rice flour and coconut milk cake)

Cambodia

52 K'tieu Phnom Penh (Khmer noodles)
54 Nhoam krauch th'long (Pomelo salad)
55 Pleah trey (Fish salad)
56 Chuchi pra kong (Chhouchi fragrant shrimp)
58 Kang-kep baob (Fragrant stuffed frogs)
59 Cambodian beef stew

Indonesia

70 Rendang (Long-cooked beef in coconut milk with spices)
72 Pallu mara ikan (Hot and sour fish from Ujung Pandang)
74 Gudeg Yogya (Long-cooked chicken and jackfruit, Yogya-style)
76 Ayam mBok Berek (The original fried chicken of Kalasan)
77 Saté pentul (Minced pork satay with Balinese spice-mixture)
78 Saté babi Menado (Pork satay, Menado-style)
80 Bebek betutu (Traditional long-cooked Balinese duck)
82 Asinan Jakarta (Jakarta fruit and vegetable salad)

Lao PDR

94 Tam mak som (Pounded sour salad)
95 Larp
96 Khaow poun nam kathih (Spicy rice noodles in coconut gravy)
98 Mawk kai (Chicken steamed in banana leaf)
99 Kaeng nor mai (Bamboo shoot soup)
100 Phan sin choum (Beef wrapped in lettuce leaf)
102 Oh larm (Stew)
104 Sangkhanya mak ueh (Coconut custard steamed in pumpkin)

Malaysia

116 Beef putri manis
118 Sup ekor (Oxtail soup)
119 Dalca kambing (Mutton dalca)
120 Gulai asam pedas (Hot and sour fish)
122 Kerabu udang dan soohoon (Prawn and glass noodle kerabu)
123 Sambal sotong (Spicy squid)
124 Acar mentah (Raw salad)
126 Nasi lemak (Rice cooked in coconut milk)

Myanmar

138   Kyar zan chet (Glass noodle soup)
140   Nga hpai thoke (Fish cake salad)
141   Hta ma nai (Glutinous rice with sesame)
142   Whet thani chet (Glossy red pork)
144   Karla thar chet (Country-style chicken curry)
145   Nga pi daung (Grilled shrimp paste relish)
146   Kayan chin thee nga pi chet (Tomato and shrimp paste relish)
147   Lahpet (Pickled tea leaves)
148   Shwe yin aye (Golden heart cooler)
150   Monhinga (Fish soup and rice noodles)
151   Boo thee kyaw (Calabash gourd fritters)

Philippines

166   Bringhe (Coconut glutinous rice with chicken)
168   Pancit sotanghon (Sautéed glass noodles)
170   Menudo (Pork and liver stew)
171   Adobong baboy at manok (Pork and chicken adobo)
172   Sinigang na bangus (Milkfish in sour broth)
174   Pan San Nicolas (Saint Nicholas cookies)
176   Leche flan (Crème caramel)
177   Biko (Sweet rice cake)

Singapore

192   Yu sheng (Chinese New Year raw fish salad)
194   Popiah (Fresh spring rolls)
198   Or chor ter kar (Pig's trotters braised with black
       vinegar and ginger)
199   Nyonya birthday mee (Nyonya birthday noodles)
200   Hainanese chicken rice
202   Kuih tart (Pineapple tart)
204   Curry puffs
206   Serikaya (Egg and coconut jam)

Thailand

222   Khao tang na tang (Rice patties with pork, chicken or shrimp topping)
224   Tom yam goong (Spicy prawn soup with lemongrass)
226   Hor mok talay (Steamed seafood soufflé with creamy coconut)
228   Som tam (Spicy green papaya salad)
229   Nahm tok (Grilled meat salad)
230   Khao soi kai (Curry noodle soup with chicken)
231   Hoi lai phad nahmprik paow (Fried clams in roasted chili paste)
232   Foi thong (Sugar-coated egg yolk)

Viet Nam

244   Cha gio (Spring rolls)
246   Thit heo bam khoai nang, xuc banh trang mi nuoc dua
       (Minced pork with water chestnuts and toasted coconut tapioca paper)
248   Bun bo Hue (Hue pork and beef noodle soup)
250   Ga xao sa ot voi nuoc mau (Lemongrass chicken with caramel sauce)
252   Suong heo nau nuoc dua (Pork stew in young coconut water)
254   Chao ga and goi ga cap cai (Chicken rice porridge and chicken
       cabbage salad)
256   Banh it nhung dua (Little steamed glutinous rice cakes with
       coconut filling)
257   Muc dua (Candied coconut)

FOREWORD

Southeast Asia is renowned for its diverse and rich cultural traditions. But, without exception, what we take the most pride in is our food. From signature dishes such as *satay*, Vietnamese *pho*, Thai *tom yam* soup or Indonesian *gado-gado*, the delicious, fresh and flavorful food of Southeast Asia has become famous throughout the world.

Inside the Southeast Asian Kitchen draws together, in one volume, the region's notable food writers and culinary experts. They capture the essence of our beloved dishes and share their unique characteristics with readers through colorful pictures and heritage recipes.

Through this appetizing showcase, *Inside the Southeast Asian Kitchen* offers a truly gastronomic tour of ASEAN, the Association of Southeast Asian Nations comprising Brunei Darussalam, Cambodia, Indonesia, Lao PDR, Malaysia, Myanmar, Philippines, Singapore, Thailand and Viet Nam. Our passion for eating reveals the unity that all ASEAN citizens share in the diversity of our distinctive food and cooking.

The value of this book lies not only in its celebration of ASEAN's cuisine and kitchen secrets. It is also an expression of Southeast Asian openness and inclusiveness in the globalized family.

Bon appetit!

ONG KENG YONG
Secretary-General of ASEAN

THIS PAGE Sorting rice kernels,
Vientiane, Lao PDR.

PREVIOUS PAGE Red rice,
Vientiane, Lao PDR.

Introduction
by Tan Su-Lyn

Ask any home cook in Southeast Asia for a recipe for the scrumptious dish you've just sampled at his or her dinner table and you're most likely to be given a list of ingredients with hardly any indication of precise quantities. It will be littered with words and phrases like "a bit of," "some" and "not too much" which are bewildering to the novice cook. But don't be misled into thinking that your host or hostess is intentionally being vague. So much of what the home cook does in the Southeast Asian kitchen is based on instinct, practice and memory. The home cook learns to rely on his or her senses. Recipes are passed down orally from one generation to the next. And a daughter learns to tweak and balance the flavors in her dishes based on her memories of what her mother's tasted like to her as a child. A grandson learns to shape intricate festive cookies by watching his grandmother fashion them in the hundreds each year. Even when neighbors and members of the extended family gather to prepare a feast, much is done wordlessly. Every kitchen volunteer instinctively knows what needs to be done.

However, with the onslaught of modernization, urbanization and globalization, these traditions are slowly being eroded. We haven't lost our taste for the food of home, but many of us have certainly forgotten how to prepare them (or never got around to mastering them in the first place). Although this book is by no means an exhaustive guide to Southeast Asian cuisine, it has been written in the hope of continuing the age-old tradition of sharing that once occurred more frequently in the kitchens of Brunei Darussalam, Cambodia, Indonesia, Lao PDR, Malaysia, Myanmar, Philippines, Singapore, Thailand and Viet Nam. Each chapter has been written to include key recipes from one of the ten member countries of the Association of Southeast Asian Nations (ASEAN), as well as some explanation of the cultural significance of each dish.

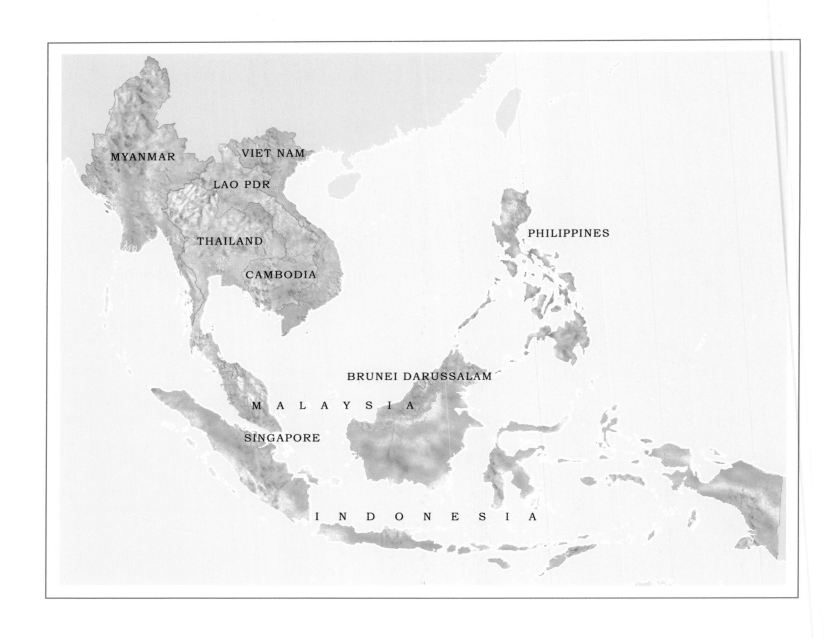

A taste of Southeast Asian home cooking

We consciously searched for special, as well as regional dishes that are served at home-cooked family dinners and celebrations rather than at restaurant meals. And wherever possible, the selection of recipes featured in each chapter contains a mixture of snacks or appetizers, main dishes, one-dish meals and desserts. The important thing to note, however, is that in Southeast Asia we rarely serve our meals in multiple courses unless they are particularly formal ones. At most family meals, we usually serve all our dishes (save for dessert) simultaneously. And we enjoy eating most of them with some rice.

The thrilling thing about collecting recipes from across Southeast Asia for this book has been the discovery that each nation in this region is at once wonderfully unique and yet so closely related to its neighbors. Even if we use them differently, we still favor similar flavors, spices and herbs. They run through our individual cuisines like charmingly familiar culinary leitmotifs. So, although recipes within each chapter have been selected so that you can create complete meals faithful to the traditions of a specific Southeast Asian nation, you can also easily create a truly regional menu by serving a combination of dishes chosen from different chapters in this book because when placed side by side, the cuisines of Southeast Asia complement one another beautifully.

THIS PAGE (left) Myanmar country contributor, Ma Thanegi hosts lunch at Maha Htu Payon monastery, Myanmar; (right) A young boy and his grandmother at a monk's ordination, Lao PDR.

OPPOSITE A map of Southeast Asia.

Soul food

However, this isn't the sole point of our book. It is equally important to note that so much of the cooking that happens in the kitchens of Southeast Asia is not merely about nourishing the body. It is about reaffirming the ties of kinship and community; salving the soul; and reinvigorating the spirit. Thus, we've endeavored to ensure that every chapter in this book offers a little introduction to what was once more commonly gleaned from sitting at a grandparent's dinner table or standing by the communal kitchen fire. This book is as much about our foodlore, what our food means to us and why, as it is about flavor and culinary technique.

You will notice as you work your way through the book that the kitchens of Southeast Asia share a lot in common. Although each country has its own distinct history, geography and culture, many other things bind the ten nations. For one, the importance and significance of shared meals is something that all communities hold very dear. Families eat together. Food is central to the way we look at ourselves in Southeast Asia. Our attitudes toward cooking and eating reveal our feelings about our place in the world. Our meals are always constructed around our families, communities and societies. They mark the changing of seasons and have also become very much part of the rituals of our various religions and beliefs. Whether a feast honors a joyous or sorrowful occasion, it is always meant to be shared with family, friends and neighbors. We celebrate each milestone of our lives with a special meal or dish. And even in death, we are remembered with offerings of food.

From our kitchen to yours

We have set out to pin down our culinary traditions and histories within the pages of this book with the wholehearted intention of sharing them. Therefore, we've tried our best to provide instructions for traditional methods of preparing dishes, as well as more contemporary methods that have been made simpler with the aid of modern kitchen tools and appliances. The blender, for example, is as common in many Southeast Asian kitchens as the mortar and pestle. Most of the ingredients required in our recipes can be found in Asian grocery stores around the world.

We chose to showcase dishes that can be prepared in regular kitchens and that require few special tools because we hope that you will go into your kitchen and try your hand at preparing some of the food that has come to mean so much to us. As you feel your way around our recipes and, through them, our kitchens, we hope you experience a little of what it was like for us to learn about our cuisines, and ourselves, in our mothers' and grandmothers' kitchens.

THIS PAGE A mid-day meal at Kya Khat Waing monastery, Bago, Myanmar.

OPPOSITE A fish monger in Indonesia.

FOLLOWING PAGE Ms. Bouasonkham Sisane of the Lao Textile Museum in Vientiane, Lao PDR, preparing a traditional meal.

Brunei Darussalam

Introduction and Recipes
by Reda Jasmine Abdul Rahman Taib

Tapai *or sweet fermented rice wrapped in palm leaves.*

Brunei Darussalam, or Brunei, Abode of Peace, sits northeast of Borneo and is flanked by two Malaysian states — Sarawak to its east and Sabah to its west — as well as Kalimantan, Indonesia, to its south. Facing the South China Sea, it has a rich history and is famed for being a major trading post along the important trade route linking China to the West. Although its land area has diminished (largely due to European expansionism in the early twentieth century), Brunei has remained one of the oldest Malay monarchies in Southeast Asia.

Because of its rich heritage and importance as a trading port in the Malay Archipelago, Brunei's culinary tradition has been very much influenced by the introduction of aromatic spices imported by merchants from India and Africa, as well as noodles, tofu, bean sprouts and soy sauce that Chinese merchants brought with them. Over the years the integration of these immigrants into Bruneian society has encouraged a rich variety of food to develop across the country. Brunei's population today is largely made up of Malays, but several indigenous communities from districts such as Tutong and Beliat also exist. There are also the Bisayas, Dusuns and Muruts. In addition, there are Chinese, Indian and other expatriate communities. This ethnic mix has helped develop a diverse food scene and yet still retain the traditional dishes we all love and identify as truly Bruneian.

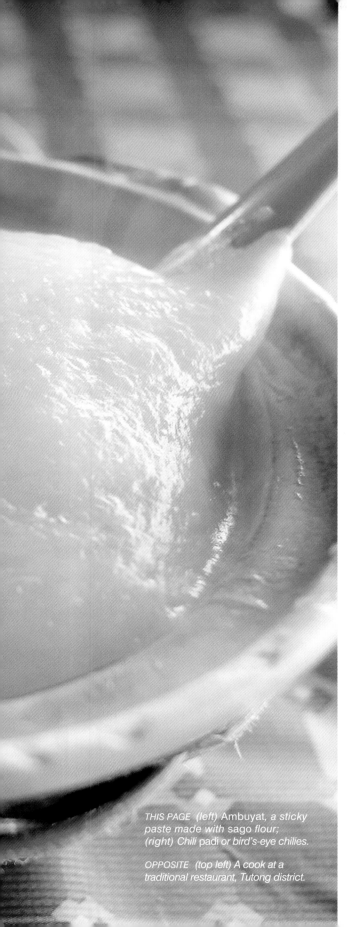

Everyday food eaten in Brunei is very simple and very healthy. Not much oil is used in its preparation. Seafood, which can be found aplenty in the Brunei Estuary and the rivers entering it, is widely enjoyed. The most popular way of preparing prawns and freshly caught fish is to boil them with a variety of seasonings such as turmeric, lemongrass, chilies, tamarind and the important locally-produced *belacan* (shrimp paste). Shrimp paste is a key ingredient in the Bruneian kitchen and can be stored for long periods of time. Fresh herbs and local leaves such as *pengaga* (Indian pennywort leaves; *Hydrocotyle asiatica*), *daun rancah-rancah* (cosmos) and cashew leaves, as well as sliced winged beans, blanched lady's fingers or sliced cucumbers are eaten raw in salads called *ulam*, which are served with *sambal belacan*. *Sambal belacan* in Brunei consists of fresh chilies pounded in the *lasong* (granite pestle and mortar) with a tablespoon of shrimp paste (it should be roasted ahead of time), some *kalamansi* juice, sugar and salt to taste. To make it even hotter, bird's-eye chilies, or chili *padi*, are thrown in!

Staples widely eaten

Rice is, of course, a staple dish. On important occasions such as weddings and *makan tahun* (the feast held to celebrate a new harvest), long-grain rice is cooked with saffron and laced with beef strips to produce a wonderful dish called *nasi kebuli*. When moving into a new home, most Malays traditionally first place a container of rice, sugar, salt, *asam jawa* (tamarind pulp) and other essentials such as onions in their pantry. This is believed to ensure continued wealth and plentiful gains, or *rezeki*. The *chupak* (traditionally made from a small hollowed-out coconut shell), used to scoop rice grains from the rice container into the cooking pot, should always be full of rice to ensure that your *rezeki* are always plentiful. It is still taught to the younger generation that rice is important and cannot be wasted. One story that is still told today concerns a young woman who threw away her half-eaten *tapai* (sweet fermented rice) into the river. The *tapai* floated by a mountain of gold that was about to float toward the woman's village. The rice warned the gold not to go to the village because the people were wasteful and unappreciative

THIS PAGE (left) Ambuyat, a sticky paste made with sago flour; (right) Chili padi or bird's-eye chilies.

OPPOSITE (top left) A cook at a traditional restaurant, Tutong district.

of what they had. Thus, the gold went elsewhere. The story reminds young Bruneians not to waste anything — especially food, which should always be appreciated and eaten, not thrown away — for fear that other riches will not come their way.

Another staple widely eaten in Brunei is *ambuyat*, a sticky paste made with *sago* flour locally referred to as *ambulung*. Eaten on its own, *ambuyat* is quite tasteless and starchy. It has to be enjoyed with a variety of other dishes and sauces. There is a special technique of eating *ambuyat*; we twist it around locally made chopsticks called *candas* and then dip it into *cacah*, a sweet and sour, slightly spicy sauce that is a blend of tamarind juice, prawn stock, *sambal belacan* and preserved *binjai* (a local fruit). It is swallowed — not chewed — making it a popular dish among the old! Other dishes normally eaten with *ambuyat* are smoked grilled fish; freshwater prawns boiled with tamarind, *belacan*, onions, chilies and *serai* (lemongrass); a salad made with *pakis* (green fiddlehead fern shoots) topped with a dressing of pounded dried prawns, chilies and *kalamansi* juice; thin slices of soy marinated beef that is first grilled and then pounded further to produce a dish similar to that of beef jerky; and local vegetables cooked in coconut milk or simply sautéed with a bit of *belacan* and chilies. Many restaurants in Brunei specialize in serving *ambuyat*.

Bruneians eat fish every day and serve meat, such as buffalo and chicken, only on special occasions. When fish or prawns are plentiful, they are either smoked or dried so that they can be stored for a longer time. The art of drying fish continues to be practiced today, as evidenced by the popularity of *tahai* — sardines smoked and then dried in the sun. Once dried, *tahai* can be kept for months. It is a key ingredient in the wonderful souplike dish called *tahai masak api*, where it is simply boiled with onions, sliced chilies and shrimp paste. Small prawns are also dried and then made into shrimp paste. When krill is in season, *cencalu* is also made. Similar to the *cencalu* found in west Malaysia, krill is essentially cleaned and washed, then mixed with salt and sugar. This mixture is bottled and left to ferment for several days before it can be eaten. *Cencalu*, like *sambal belacan*, can be eaten as a side dish. It is usually served with rice, fried fish and sliced cucumbers. Bruneians also produce a variety of crackers made with prawns and fish. The prawns are pounded and then mixed with flour and water into a dough. The dough is rolled into long cylindrical portions before it is steamed and cut into thin slices. In turn, these slices are dried in the sun. Once fried, they make wonderful snacks.

THIS PAGE Aromatic wild beans also known as twisted cluster beans. They are also called petai *in Brunei.*

OPPOSITE Barbecued smoked fish at Jerudong Market.

Buffalo is traditionally a meat served at large functions. As in other parts of Southeast Asia the buffalo has long been revered as the animal with which one displays one's wealth. Nowadays with the introduction of imported cattle, buffalo continues to be eaten, but most people prefer the subtle flavor of beef or chicken. Many curry, *korma* (braised, mildly spicy dishes of Indian origin) and *pindang* (long-cooked dishes called *rendang* in other parts of Southeast Asia) recipes have been developed to showcase buffalo meat. Chicken and a variety of other fowl, such as pigeon and quail, are also widely eaten. In the interior areas, other game meats are also commonly found on the menu. These include *pelanduk* (mouse deer) and *kijang* (another variety of deer indigenous to Borneo). Here, freshwater fish and prawns are cooked simply — with the freshest of herbs and either boiled or steamed in bamboo over the open fire, a tradition somewhat similar to that found among indigenous tribes across the Malay Archipelago.

Desserts and cakes

Bruneians also love desserts and cakes. However, the desserts in Brunei are often very similar to the ones found in the rest of the Malay Archipelago. Sometimes, the only difference is their names! Desserts in Brunei often have ingredients such as glutinous (sticky) rice, rice flour, *ambulung* (*sago* flour), palm sugar, eggs and coconut milk. Some favorites include *tapai* (sweet fermented rice wrapped in palm leaves), *serimuka* (custard and sticky rice cake) and *wajid* (palm sugar and coconut sticky rice cake), as well as the numerous types of *bingka*, a soft, custardlike cake. A host of *kuih kering* (biscuits) are also widely served. These include *kuih sapit* (paper-thin rolled biscuits also called love letters), *kuripit* (a biscuit made from coconut milk and *sago* flour), *makanan cincin* (a fried palm sugar biscuit) and *bahulu* (mini sponge cakes baked in special molds). A number of the traditional wooden molds and brassware used in making some of these cakes are displayed in Brunei's Malay Technology Museum. Nowadays, these cakes and desserts are commonly sold at the famous *tamu* or open market beside the Brunei River. They are most popular during the fasting month of Ramadan. In addition, fruits are eaten daily in Brunei owing to an abundance of locally grown ones such as the countless varieties of bananas, as well as jackfruit, rambutans, mangosteens, and mangoes and other fruits found only in Borneo. There is also a great variety of sweet potatoes which come in different colors and sizes. These have all been incorporated into desserts such as *pisang goreng* (banana fritters), *bubur kacang* (boiled green split beans served in a soup of coconut milk and sugar with *sago* pearls), *bubur ubi* (sweet potato cubes and *sago* pearls in coconut milk) and *pengat pisang* (boiled coconut milk served with sugar and sliced bananas). In these desserts pandan leaves play a major part in helping to accentuate aromas and flavors.

THIS PAGE A couple making wajid, *a sweet cake made out of millet, Temburong district.*

OPPOSITE (top) Dried asam keping; (bottom) Celurut, a Bruneian dessert steamed in cigar shaped molds of palm leaves.

In the past the preparation of daily meals was traditionally done by women. It was also fairly common for neighbors and family members to exchange portions of dishes they had prepared for the day, since everyone lived close to each other. The sharing and receiving of food created a strong sense of kinship among villagers. Thus, villagers often regarded their neighbors as *bersaudara* (family). However, this convivial exchange is not so widely practiced today, owing to the disintegration of rural communities and growing consciousness of security and hygiene.

For special occasions such as weddings, *makan tahun* (feasts celebrating the new harvest), *makan doa arwah* (annual prayers and feasts commemorating members of the family who have passed on) or funerals, it used to be common for the community to come together for *memucang-mucang* in the spirit of helping each other. In the old days this meant that the home where the feast was to be held was cleared and cleaned, and a canopy erected. Neighbors and relatives would assist in doing this and help each other out in whatever way or form they could. The womenfolk would prepare all the dishes, but it was also not uncommon to find men helping out with the cooking, since it required great strength to stir the large pots and huge woks which were usually placed over hot open fires. Today, feasts are held in hotels, halls or hired canopies set up within and around the home compound, and most families hire caterers to prepare the meals. The spirit of giving, however, remains evident as family members and close friends will donate a dish to the meal or contribute cakes or desserts.

While Brunei's geographic location and history have led its rich and diverse cuisine to develop very much in parallel with those of its neighbors in the Malay Archipelago — resulting in many shared culinary styles and preferences — a few key ingredients such as *belacan*, spices like coriander, cumin, cardamom, turmeric, nutmeg and star anise, as well as indigenous fruits and vegetables favored in the Bruneian kitchen, make our dishes taste a little different.

THIS PAGE (left) Wild rosella, from the hibiscus family; (right) A variety of the local Brunei durian which is small but exquisite.

OPPOSITE A vendor at Gadong Night Market.

Daging dinding
Spicy braised beef curry

Four dishes — daging dinding, daging pindang (another type of beef curry similar to a rendang), kalia hati (kalia beef liver) and nasi minyak (saffron rice) — are normally served at weddings or on special occasions such as harvest celebrations and annual remembrance prayers. In the past it was common that whenever a wedding or celebratory feast took place a cow or buffalo (or several of them, depending on your status in the community) would be slaughtered. All parts of the animal would be used and the whole community would come together for memucang-mucang. This meant that all members of the community would help out in whatever way they could to clean, prepare and cook dishes for the occasion.

Owing to the lack of refrigeration in the old days, a lot of meat dishes and hardly any fish, vegetable or chicken dishes were consumed at feasts. Even the rice would have beef strips added to it. The introduction of spices to Brunei by traders and other visitors has influenced many recipes, especially dishes that are prepared on special occasions. The use of spices such as cumin, coriander, fennel and candlenuts adds to the richness of the dish and helps to preserve the beef. Traditionally, all spices are blended using a batu giling (flat granite grinding stone). Nowadays the introduction of commercially produced curry powders as well as electric blenders has made the preparation of the spices for such dishes a lot simpler and faster.

Serves 10

10 shallots, peeled
1 large onion, peeled
2 cloves garlic, peeled
5-centimeter piece ginger, peeled
5 tablespoons beef curry powder
2 tablespoons dried chili paste
3-4 tablespoons cooking oil
2 stalks lemongrass, bruised

3-4 sprigs curry leaves
1 kilogram beef topside, sliced thinly
1 liter coconut cream
3-4 tablespoons tamarind pulp juice
2 tablespoons *kerisik* (freshly grated coconut fried over low heat until dark brown)
salt and sugar to taste

Chef's note:
To make 3 to 4 tablespoons tamarind pulp juice, add 75 milliliters of water to 2 tablespoons tamarind pulp. Mash softly using a spoon. This helps to loosen the pulp from the seeds. Discard seeds. What remains is considered pulp juice.

To make dried chili paste, soak 20 dried chilies in hot water for 10 minutes. Drain and purée them in an electric blender.

1. Grind or blend shallots, onions, garlic, and ginger into a paste. Add curry powder and dried chili paste.

2. Heat oil in a wok. Fry lemongrass and curry leaves (without removing them from the stem) for 1 to 2 minutes. Add paste and stir constantly until you see a ring of oil around the paste.

3. Add beef and stir, ensuring that the mixture evenly coats the beef. Fry for another 4 to 5 minutes. Add 250 milliliters water and let mixture boil before turning it down to a simmer for a further 1 to 2 hours. Add water constantly once mixture looks dry.

4. Once beef is tender, add coconut cream and allow to boil before turning down the heat. Let it simmer for another 30 to 45 minutes. Finally, add tamarind pulp juice and *kerisik*. Adjust flavor with salt and sugar to taste.

Kalia hati

Kalia beef liver

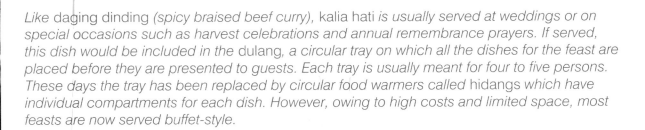

Like daging dinding *(spicy braised beef curry)*, kalia hati *is usually served at weddings or on special occasions such as harvest celebrations and annual remembrance prayers. If served, this dish would be included in the* dulang, *a circular tray on which all the dishes for the feast are placed before they are presented to guests. Each tray is usually meant for four to five persons. These days the tray has been replaced by circular food warmers called* hidangs *which have individual compartments for each dish. However, owing to high costs and limited space, most feasts are now served buffet-style.*

Serves 10

3-centimeter piece ginger, peeled
5 shallots, peeled
2 cloves garlic, peeled
2 candlenuts
75 grams beef curry powder
3-4 tablespoons cooking oil

1 kilogram beef liver, sliced thinly
750 milliliters coconut cream
2-3 tablespoons tamarind pulp juice
  (see Chef's note on page 32)
salt and sugar to taste

1. Grind or blend ginger, shallots, garlic and candlenuts to a paste. Add to curry powder.

2. Heat oil in a wok over medium-high heat. Add curry paste. Fry until fragrant and oil breaks on top of the mixture. Add beef liver and 250 milliliters of water. Lower heat and simmer for 1 hour. Constantly add water if the mixture becomes dry.

3. Once the liver is cooked and tender, add coconut cream and simmer again for another 30 minutes before adding tamarind pulp juice, salt and sugar to taste.

Lemak pucuk labu

Pumpkin leaf shoots cooked in coconut cream

In the old days, vegetables were not commonly served at celebrations or special events. This was probably because they were considered too common. However, ethnic groups such as the Muruts and Ibans living in the interior parts of Brunei include vegetables in their celebratory feasts. A variety of vegetables found in the lush Bruneian forests are consumed regularly. Bamboo shoots are a favorite.

This dish is very easy to prepare and the pumpkin leaf shoots can be replaced by other vegetables such as long beans, fiddlehead greens or kale. Belacan (shrimp paste) gives the dish a distinctive aroma and piquant taste.

Pumpkin leaf shoots and flowers

Serves 10

1 kilogram young bamboo shoots
1 kilogram young pumpkin leaf shoots
4 shallots, peeled
2 cloves garlic, peeled
1/2 teaspoon *belacan* (shrimp paste)
2 tablespoons cooking oil
500 grams prawns, peeled

1 liter coconut milk
500 grams baby corn, cut in half lengthwise
3 red chilies, cut in half lengthwise, deseeded
salt and sugar to taste

1. Slice bamboo shoots thinly and place them in boiling water. Boil for 6 minutes and make sure to drain thoroughly.

2. Clean pumpkin leaf shoots. Discard thorns and hairs on the stems. Wash and drain thoroughly.

3. Blend shallots, garlic and *belacan* to a paste.

4. Heat oil and fry paste with prawns. Add coconut milk, then bamboo shoots and baby corn. Once baby corn becomes tender, add pumpkin leaf shoots, red chilies, salt and sugar to taste. Bring to a boil, then remove from heat immediately to prevent the coconut milk from curdling.

Ikan masak ampap

Grilled or boiled spicy fish

Seafood abounds in Bruneian waters. Therefore, it is eaten daily and prepared simply to showcase the freshness of the fish. Fish are often barbecued, fried or boiled. However, whenever a fisherman returns with an unusually large catch, some of the fish are also dried. This preserves them and prevents them from going to waste.

Smaller fish such as rumahan *(short-bodied or Indian mackerel),* kembura *(mullet),* bilis *(ponyfish) and* tamban *(spotted sardinella) are eaten everyday. For curry dishes, bigger fish such as Spanish mackerel, mangrove snapper, sea bream and sea bass are used. A great variety of shellfish is also consumed daily.* Cencalu *(krill) and* budu lukan *(shellfish) are even preserved in a vinegar and sugar mixture. The dish below can be prepared in the oven, with the fish placed on top of a banana leaf. Alternatively, the fish can also be boiled.*

Serves 4

8 small fish (*rumahan* or *kembura*)
3 tablespoons tamarind pulp juice
(see Chef's note on page 32) or
kalamansi juice
3 shallots, peeled
1 clove garlic, peeled

3-centimeter piece turmeric, peeled
1 tablespoon *belacan* (shrimp paste)
2 tablespoons dried chili paste (see Chef's
note on page 32)
salt to taste
3 fresh chilies, deseeded and sliced

1. Clean, gut and scale fish. Pat dry and rub with salt, or soak them in either tamarind or *kalamansi* juice.

2. Grind or blend shallots, garlic, turmeric, *belacan* and dried chili paste.

3. If grilling, rub the blended spices on the fish, place on banana leaves and grill until fish are cooked before sprinkling sliced chili over them. If boiling, bring 300 to 400 milliliters of water to a boil. Add blended spices, fish and salt to taste.

4. Once the fish are cooked, sprinkle them with sliced chili and serve. Please note that this dish is not meant to have much gravy and the spices should coat the fish once they are cooked.

Kelupis

Steamed glutinous rice parcels

These steamed glutinous (sticky) rice parcels with a hint of coconut milk are a local favorite. Daun nyirek (Carapa moluccensis) is a local leaf widely used for wrapping all types of food. It often serves as an alternative to banana leaves. Once steamed, the aroma of the coconut-infused rice develops a subtle and very satisfying aftertaste. Kelupis has long been served and eaten by Bruneians. It is handy for travelers and fishermen because the rice lasts longer wrapped in the leaves. It is also served at weddings, celebrations announcing the birth of a child and engagement ceremonies.

Kelupis can be served without a filling. However, if you wish, you could add a stuffing of minced beef curry or minced chili prawns to the middle of the rice parcel. This dish can be eaten with your favorite sauce or curry.

Makes 8 - 10 parcels

600 grams glutinous rice
300 milliliters coconut milk
1/2 teaspoon salt

daun nyirek, **banana leaves or pandan leaves for wrapping**

1. Wash rice several times until water runs clear. Rinse, drain and set aside.

2. Over a medium fire, heat coconut milk to almost boiling point, then add salt. Add rice and stir constantly until all the coconut milk is absorbed. Remove from heat.

3. Prepare *daun nyirek,* banana leaf or pandan leaves by dipping them into hot boiling water. Wipe them well. Cut to desired length if using pandan

leaves. If using banana leaves, cut into rectangles roughly measuring 30-by-12 centimeters. Place 3 to 4 tablespoons of the cooked rice mixture in the middle of your leaf. Fold the leaf into a parcel, tucking each end underneath. Secure with toothpicks.

4. Lay the rice parcels in a single layer in a steamer and steam for 20 to 30 minutes. Leave to cool overnight and serve at room temperature with your favorite curry or sauce.

Nasi minyak

Saffron rice

This is usually served alongside other dishes at special functions or feasts. The yellow rice can be presented in several ways. Sometimes, it is laced with beef strips and called nasi kebuli. *The recipe below is more traditional.*

Serves 10

60 grams butter or margarine
40 grams ghee (clarified butter)
3-4 cinnamon sticks
2-3 cloves
2 star anise
4 *pelaga* (cardamom) pods
2-centimeter piece ginger,
   peeled and julienned
1/2 large onion, sliced thinly
1 stalk lemongrass, bruised
1.4 kilograms rice, washed
   and left to dry

1/2 tablespoon salt
120 milliliters evaporated milk mixed
   with 2 liters water
a few saffron strands soaked in 2-3
   tablespoons water
50 grams shallots, peeled, sliced
   and fried
60 grams cashew nuts, fried
50 grams sultanas, fried

1. Heat butter (or margarine) and ghee. Lightly fry cinnamon sticks, cloves, star anise, *pelaga* pods and ginger until fragrant. Next, add onion and lemongrass. Fry for a further 2 to 3 minutes.

2. Add rice and stir, mixing well. Add salt, and milk and water mixture. At this point you can choose to transfer the mixture into a rice cooker.

3. Once all the liquid has been absorbed, stir in the saffron and water mixture.

4. Garnish with fried shallots, cashew nuts and sultanas just before serving.

Penyaram
Palm sugar pancakes

These pancakes are usually served as mid-morning or teatime snacks and are best enjoyed with a cup of strong, sweet black coffee. They are now sold alongside other local sweets and snacks at numerous open-air stalls across Brunei.

These turn out nice and fluffy when you leave the mixture to rest for about 6 hours or overnight.

Makes 10 - 12 pancakes

220 grams plain flour
220 grams rice flour
200 grams sugar
100 grams palm sugar, grated
oil for frying

1. Combine all the ingredients, except the oil, with 500 milliliters of water. Stir until smooth.

2. Heat some oil in a small wok. Once hot, drop 4 tablespoons of batter into it. Fry for 2 to 3 minutes on each side. It should develop a curled, crispy outer rim. *Penyaram* should be fried one at a time. Drain well and serve.

Bingka dadak

Baked rice flour and coconut milk cake

Bruneians love eating sweets. In Bruneian kitchens cakes and biscuits are always on hand, ready for the unexpected guest. After all, a good host has to ensure that all guests are served a drink and a snack. Interestingly though, at big feasts, dessert normally consists of a plate of seasonal fruits such as rambutans or a plate of pisang emas *(small, golden yellow local bananas).*

This dessert and the one on the previous page are made using rice flour. Working out the precise quantities for these recipes was difficult, because the Bruneian cook instinctively measures ingredients by look and touch. If the mixture is too watery, add a little more flour. Nonetheless, I have tried to be as precise as possible.

Serves 8 - 10

500 milliliters coconut milk
220 grams rice flour
220 grams sugar

salt
1 pandan leaf, knotted

1. Pre-heat the oven to 350 degrees Fahrenheit (175 degrees Celsius) and grease a 20-centimeter square tin.

2. Combine half of the coconut milk with all of the rice flour, sugar and a pinch of salt. Mix until smooth.

3. In a pot, bring the rest of the coconut milk and the pandan leaf to a boil over medium heat. Add the flour mixture and stir slowly until mixture thickens. Discard pandan leaf.

4. Pour mixture into the cake tin and bake for 40 minutes until it turns golden brown. Cool cake completely before cutting.

Cambodia

Introduction and Recipes
by Her Royal Highness Princess Marie Ranariddh Norodom

Decades of war and genocide have ravaged Cambodia, stealing over two million lives including those of the keepers of the nation's ancient culinary wisdom — its cooks and master chefs. Yet, nothing can truly quell the delicate flavors and aromas of this sophisticated, thousand-year-old culinary tradition which dates back to the great Angkor Empire of the seventh to fourteenth centuries. Like a phoenix rising from its ashes, Cambodian cuisine is re-emerging not only in homes, markets and restaurants within the country but in cosmopolitan cities around the world.

Cambodian food is unique. His Majesty the King Father Norodom Sihanouk's aunt, Her Royal Highness Princess Kanitha Norodom Rasmi Sobbhana, spent most of her life learning and practicing the art of cooking. She once described Khmer cuisine as a cuisine of details. Small quantities of many ingredients are first finely pounded, then cooked individually and eventually added to the main dish. Its distinctiveness cannot be overemphasized. Contrary to popular belief, it is not Thai food without the chilies, not Vietnamese, and certainly not Chinese. Cambodian cuisine, like that of many other nations, has undeniably been influenced by its exposure to civilizations other than its own. India, China, Portugal and France, four great exporters of their own cultures and beliefs, have all contributed their own culinary nuances via commercial, religious, cultural and political interaction with the Angkor Empire and the kingdoms that followed it. The process of nation building, with its complex balance of give and take between conqueror and conquered, good neighbors and even enemies, also added to the blend of foreign and indigenous flavors. However, Cambodians chose to assimilate only what stimulated their taste buds and complemented native ingredients. In certain situations, they adopted dishes unaltered — why create a new dish when the original, albeit foreign, one already tasted good? Two of Cambodia's most well-known imports are the Chinese noodle soup (*k'tieu*) and the French baguette.

The lotus is very much part of everyday life in Cambodia. Various parts of the plant are used in the preparation of soups, stews, desserts and even traditional medicine.

2,000 indigenous rice varieties

As with the rest of Southeast Asia, rice accompanies almost every Cambodian meal. The country has over 2,000 documented indigenous rice varieties which were developed by farmers over the centuries in order to be able to grow rice all year round in all sorts of terrain and water conditions. Hundreds of these varieties became extinct as a result of the Khmer Rouge's policy of collectivization, which dramatically reduced rice acreage and replaced indigenous varieties with foreign ones from China with disastrous results. Rice cultivation today has yet to match the levels attained in the 1960s, but Cambodian farmers all over the country have demonstrated their resilience and determination to return rice to its rightful place in Cambodians' lives.

To Cambodians, rice symbolizes life itself. It is used to mark every milestone from birth to death and is both a staple food as well as a central component of rituals, ceremonies and religious offerings. Cambodians feature rice in their songs, dances and theater performances; it frames so much of how the community defines itself. While rice is primarily served as the dish upon which side dishes are spooned over or eaten with, it is also cooked using a wide variety of methods. It can be boiled, steamed, fried or grilled, and is incorporated into desserts and snacks. When fermented, it is savored as rice wine.

THIS PAGE (left) Selling French baguettes; (right) A ginger vendor samples her wares alongside her mid-morning meal of grilled fish with mango slices and fish sauce.

OPPOSITE Rice gruel is a popular comfort food.

INSIDE THE CAMBODIAN KITCHEN

Fresh mint, lemongrass, coriander, garlic and ginger are central to the Cambodian pantry. To give dishes the authentic Cambodian flavor, *prahok* (fermented fish paste), *touk trei* (fish sauce) and *kapi* (shrimp paste) are also vital.

ESSENTIAL COOKING TECHNIQUES

All food is cooked fresh daily according to the Buddhist religion. The most important cooking technique remains the pounding of *kroeungs*. Lemongrass and kaffir lime leaves have to be sliced thinly before they are thrown into the mortar because they are fibrous. *Galangal* (blue ginger) and turmeric also need to be cut into small pieces. These are pounded into a smooth consistency before the garlic and shallots are added toward the end.

ESSENTIAL KITCHEN IMPLEMENTS

The typical Cambodian stove is a charcoal brazier. Multiple braziers are used to provide the different heat intensities required for cooking different dishes. Most dishes are prepared in a *chhnang khteak*, a wok-like pan. Earthenware pots are used for cooking rice and soup, although aluminum pots have been appearing in modern kitchens. A mortar and pestle are needed for making *kroeungs*, while a bamboo sieve is essential for straining liquids. Also useful is a coconut grater.

Equally important to the cuisine is freshwater fish. Cambodia abounds with fish from the Tonle Sap Great Lake, the largest freshwater lake in Southeast Asia. The Tonle Sap is one of the most unique geographic wonders of the world. It is 160 kilometers long and 36 kilometers wide. During the dry season, it can cover as little as 3,000 square kilometers and its depth drops to 1 meter in some areas. However, during the wet season, it swells to 10,000 square kilometers and rises to a depth of 12 meters. For centuries the people living along the Tonle Sap have been able to catch an average of 10 tons of fish per square kilometer, providing a major source of protein for the sustenance of the Khmers. Cambodians also fish from the country's rivers, lakes, ponds and even rice fields. They have a saying, "*mean tek, mean trei*," which means where there is water there is fish. Fish is most often boiled, grilled or steamed. The abundance of fish and the need for a secure food source that will last throughout the year have led to the development of sophisticated techniques of preserving fish. The most famous are *prahok* (fermented fish), *trei chha-ae* (smoked fish), *trei ngiet* (dried fish), *touk trei* (fish sauce), *trei prama* (salted fish) and *kapi* (shrimp paste).

Three elements of distinctive taste

Attaining the distinctive taste of Cambodian dishes hinges upon three elements: *prahok* or *kapi* (fermented fish or shrimp paste); fresh local herbs which accent salads, soups and curries; and *kroeungs* (herb pastes), which form the basis of curries, stir-fries and soups. *Prahok* and *kapi* are defining flavors of Khmer cuisine. The methods used to prepare both are fairly similar and have been fine-tuned over the centuries (*prahok* is said to have existed in the region even before the establishment of the Angkor Empire). These preparation techniques are secrets carefully passed down from generation to generation. *Prahok* season begins with the onset of the monsoon and entire villages come together to prepare it. The air is first filled with the fragrance of fresh fish, but as the salting and months of fermentation ensue, a very different aroma pervades the villages. Villagers have learned to identify the stages of fermentation based on the distinct scents the *prahok* releases. The pungent, protein-rich pasty gray *prahok* from Siem Reap is considered the best in the country.

Cambodians also enjoy an abundance of fruits, vegetables and herbs which are served fresh at every meal. *Kanthrup* leaves (curry leaves) are toasted on the branch over an open flame before they are removed and added to soups, contributing a smoky, mildly bitter flavor. *Chi van suy* (coriander) stems are added to *kroeungs*, while the leaves are used as a garnish. *Chi ang kham* (mint) and *chi neang vong* (Asian basil) leaves are left whole and used in *nhoams* (salads). In Cambodian markets the five key herbs used in *nhoams* — Asian basil, mint, *chi ta-puo* (also known as *chi ma luong*), *chi sang hom* (Cambodian mint, also known as Vietnamese mint, or polygonum although it is not actually a member of the mint family) and *chi ma hao* (spearmint) — are sold packaged together, wrapped in lotus leaves.

Kroeungs, which are traditional herb pastes, form the cornerstone of most Cambodian dishes. The basic ingredients of a *kroeung* are lemongrass, *galangal* (blue ginger), *khchiey* (finger root, which is not to be mistaken for lesser *galangal*), turmeric, kaffir lime zest, garlic and shallots. To these basic ingredients, the chef may choose to add or replace ingredients to meet his or her specific needs. General *kroeungs* are divided into three categories: green, yellow and red. Each is named according to its color, which it derives from the primary herb it is made of. These *kroeungs* are used to make most curries, stir-fries and stuffings. Individual *kroeungs* include special ingredients specific to the dish being made; royal *kroeungs* include additional herbs like kaffir lime leaves and coriander stems. *Kroeungs* are pounded in stone, clay or wooden mortars, and the toughest ingredients are always added in first. When done, it should have a smooth consistency, which can be achieved only with great skill. In the past, Cambodians gauged a woman's potential as a wife by the quality of her *kroeungs*.

THIS PAGE A young vendor selling pickled vegetables.

OPPOSITE Fresh turmeric is ground daily in Cambodian homes.

Royal, urban and rural

Cambodian cuisine can be further classified as royal, urban (the food eaten in the cities) and rural (the diet of the country's peasants). While there are also the regional cooking traditions of Siem Reap and the mountain regions to the east of the country, the starkest contrast lies between the urban and rural culinary traditions. In terms of royal cuisine, two names stand out: Her Royal Highness Princess Mom Ket Kanya and Her Royal Highness Princess Kanitha Norodom Rasmi Sobbhana. Both were aunts of His Majesty King Father Norodom Sihanouk. HRH Princess Mom continues to be regarded as the keeper of traditional Khmer cuisine, while HRH Princess Rasmi Sobbhana is revered as the force behind nouvelle royal cuisine. Both have left indelible marks on the history of Cambodian culinary art. HRH Princess Mom's recipes were recorded in HM King Father Sihanouk's monthly bulletin, *Le Bulletin Mensuel de Documentation* and she is still remembered for her passion for preparing authentic Cambodian meals for His Majesty's guests. HRH Princess Rasmi Sobbhana devoted her life to studying Cambodian cuisine. She also worked with the American Women's Club to put together the first Cambodian cookbook, *The Cambodian Cookbook of HRH Princess Rasmi Sobbhana* in the 1960s. The cosmopolitan Princess is noted for her creativity and talent for blending East and West in the kitchen, as well as her tireless efforts in promoting women's education, creativity and freedom of expression. Cambodian royal cuisine is refined and highly detailed. Special dishes are not only served to reflect the changing seasons. They are also created to mark significant milestones of a king's reign, celebrate a royal wedding or birth and serve as religious offerings.

The country's peasants eat very simply, often depending purely on what they can cultivate, gather or catch themselves. Small paddy birds that can be found in the rice fields are caught with nets and eaten grilled. Spices are a luxury and curry dishes which are time-consuming to prepare are usually reserved for holidays and special celebrations. It is nonetheless a hearty, flavorful cuisine that focuses on indigenous ingredients. But in the bustling capital city, Phnom Penh, street vendors make for a colorful sight as they hawk their barbecued squab, deep-fried cicadas, frog's legs in ginger, catfish with chopped green mango and fish sauce, skewers of fish balls and French baguettes lined with homemade pâté and papaya pickle. It seems as if at every corner and certainly along every street, there's always something to eat, someone eating or someone in the midst of cooking. From as early as 5:30 a.m. until 9 a.m., many Cambodians can be found tucking into the iconic dish now famously referred to as Phnom Penh noodles at street stalls and minuscule hole-in-the-wall eateries. Thin rice noodles are topped with meat, shrimp, fresh vegetables and other garnishes, and then covered with a flavorful pork or chicken broth. At sundown it's time for a small snack of beef brochettes or stir-fried noodles (*k'tieu cha*) before dinner, which is usually a more traditional meal shared with the family.

At a Cambodian meal all dishes are served simultaneously and eaten with rice. There is usually a *samla* (a soup or stew), and a selection of other items such as a *cha* (a sautéed or stir-fried dish of meat or poultry with vegetables, rice vermicelli or just flavorings), an *aing* (grilled or roasted fish, meat or poultry) and a *chion* (fried fish, meat or poultry). Food is eaten with a fork and spoon, unless a noodle dish is served and chopsticks are required.

THIS PAGE Buddhists revere the lotus blossom for its purity. Thus lotus plants are cultivated all over the country.

OPPOSITE A personalized system of organizing prepared ingredients developed over the course of years spent working in the kitchen leads to calm cooking and nuanced flavors.

K'tieu Phnom Penh

Khmer noodles

There are numerous variations on Cambodian rice noodle dishes. This one is the most famous among them. In Cambodia noodles are served only in the morning.

Rice noodle dish served in market

Serves 10

For the broth and pork
1.3 kilograms pork leg bones
1/4 of a large yam bean
1 head garlic, cut in half
1 onion, peeled and quartered
60 grams dried shrimp
1 dried cuttlefish
2 tablespoons preserved mustard greens
5-centimeter piece ginger, sliced
1 tablespoon white peppercorns
a handful of coriander stems
2 tablespoons fish sauce
1 tablespoon sugar
1 tablespoon salt
1.3 kilograms pork (preferably heart
  and tongue, but pork loin cut into
  2 pieces also works well)

For the garnish
90 milliliters vegetable oil
8 cloves garlic, peeled and chopped
450 grams minced pork
1.3 kilograms large shrimp, peeled and
  deveined, or 900 grams shrimp and 400
  grams squid sliced into rings
285 grams fresh or dried rice noodles
360 grams bean sprouts
5 teaspoons preserved cabbage
50 milliliters soy sauce
freshly ground white pepper to taste
10 grams cilantro leaves, chopped
10 grams parsley leaves, chopped
15 grams spring onions, chopped
chinese hot sauce or chilies in vinegar
hoisin sauce
4 limes, quartered

1. Prepare the broth and the pork:
a) Place the bones in a large stockpot. Cover with 11 liters of cold water. Bring to a boil and simmer, uncovered. Remove and discard any scum that accumulates on the surface of the liquid.
b) Meanwhile, in a large square of cheesecloth or muslin, tie together the yam bean, garlic, onion, dried shrimp, dried cuttlefish, mustard greens, ginger, white peppercorns and coriander stems and add them to the pot.
c) Add fish sauce, sugar and salt. Simmer for 2 hours. Season to taste.
d) Strain the broth and discard the cheesecloth and bones.
e) Return broth to the pot, bring back to a boil and add the pork. Simmer until just cooked through, about 30 minutes. Lift out the pork and slice thinly.

2. Prepare the garnishes:
a) In a small frying pan, heat 75 milliliters of the oil over medium heat. Add the garlic and cook, stirring occasionally, until just golden, about 5 minutes. Set aside.
b) Heat remaining oil in a frying pan over medium heat. Add minced pork and cook until no longer pink (be sure to break up the larger pieces of meat). Set aside in a bowl.
c) Lower shrimp into the broth using a colander or strainer (you may have to do this in batches) and simmer for 1 to 2 minutes. Do the same with the squid if you are using it. Set aside in a bowl.
d) Bring a large pot of water to a boil. Add noodles and cook, stirring with chopsticks, until soft, about 1 minute for dried (less for fresh). Drain.

3. Divide half the bean sprouts among 10 large soup bowls. Divide the noodles between the bowls. Toss the noodles with a teaspoon of the garlic and oil mixture. Top each with half a teaspoon of preserved cabbage, 1 teaspoon soy sauce and a sprinkle of ground white pepper. Add a few slices of pork meat, 1 tablespoon minced pork, a few shrimp and squid (if using) to each bowl. Fill each bowl with hot broth.

4. Combine the cilantro, parsley and spring onions. Top each bowl with about a tablespoon of the herbs. Top with bean sprouts.

5. Bring bowls to the table and serve with soy sauce, hot sauce and *hoisin* sauce. Guests should squeeze lime juice over their soups and season them with condiments of their choice.

Nhoam krauch th'long

Pomelo salad

This is a common Khmer salad most often served at home for lunch. It is very refreshing and the fruity taste mixes well with flakes of grilled fish or thinly sliced boiled pork.

Freshly peeled pomelo segments

Serves 4

500 grams pomelo
100 grams sugar
1 teaspoon white vinegar
3 tablespoons fish sauce

6 cloves garlic, peeled, smashed and chopped
6 shallots, peeled and thinly sliced
salt and pepper to taste

1. Prepare the salad: Peel pomelo, removing the membrane around each segment. Crumble the pomelo flesh so that it is separated into individual sacs. Add some grilled and flaked fish or thinly sliced boiled pork (traditionally, pork belly is preferred) if you wish. Set aside.

2. Prepare the dressing: Combine sugar, vinegar and fish sauce in a small pot. Dilute with water to

taste and boil for 5 minutes. Let the mixture cool before adding garlic, shallots, salt and pepper.

3. Toss the salad with the dressing and then serve immediately.

Pleah trey

Fish salad

The Tonle Sap Great Lake is home to possibly the greatest variety of fish in Southeast Asia. As such, fish represents more than half of the protein most Cambodians consume. This dish is often served with rice.

Serves 4

500 grams catfish or other fresh
   fish fillets
3 tablespoons lemon juice
2 teaspoons sugar
3 tablespoons fish sauce
7 cloves garlic, peeled and pounded
2 large shallots, peeled and pounded

1 stalk lemongrass, thinly sliced
1 head of lettuce, leaves separated and
   torn into wide strips
200 grams bean sprouts
1 carrot, peeled and sliced
a few mint leaves
1 teaspoon crushed peanuts

1. Slice fish. Marinate with lemon juice, sugar and fish sauce for 20 minutes.

2. Drain the fish and boil the remaining marinade mixture with the pounded garlic and shallots for 5 minutes to create a sauce.

3. Combine the fish with the lemongrass, lettuce, bean sprouts, sliced carrots, mint leaves and crushed peanuts. Toss in the sauce before serving.

Chuchi pra kong

Chhouchi fragrant shrimp

Fresh shrimps

As in many Cambodian delicacies, this dish is simmered. It is enjoyed on special occasions such as large family gatherings.

Serves 4 - 6

80 grams dried red chilies
3 stalks lemongrass, finely sliced
200 grams garlic, peeled and diced
200 grams shallots, peeled and diced
salt to taste
1 teaspoon ground coriander seeds

1 teaspoon *kapi* (local shrimp paste)
500 milliliters coconut milk
3 tablespoons fish sauce
1 kilogram *demoiselle du Mekong*
   (Mekong shrimp) or fish
fresh coriander leaves for garnish

1. Remove the seeds of the red chilies, then soak the chilies in water for 20 minutes before squeezing them dry and chopping them.

2. Pound the sliced lemongrass with the chopped red chilies, garlic, shallots and some salt. Add ground coriander seeds and *kapi,* mix well to create chili paste.

3. Bring coconut milk and chili paste to a boil. Add the fish sauce and simmer for 20 minutes. Add shrimp and cook for about 4 minutes until they turn red. Do not overcook or they will become tough.

4. Garnish with fresh coriander leaves and serve with rice.

Kang-kep baob
Fragrant stuffed frogs

The croaking of frogs living in ponds and rice fields is associated with the start of the rainy season. Cambodians are fond of frogs and enjoy savoring them at weddings and on other special occasions. This is a countryside delicacy.

Grilled frogs

Serves 5 - 6

5-6 medium frogs

For the stuffing
400 grams minced pork
100 grams lemongrass

50 grams kaffir lime leaves, finely sliced
50 grams crushed peanuts
3 teaspoons fish sauce
3 tablespoons sugar
salt and pepper to taste

1. The frogs should be cleaned, and their heads and skin removed.

2. Mix the stuffing ingredients and stuff them into the frogs.

3. Grill the stuffed frogs until well cooked (approximately 20 to 25 minutes, depending on the size of the frogs).

Cambodian beef stew

A typical Cambodian meal consists of a stew like this served with rice. People love eating stew because the heady flavors of its abundant sauce pair perfectly with rice.

Serves 4

40 grams dried red chilies
5 tablespoons oil
100 grams garlic, peeled and chopped
100 grams shallots, peeled and chopped
1 kilogram stewing beef, cubed
3 tablespoons tomato paste
3 pieces star anise
1 tablespoon palm sugar
5 tablespoons fish sauce
salt and pepper to taste

Star anise

1. Soak dried red chilies in water for 20 minutes, then squeeze them dry and chop them until they form a paste (alternatively, do this in a blender).

2. Heat oil and add chili paste, garlic and shallots. Add the beef and stir for 10 minutes before adding the tomato paste, star anise, palm sugar, fish sauce, salt and pepper. Add 250 milliliters of water and simmer for 20 minutes until the beef becomes tender.

Indonesia

Introduction and Recipes

by Sri Owen

More than any other Southeast Asian country, Indonesia is a world in itself: a quarter of a billion people, an archipelago of 18,000 islands. Lying right across the Equator, its climate is easily influenced by small changes in the pattern of monsoon winds, and by El Niño events far away in the Pacific. Despite this, the western islands are rarely short of rain to fill their paddy fields, while those on the east do not get enough to make rice their staple food, and instead eat maize, tubers and *sago*. Fertile soils produce abundant vegetables and fruit. Seas, lakes and rivers still teem with fish, despite recent overfishing. Indonesia is by far the largest and most populous member of ASEAN, and therefore should have the greatest variety of foods and food traditions.

Its regional foodways are indeed influenced by what ingredients are available, but history and contacts with the outside world have also played a big part. Indonesians have always been seafarers and traders as well as fishermen, and for centuries they have been exporting precious resins and spices to China, India and beyond. In return they have received new faiths, new food crops and new ways of cooking, without forgetting what they inherited from their ancestors. It will be interesting to see how many of their traditions they can retain as they move from the countryside to the city and enter the global marketplace.

Chicken satay.

It is often hard to tell in which direction knowledge, ideas and ingredients have traveled; more likely there has been a continual dialogue of influences along the trade routes. For example, almost nine Indonesians out of ten today are Muslims, and observe Islamic dietary rules. But these allow plenty of scope for good food and for novelty. We cannot be sure where the idea of grilling meat and fish on wooden skewers originated, but *satays*, in one shape or another, are popular across a wide area and will survive in the age of the barbecue.

Similarly, we have many curry-type dishes (meat, fish or vegetables cooked in a spiced sauce), but whether these were first developed in India, or further east in Southeast Asia, or whether they originated in different places quite independently, we cannot tell. A harder question: most Indonesians use tamarind for its sour yet subtly sweet taste, but have we always done this, or was it introduced, say, a thousand years ago, brought by Arab or Indian traders? Its English name derives from Arabic, and certainly the tamarind tree came originally from India, but its Indonesian names mean simply "sour." Even a custom that seems to be purely Islamic may have its roots in earlier beliefs. For example, we celebrate almost every important event, in the family or the community, with a love-feast which, in most areas, is called *selamatan*, an Arabic term for what is indeed a religious ceremony, with prayers. But this convention of food sharing could be pre-Islamic. Other ritual feasts, often very elaborate and closely linked to the status of community leaders, take place in parts of Indonesia where animist beliefs are still strong.

The recipes that represent Indonesia here can all be described as "mainstream," even classic, dishes that are widely popular and have become familiar outside the country. They can all be made pretty well anywhere in the world, with easy substitutions for ingredients that might be hard to find in Europe or America. They are not, for the average Indonesian, everyday dishes. In the villages and *kampungs* (the back blocks of the cities), the daily fare is standard Southeast Asian: rice, vegetables, some fish or perhaps a little meat, cooked with shrimp paste and chilies. Even among the many-layered middle-classes of the cities, meals are usually quite simple, often bought from itinerant street traders — husband and wife both have jobs, and office workers don't have time or (perhaps) inclination to cook when they get home. Though the family may eat the evening meal together, they eat quickly, and usually in silence.

Social eating goes on outside the home, with casual visits to the street food stall, and formal attendance at family or communal meals such as the *selamatan*; these are places where food of this type might be encountered. Despite their general recognition, each has links to a particular region or city in one of five of the principal islands: Sumatra, Java, Kalimantan, Sulawesi — and Bali. The first four are the four largest islands of this vast archipelago. Bali is nowhere near as big, but is known to the world at large for its Hindu culture, which has survived in isolation from the sixteenth century. Each island has its own history, languages, customary laws and internal divisions, which lurk enticingly beneath the smooth surface of national and religious unity.

THIS PAGE (left) Dessert stall; (right) A palm wine vendor.

OPPOSITE At Koffie Aroma, Mr. Widyapratama continues to roast coffee in the same way his grandfather, one of Bandung's first koffiebranderij (coffee roasters), did. The beans come from all parts of Indonesia (Sulawesi, Sumatra, Java, Timor, Flores) and are aged for seven to eight years.

LEFT In Padang eating houses, as soon as you sit down, an array of perhaps a dozen small plates of cooked dishes is set before you, with a larger plate of steamed white rice.

RIGHT Stir-frying, usually in coconut oil in a wok over glowing charcoal, is an everyday activity.

INSIDE THE INDONESIAN KITCHEN

The underlying principles of Indonesian cooking are similar to those of other Southeast Asian cuisines. Good food requires a balance among at least three of the five basic tastes: hot, sweet, bitter, sour and salty. Hotness comes from chili, ginger and peppers. Sweetness derives not only from various kinds of sugar but from onions, ripe fruit and coconut milk. Salt is given pungency and variety by its use in shrimp paste and fish sauce. For sourness, unripe fruit such as green mangoes for example, and the natural sourness of tamarind, are supported by a long list of more or less acid wild and cultivated plant produce. While the bitterness that we all love, in proper measure, is found in root herbs [galangal (blue ginger), turmeric root], certain leaves and flowers such as those of the papaya tree, and in several tropical vegetables, of which our favorite is perhaps the bitter gourd. In short, the five tastes are not just simple primary colors: each is a whole palette of shades and tints, some delicate, some strident.

Halfway down the west coast of Sumatra, the old port city of Padang has given its name to an informal network of small restaurants that have long thrived in every town of any size throughout Indonesia. They cater for travelers and are businesslike in their approach: as soon as you sit down, an array of perhaps a dozen small plates of cooked dishes is set before you, with a larger plate of steamed white rice. You help yourself to what you want from the side dishes, and at the end you pay for every dish from which you have taken food. The cooking may be excellent, or it may be indifferent, but in any case you are likely to find that Indonesians love offal, and believe no edible part of the animal should be wasted. They also expect all dishes to be chili-hot, often fearsomely so. These *rumah makan* Padang — Padang eating houses — reflect the local tradition that sent young men from the region out into the world to seek their fortunes before they returned to marry and settle down; the restaurants, where the cooking and the service were pretty much what they'd been used to at home, must have comforted many a homesick youngster, but also attract local people (mostly men) because of their help-yourself menu.

About 60 kilometers inland from Padang, and 1,000 meters or so above the sea, is the town of Bukittinggi (literally, "high hill"), with its famous food markets: Pasar Atas (on top of the hill) and Pasar Bawah (lower down), where you can find every kind of fresh food, an astonishing variety of snacks (all Indonesians love to snack between meals, or in place of meals), and food stalls offering hot fresh-cooked dishes to eat on the spot or take away. These work to the formula of steamed white rice (*nasi*) plus a selection of side dishes, meat, fish and vegetables; here the local name is *nasi kapau*. Among what's on offer, you may see some generic dishes, such as *soto*, a soup with plenty of meat and vegetables in it; *gulai*, a meat dish, usually goat or beef, or else chicken or duck, with a fairly thick, spiced sauce, very similar to a curry; *pangek*, fish cooked in spiced coconut milk, usually with fiddleheads (small green edible fern-shoots); and *rendang*, the classic west Sumatran dish (also claimed by Malaysians whose ancestors migrated from Sumatra), a rich long-cooked mass of beef infused with coconut milk and spices — a dish for a feast indeed, or for taking on a journey, since it will keep for a fortnight, unrefrigerated, as long as it is reheated each day.

Over 3,000 kilometers eastward, but still very close to the Equator, lies the town of Manado, near the outflung northern arm of Sulawesi. Most people here are Christians and therefore eat pork. The Portuguese were here for a century or so from about 1540; a few words from their language, and recipes derived from their cuisine, are still in use, for example they continue to enjoy a pasty called *panada*, made with yeast-raised dough and filled with smoked tuna. The flavoring is fairly standard: onions, garlic, ginger and chilies, with red tomatoes for sourness and plenty of chopped basil or mint. Here as elsewhere in Southeast Asia, the aromatics have to fit into the framework of the basic tastes — sweet, sour, salty, bitter, savory and chili-hot. The local pork *satay* is made with a spice mix called *rica rica* (pronounced reach-a reach-a), in which lime juice is the souring agent; it is eaten with an uncooked "sweet and hot" sauce with, once again, shallots, chilies, lime juice, tomatoes, basil or mint, and sugar.

THIS PAGE A vendor selling breakfast at a market in Bandung.

OPPOSITE A halal restaurant in Jakarta.

ESSENTIAL COOKING TECHNIQUES

Many millions of Asians still do all their cooking over wood fires and charcoal stoves, so they choose cooking methods that transfer heat efficiently and save fuel. To start with the simplest: we boil and poach meat, fish, and vegetables. Steaming is also a basic technique for cooking rice, vegetables, and fish; even our cakes are steamed, for few people in the countryside have gas or electric ovens, though these are becoming common now in the towns. Deep-frying and stir-frying, usually in coconut oil in a wok over glowing charcoal, are everyday activities, and the embers of the fire are fanned to grill meat or fish on bamboo skewers.

ESSENTIAL KITCHEN IMPLEMENTS

A middle-class big-city household will, of course, have a fully equipped high-tech kitchen, but the virtues of the old ways are not yet entirely forgotten. Traditional utensils are simple and practical, and may be made of the cheapest materials — an empty coconut shell for a ladle, unglazed pottery for cooking. In Indonesia these round-bottomed pots are called *belanga*. They sit snugly on three bricks over the open fire, and with repeated use they develop their own internal glaze of ancient sauces and spices. But every household has at least one wok, for frying, and a few saucepans, for boiling and steaming, and for cooking rice. Many people, especially in Java, still use the traditional *dandang* rice-steamer with its *kukusan*, a conical woven bamboo basket. This can also be used for steaming meat, fish, vegetables and cakes wrapped in banana leaf packets. However, most people, especially in or near a town, now have sufficient electricity to power an electric rice cooker.

In the opposite corner (so to speak) of Sulawesi is Ujung Pandang, formerly Makassar, a great fishing as well as trading port, and still famous for its seafood. The place to be in the evening is the west-facing esplanade, first to watch the sun set over the ocean, then to eat charcoal-grilled shellfish, or *pallu mara ikan*, made with skipjack (also known as little tunny or mackerel tuna) poached with the usual onions and garlic and a lot of lemongrass and tamarind. Almost everyone in Indonesia lives on the coast or near a lake or river, so fish — fresh, dried or made into *terasi*, a wonderfully pungent flavoring of pounded, fermented shrimp — appears on the table more often than meat, and is most people's best source of protein.

From Ujung Pandang to Banjarmasin on the south coast of Kalimantan (Indonesian Borneo) is some 1,000 kilometers across open ocean. On this voyage we pass from the relatively deep waters of the Makassar Strait to the shallower Java Sea, and we cross Wallace's Line, the boundary that separates (more or less) the plants and animals of Asia from those of Australasia. Banjarmasin is a busy port at the mouth of the Barito River, down which come various jungle products from the interior. Banjar food is considered the premier culinary tradition in Kalimantan, celebrated for its *soto*, *satay*, and *ikan asam pedas* (hot and sour fish).

Further round the coast to the east, you come to the oil town of Balikpapan and, a few kilometers up the Mahakam River, to Samarinda, the home of *gang asam*, short ribs of beef braised in a sauce that balances chilies with the acidity of tamarind water and the leaves of the *kedondong* (ambarella) tree. Go west from Banjarmasin and you will find yourself in Pontianak, essentially a town of immigrants from Java, Sumatra, the Philippines, China — any place from which Pontianak can be seen to offer the promise of a better life. The indigenous people of this part of Borneo are the Dayak, who, besides eating game that they hunt in the jungle, also eat pork. As it's customary to cook outdoors, they have a traditional way of cooking meat, and also fish, wrapped in banana or teak leaves and stuffed inside a green bamboo segment. You can see rows of these, propped on metal stands near a wood or charcoal fire; someone turns them from time to time so that their contents of well-chopped spiced pork or fish are cooked evenly. The Minangkabau people in west Sumatra cook their glutinous (sticky) rice in the same way. Rice thus cooked is called *lemang*, and the traditional accompaniment is *rendang*.

From Padang in west Sumatra, or from Ujung Panjang or Menado in Sulawesi, a flight to Denpasar, capital of Bali, will probably take less time than you spent in the departure lounge. Bali has been much changed by the impact of mass tourism, but it has not been spoiled — the Balinese are too resilient for that. If anything, it has become more interesting, and the food has improved. Visitors can eat well at the big tourist hotels and at many small hotels, homestays and restaurants (and it is worth noting that Balinese are being appointed executive chefs and food and beverage managers in

hotels outside Bali and outside Indonesia). Most tourist food, here as elsewhere, is beyond the reach of the average villager, but two recipes are included here which first appeared in my book, *Indonesian Regional Food and Cookery*, in 1995. They will at least give you a taste of how Balinese food is spiced and prepared.

Yogyakarta, the eighteenth-century principal town in Central Java, is the seat of the island's surviving sultanate. Here we might expect to find a court cuisine to go with the elaborate ceremonial of the palace, the dress of its courtiers, the refined subtlety of court dancers and the music of the gamelan. In fact, no such cuisine has ever developed, perhaps because successive sultans appreciated popular local tradition and preferred to have their palace food cooked by a rota of trusted noble families in the town, then carried inside the gates to be served by yet more faithful family retainers.

Yogyakarta, or Yogya for short, is known principally for two dishes: fried chicken and *gudeg*. Both are, essentially, street food. Fifty years ago, a local lady called *mBok Berek* (*mBok* is Javanese for "mother" or simply "Mrs") hit on a way of marinating chickens in coconut water (water, not milk) with shallots, ginger, *galangal* (blue ginger), turmeric, *salam* leaves and a little salt for about 4 hours, then putting the whole lot on the boil for at least an hour, and leaving it all to cool. The chicken, whole or chopped into pieces, is then deep-fried in coconut or peanut oil. The flesh should then be crisp outside, beautifully tender inside; even an *ayam kampung*, a local chicken whose free range is the village street, can be tenderized in this way. *Gudeg* is also, in part, a chicken dish, or rather a one-dish meal consisting, in the form I give it here, of a well-roasted chicken, cut into pieces, then simmered in coconut milk with green jackfruit, *terasi*, candlenuts, the usual shallots-garlic-ginger, and one or two spices, garnished with hard-boiled eggs. Making this sort of street food is a major cottage industry in a town with several universities and thousands upon thousands of hungry students, for whom "*gudeg Yogya*" is synonymous with the good life.

Visits to Indonesia tend to start and finish either in Bali or in Jakarta. Most visitors dislike Jakarta at first sight, and it does sometimes seem to be a black hole into which the rest of Indonesia is being sucked, but it improves greatly on closer acquaintance, especially when you begin to meet people and make some friends. It is cosmopolitan and has excellent Chinese, Thai, Japanese, Korean, Italian and even Indonesian restaurants; its regional specialties are correspondingly widely known. *Nasi goreng* (fried rice) is a cliché, but a good one is still worth eating. *Gado-gado*, a cooked salad of mixed vegetables with a peanut sauce, is a gourmet dish if the vegetables are not overdone. *Sambal goreng daging* (beef in a rich coconut sauce) is a classic known throughout Southeast Asia. *Asinan Jakarta* is a deliciously fresh-tasting salad, mingling vegetables with pineapple and other sour-tasting fruit and dressed with a mixture of vinegar, sugar, shrimp paste, dried shrimps, and of course chilies and a few peanuts.

Rendang

Long-cooked beef in coconut milk with spices

Rendang *is a traditional dish of west Sumatra. It was probably developed out of the need to preserve the meat from a newly-killed buffalo for as long as possible in a tropical climate with no refrigerators. The meat is cut into chunky cubes and is then boiled in large pots, not in water, but in spiced coconut milk, which slowly penetrates the meat and incidentally gives it a delicious flavor. My recipe is the recipe that was dictated to my mother by my paternal grandmother, who used to cook buffalo* rendang *for large family gatherings.* Rendang *is traditionally eaten with glutinous (sticky) rice cooked in coconut milk, or with* lemang, *the same glutinous rice but cooked in a bamboo segment. However, it is just as good with plain boiled rice.*

Serves 8 - 10

6 shallots
4 cloves garlic
6-10 red chilies, deseeded,
   or 3 teaspoons chili powder
2.5-centimeter piece ginger, peeled
2.5-centimeter piece turmeric, peeled
   or 1 teaspoon turmeric powder
2.3 liters coconut milk
1.35 kilograms buffalo meat or beef,
   preferably brisket, otherwise chuck
   steak or silverside, cut into 2-centimeter
   cubes

1 teaspoon chopped *galangal* (blue ginger)
   or 1/2 teaspoon *galangal* powder
1 *salam* leaf or bay leaf
1 fresh turmeric leaf or 1 stalk lemongrass
2 teaspoons salt

1. Peel and slice the shallots and garlic finely, and roughly chop the chilies, ginger and turmeric. Put them in a blender with 4 tablespoons of the coconut milk, and blend until smooth. Put all these ingredients with the coconut milk, into a large wok or saucepan. (It is generally more convenient to start in a pan, and transfer to a wok later.) Put the meat and the rest of the ingredients into the pan also, making sure that there is enough coconut milk to cover it.

2. Stir the contents of the pan, and start cooking, on medium heat, uncovered. Let the pan bubble gently for 90 minutes to 2 hours, stirring from time to time. The coconut milk will by then be quite thick, and of course much reduced.

3. If you started in a large saucepan, transfer everything to a wok and continue cooking in the same way for another 30 minutes, stirring occasionally. By now the coconut milk should begin to reduce to oil, and the meat, which has so far been boiling, will soon be frying. From now on, the *rendang* needs to be stirred frequently. Taste, and add salt if necessary. When the coconut oil becomes thick and brown, stir continuously for about 15 minutes, until the oil has been more or less completely absorbed by the meat. Take out and discard the turmeric leaf or lemongrass. Serve hot with lots of rice.

Lemongrass

Pallu mara ikan

Hot and sour fish from Ujung Pandang

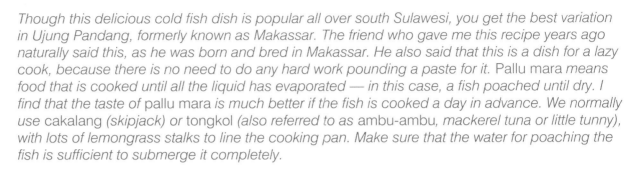

Though this delicious cold fish dish is popular all over south Sulawesi, you get the best variation in Ujung Pandang, formerly known as Makassar. The friend who gave me this recipe years ago naturally said this, as he was born and bred in Makassar. He also said that this is a dish for a lazy cook, because there is no need to do any hard work pounding a paste for it. Pallu mara means food that is cooked until all the liquid has evaporated — in this case, a fish poached until dry. I find that the taste of pallu mara is much better if the fish is cooked a day in advance. We normally use cakalang (skipjack) or tongkol (also referred to as ambu-ambu, mackerel tuna or little tunny), with lots of lemongrass stalks to line the cooking pan. Make sure that the water for poaching the fish is sufficient to submerge it completely.

Serves 6 - 8

about 1.5 kilograms fish
1 teaspoon salt
1/4 teaspoon ground turmeric
2 tablespoons lime juice
225 grams lemongrass, each stem washed
  and split in half lengthwise
1 1/2 tablespoons coarse sea salt

10 shallots or 3 large onions, sliced
5-10 large red chilies, deseeded
  and sliced
4 cloves garlic, sliced
5-centimeter piece ginger, peeled
  and thinly sliced
225 milliliters tamarind water

1. Clean the fish well and rub all over with salt, ground turmeric and lime juice. Keep in a cool place for at least 1 hour before cooking.

2. Line the bottom of the saucepan with the lemongrass, and sprinkle about half a tablespoonful of sea salt over it. Spread half of the sliced shallots or onions on top of the lemongrass, followed by half of the chilies, garlic, and ginger. Sprinkle on another half-tablespoonful of coarse salt. Lay the fish on top of this in one layer, then spread the rest of the onions, garlic, chilies and ginger, and the rest of the salt, on top of it. Pour in the tamarind water and add 570 milliliters of cold water (or more) to submerge the fish.

3. Cover the pan and cook on low heat for 40 to 50 minutes, or until all the water has been absorbed. The lemongrass may get a little burned but this will only give a nice smoky taste to the fish. Leave the fish to cool in the pan unless the lemongrass is too burnt, in which case transfer the fish with the rest of the solids, (except lemongrass, which you can now discard) into a glass container to cool. When cold, store in the refrigerator. Just before you serve the fish the next day, discard all the solids and serve the fish carefully filleted.

Chef's note:
To make tamarind water, combine about 40 grams of tamarind pulp with 3 to 4 tablespoons of warm water, then squeeze and mix until the water turns brown. Repeat this process until you have as much tamarind water as you need. Pass the liquid through a sieve and discard the solids.

Gudeg Yogya

Long-cooked chicken and jackfruit, Yogya-style

This is the most satisfying and delicious of all meals for the Yogyanese. And for students studying and living in Yogya, gudeg is their staple food. When I was a high school student, there was a famous roadside stall that I would go to every morning for breakfast with my fellow students who were living at the same students' house. When I visited Yogya again more than 35 years later, providing gudeg to students had become a vast catering business. Gudeg has now become synonymous with good living for students in Yogya. I miss gudeg a lot, so I am putting my recipe here, in this book, to get more people to know and appreciate it.

Jackfruit

Serves 6 - 8 for breakfast

1 medium chicken, ready for roasting
1 teaspoon salt
1 lemon, juiced
850 milliliters thick coconut milk
1.1 liters thin coconut milk
3 *salam* leaves or bay leaves
5-centimeter piece *galanga*l (blue ginger)
900 grams parboiled jackfruit segments,
   or canned green jackfruit, drained
   and rinsed
6-8 hard-boiled eggs, peeled

For the bumbu *(paste)*
5 shallots, chopped
4 cloves garlic, chopped
1 teaspoon chopped ginger
8 *kemiri* (candlenuts) or macadamia nuts,
   or 10 blanched almonds, chopped
2 teaspoons ground coriander
1 teaspoon crumbled *terasi* (shrimp paste)
1 teaspoon ground white pepper
1 teaspoon sugar
1 teaspoon salt

Chef's note:
The main ingredient for *gudeg* that might be difficult to find in Europe and America is the fresh jackfruit (only occasionally available in some Thai and Indian shops). You can use canned green jackfruit, available from almost any Oriental store.

1. Rub the outside of the whole chicken with the salt, then liberally rub the juice of the lemon all over the chicken. Wrap the chicken loosely in aluminum foil, and roast in a pre-heated oven, at 330 degrees Fahrenheit (165 degrees Celsius) for 1 hour. Unwrap and chop the chicken into 8 or 10 portions, discarding some of the large bones. (Alternatively, the whole chicken can be boiled with water in a separate saucepan, for 50 minutes from the time the water starts to boil.)

2. Blend all the ingredients for the *bumbu* with 8 tablespoons of the thick coconut milk until smooth and transfer it to a saucepan. Bring to the boil and simmer, stirring often, for 6 minutes. Add the thin coconut milk, the *salam* or bay leaves and *galangal*, and continue to simmer for 10 minutes. Add the jackfruit, increase the flame and boil for 40 minutes. Now add the remaining thick coconut milk, the chicken and eggs. Continue to simmer, stirring often, for 30 to 40 minutes or until the sauce becomes quite thick. Serve hot with plenty of boiled rice.

Ayam mBok Berek

The original fried chicken of Kalasan

Every visitor to Yogyakarta goes to see the temple complex at Prambanan, in Kalasan, about 15 kilometers out of town on the Solo road. In the early 1960s, there was a fried chicken restaurant near the temples called Warung mBok Berek *(mBok means "mother" in Javanese, but like the Indonesian word* ibu *it is used as a polite term of address for any lady over the age of about 25). This* warung *was rapidly becoming famous all over Yogya — soon, all over Java. Before long, so it was said, airline pilots were taking packages of* mBok Berek's *chicken to Indonesian expatriates in New York.*

The ingredient that makes this fried chicken so special is the absolutely essential coconut water. Water out of thick-shelled old coconuts from the supermarket will do well enough, but you need 850 milliliters of it — the contents of several nuts. In Indonesia, of course, the water is from kelapa muda, *the young coconuts that grow profusely everywhere and are full of water because their flesh has not begun to form. Here I can suggest using the canned coconut juice with no added sugar that is often available in Chinese supermarkets. However, fresh young coconut is sometimes available in Thai and Indian shops.*

Serves 2 - 4

850 milliliters coconut water
5 shallots, finely chopped
2 teaspoons finely chopped ginger
3.5-centimeter piece *galangal*
   (blue ginger)
1/4 teaspoon ground turmeric
2 *salam* leaves or bay leaves

1 teaspoon salt
1 free-range chicken, cut in half or
   into 4 pieces
2 tablespoons plain flour
salt and pepper
vegetable oil for deep-frying

1. Put the coconut water in a deep saucepan, and add to it the shallots, ginger, *galangal*, turmeric, *salam* or bay leaves and 1 teaspoonful of salt. Mix these well, then put in the chicken. Leave to marinate for 2 to 4 hours, then boil the chicken in this marinade on medium heat for 45 to 60 minutes. Leave to cool in the remaining cooking juices. When cold, take the chicken pieces out and dry them with kitchen paper.

2. On a large plate or a tray, season the flour with salt and pepper. Rub the flour all over the chicken pieces. Heat the oil in a deep-fryer or a wok to 325 degrees Fahrenheit (165 degrees Celsius) and fry the chicken until golden brown. The pieces should be crisp outside and still soft and tender inside. Serve hot straightaway, or cold for a picnic.

Saté pentul

Minced pork *satay* with Balinese spice-mixture

You can find saté pentul *everywhere in Bali, especially on holy days, when there are Balinese religious ceremonies in the major temples. The road or path, usually steep, that leads to the temple will be lined on both sides with vendors of all sorts of food, including a great variety of satays. Each has his or her small charcoal stove, some quite modern-looking, not dissimilar to the Japanese* hibachi, *others very primitive, made from thin sheet aluminium, often stained and battered; but as long as the fire is really hot, you will get good spicy minced satays.*

Made at home, saté pentul *can be as hot and spicy as in the recipe below, or as mild as a hamburger. If you want it mild, leave out the chilies.*

Serves 4 - 6

1 teaspoon salt
2 teaspoons lime juice
500 grams loin of pork, minced

For the bumbu *(paste)*
4 shallots or 1 large onion, chopped
4 cloves garlic, chopped
3-6 red chilies, deseeded, and chopped;
    or 1 to 2 teaspoons chili powder
2 teaspoons coriander seeds, roasted
1 teaspoon cumin seeds, roasted
2 cloves
2 cardamom seeds

2.5-centimeter-long cinnamon stick
1 teaspoon finely chopped ginger
1 teaspoon finely chopped turmeric
several pinches of grated nutmeg
4 tablespoons tamarind water (see
    Chef's note on page 72) or lime juice
3 tablespoons peanut oil
1 teaspoon salt
1 teaspoon soft brown sugar
1 teaspoon crumbled *terasi*
    (shrimp paste)
90 milliliters thick coconut milk
    (optional)

1. In a bowl, rub the salt and lime juice into the minced pork. Keep aside.

2. Put the ingredients for the *bumbu* in a blender, and blend till you get a smooth paste. Mix this paste well into the meat. Knead it for a while with your hand, then divide the meat and shape it into small balls the size of a walnut.

3. Put four meat balls on to a bamboo or metal skewer just before you are ready to grill. You can prepare the mixture up to 24 hours before, but don't mold it or put it on to skewers until the last possible moment; if you do, the balls will tend to split and fall off. Grill slowly, turning carefully from time to time. After 4 or 5 minutes, when the *satays* should be half cooked and pretty firm, brush the balls with some oil, and continue cooking for 2 to 3 minutes longer. Serve hot, as canapés with drinks, or as part of a buffet party.

Saté babi Menado

Pork *satay*, Menado-style

Pork satay in Indonesia is usually made to a Chinese recipe, except in Bali and north Sulawesi. The Balinese have their own spice mixture to marinate the meat. In north Sulawesi the spice mixture is the rica rica mixture which is always very hot, because it is made with a lot of chilies. This is usually eaten with a sauce called dabu-dabu manis, not the usual satay sauce made of peanuts.

The pork can be boiled first together with the paste, then cut up and put on skewers to be grilled on charcoal. In London I use spare ribs of pork if I am going to boil the meat first, but if you use the more tender parts, such as tenderloin, just cut the meat into small pieces, marinate the pieces in the paste, put them on bamboo or metal skewers, and grill on charcoal or under an electric or gas grill. With the ribs, of course, you don't need the skewers.

Pork satay

Serves 4 - 6

1 kilogram spare ribs of pork, cut into
   10-centimeter lengths

For the paste
3-5 red chilies, deseeded and chopped
5-centimeter piece ginger, peeled and
   chopped
4 shallots, chopped
4 cloves garlic, chopped
2 tablespoons peanut oil
2 tablespoons tamarind water (see Chef's
   note on page 72) or lime juice
1 teaspoon salt

For dabu-dabu manis *(sweet and hot sauce)*
2 shallots, finely sliced
2 large red chilies, deseeded and
   finely sliced
2 tablespoons *kalamansi* juice or
   lime juice
3 medium tomatoes, skinned and deseeded
   then quartered and thinly sliced
1 teaspoon salt
2-3 teaspoons sugar
2 tablespoons chopped basil leaves

1. Put all the ingredients for the paste into a blender and blend until smooth. Transfer this paste to a saucepan and simmer for 4 minutes. Add the spare ribs, and stir until all of them are well coated with the paste. Then add 570 milliliters of hot water, bring to boil, and simmer for 1 hour. By this time the water should have reduced considerably.

2. Continue to cook the spare ribs on higher heat until all the water has evaporated. Take care not

to burn the ribs. Up to this point the dish can be prepared in advance. Keep the boiled ribs in a cool place. When you are ready to serve them, grill them for a few minutes on each side or until they start to char. Serve hot with the *dabu-dabu manis* as a dip.

3. To prepare the sauce, mix all the *dabu-dabu manis* ingredients in a small glass bowl, and serve immediately.

Bebek betutu

Traditional long-cooked Balinese duck

Chili paste

I was hoping very much that during my trip around Bali a few years ago I would find this delicious duck on restaurant menus. But no, it was nowhere to be found. Bebek betutu is considered so old-fashioned now. In the old days, bebek betutu as cooked by the monks in Ubud was a real delicacy, long-cooked in a shallow trench that was covered with the embers of a wood fire. I was not lucky enough to see the monks' version of the bebek betutu, but a noble lady in Bangli, the mother of one of my Balinese friends, once served me this delicious duck. The duck was stuffed with cassava leaves and spiced with a Balinese spice-mixture. The wrapping, which consisted of layers of banana leaves and seludang mayang (the hard outer sheath of the coconut flower) opened to reveal a mass of black and tender meat. The color of the stuffing had become black as well. Not very appetizing to look at, maybe, but the taste was exquisite.

Serves 4

170-225 grams curly kale, vine or
 courgette leaves, or spinach, blanched,
 squeezed dry, and shredded
1 duck (1.5-2 kilograms), cleaned and
 ready for roasting

For the bumbu *(paste)*
5 shallots or 2 medium onions, chopped
4 cloves garlic, chopped
5 red chilies, deseeded, chopped; or
 1 teaspoon chili powder
2 *kemiri* (candlenuts) or macadamia nuts
 (optional)
2 teaspoons coriander seeds
1 teaspoon cumin seeds
2 cloves
2 green cardamom pods

2.5-centimeter-long cinnamon stick
1/4 teaspoon ground or grated
 nutmeg
1/2 teaspoon ground turmeric
1/4 teaspoon *galangal* (blue ginger)
 powder
1/4 teaspoon ground white pepper
5-centimeter piece lemongrass, cut
 from hard root end, outer leaf
 discarded, chopped, or 1/4 teaspoon
 lemongrass powder
1 teaspoon shrimp paste
3 tablespoons tamarind water (see
 Chef's note on page 72) or lime juice
2 tablespoons peanut oil
2 tablespoons water
1 teaspoon salt

1. Blend all the ingredients for the *bumbu* together until smooth. Transfer the mixture to a saucepan and simmer for 6 to 8 minutes, stirring often. Then transfer it to a bowl and leave it to cool. Adjust the seasoning by adding more salt as necessary.

2. When the paste is cold, mix half of it in a bowl with the shredded leaves. Then rub the remaining paste on the duck, inside as well as outside. Stuff the shredded leaves into the duck. Wrap the duck first with some banana leaves, then with 2 or 3 layers of aluminum foil, quite loosely, but sealing the top well. Everything up to this point can be done the day before and the parcel can be left in the refrigerator overnight so that the duck marinates thoroughly.

3. To cook, pre-heat your oven to 320 degrees Fahrenheit (160 degrees Celsius) and put the parcel on a baking tray in the middle of the oven. Cook for 1 hour, then reduce the heat to 250 degrees Fahrenheit (120 degrees Celsius) and continue cooking for a further 3 to 4 hours.

4. To serve, unwrap the parcel and transfer the duck to a large dish. Separate and discard the oil from the cooking juices. Put the cooking juices in a small saucepan, add to this all the stuffing, which has now become a dark-colored purée (but tastes delicious). Heat, and serve it as a thick sauce. The duck has become very tender, and the meat will come off the bones very easily. With a fork, transfer the meat to a well-heated serving platter. Serve straightaway with plenty of hot boiled white rice, with the sauce poured over the duck meat or in a sauceboat for everybody to help themselves.

Asinan Jakarta

Jakarta fruit and vegetable salad

Asinan is a generic name for a hot, salty, sour and sweet salad, which is considered a refreshing dish. The equivalent dish but without vegetables is called rujak. *There are rivalries between the street vendors of* asinan Jakarta *and* asinan Bogor, *a more elaborate mixture of freshly-sliced crunchy fruit and vegetables made in a hill town some distance south of Jakarta. When I bought some in Bogor recently, I found the* asinan *very tasty and refreshing, though I could not interest my English husband in it. When I make* asinan Jakarta *at home in London, however, he eats it as cheerfully as any other mixed salad. So here is the recipe for* asinan Jakarta, *with suggestions for alternative fruit.*

The well-known joke is that every young woman who shows even a slight craving for these refreshing salads must be expecting a baby. Maybe this is one of the reasons that street vendors selling asinan *are popular.*

Carrots

Serves 4 - 6

1 cucumber, peeled
2-3 medium carrots, peeled
2 *kedondong* (ambarella) or hard apples
2 small *bengkuang* (yam beans), or
   unripe pears
1 small pineapple, peeled and cored
   (optional)
115 grams bean sprouts, cleaned
115 grams white cabbage, finely shredded
60 grams Chinese cabbage, finely
   shredded

For the dressing
60 grams brown sugar
4 tablespoons water
1 tablespoon caster sugar

1 teaspoon fried or grilled *terasi*
   (shrimp paste)
2 tablespoons dried shrimps, soaked in
   hot water for 5 minutes, then drained
3-5 *cabe rawit* (bird's-eye chilies), or
   2 small dried red chilies
1 large red chili, deseeded and chopped
225 milliliters distilled malt or
   white vinegar
2 teaspoons salt

For the garnish
85 grams peanuts, fried or roasted
3 or 4 *krupuk udang* (prawn crackers)
some mixed lettuce leaves

1. Cut the cucumber and carrots into matchsticks, taking care not to make them too small. Peel the *kedondong* and *bengkuang,* then slice them into irregular wedges, but not too thinly. Cut the pineapple, if used, into small pieces.

2. To make the dressing, melt the brown sugar and the water in a small saucepan. Transfer this straightaway into a large glass bowl. Set aside. Put the rest of the ingredients for the dressing into a blender and blend, but not too smoothly. Transfer

this into the bowl with the already melted brown sugar. Stir this dressing to mix well, and adjust the seasoning. Now mix all the salad ingredients in the dressing, and leave to stand for a few hours or overnight, in the refrigerator or a cool place, to let the juices penetrate.

3. Just before serving, transfer the salad mixture to a large platter, garnish with the peanuts and *krupuk udang*, and arrange the lettuce leaves around the edge of the platter.

Lao PDR

Introduction and Recipes
by Somsanouk Mixay

Laotians usually wake up early. The drums at Buddhist temples wake the monks and novices at 4 a.m. for prayers and meditation. Laypeople are up by cockcrow, especially in the countryside. The first thing the elder woman of the family does in the morning is cook *khaow neow* (glutinous or sticky rice). The previous night, before turning in, she would have covered some glutinous rice with water, leaving it to soak in order to soften the grains. To prepare *khaow neow*, she puts the drained rice in a *huad* (a plaited bamboo container), which she places on an earthen or aluminum pot partly filled with water. Steam from the boiling water slowly cooks the rice. After some time, she will shake the *huad* to bring the cooked rice to the top, letting the raw rice settle into the base. When the rice is cooked, she uses a wooden spatula to spread it out on a large, round wooden plate to ensure that the steam escapes as quickly as possible. This makes the rice less sticky. It is then placed in small bamboo boxes called *tip khaow*. Then, wearing her *sinh* (the traditional skirt Laotian women wear) and her shawl on her left shoulder, she heads toward the main street, carrying her rice box. She kneels alongside other people and places little balls of rice in the alms bowls of a row of monks and novices as they file past her.

This is the daily ritual of Laotians. It has been so for centuries. The Laotians subscribe to Buddhist philosophy, which holds generosity in high regard. They put this into practice by presenting offerings to monks and sharing what they have with other people. Each day, most families cook a dish that is sent to the local temple and served to the monks at breakfast — or lunchtime.

The khok *(mortar)* and sark *(pestle)* are frequently used in the Laotian kitchen for pounding ingredients.

The glutinous rice left over from this daily ritual is kept for the family's meals. Glutinous rice is the staple food of the majority of the 49 ethnic groups that make up Lao PDR's population. In the Laotian language, the phrase for eat is *kin khaow*, which means "to eat rice." When you visit people, the host will invariably ask you, "*Kin khaow laew bor*?" (Have you eaten?) This shows the sense of hospitality the Laotians have. The spirit of sharing is very much part of their lives. Guests are always welcome to share a meal with the family. Your host will say, "Whatever we have, let us eat it together." And should you visit people living in the countryside, the villagers will slaughter a chicken — even if it is the last one in their farmyard — just in order to present you with a culinary treat.

Traditionally, the Laotians eat seated on the floor. They sit on straw mats around a *pha khaow* which consists of a tray of rice and a round bamboo platter on which all the dishes, served in small bowls called *thuai*, are placed. The biggest bowl containing the soup (*thuai kaeng*) is positioned in the middle. Glutinous rice is served in bamboo boxes. On festive occasions several *pha khaow* are served. Each seats five or six guests. At family meals, children wait for their parents to start eating before beginning with their own meals. A meal is a time for conversation and exchange among family members. People usually drink water after they have eaten. When someone at the table has finished his meal, he joins the palms of his hands in a *nop* as a gesture of gratitude to Lord Buddha and leaves the circle without having to wait for the others to finish — unless there are guests present.

In Luang Prabang, which is in the north, the masks of Pou Nyer and Nyar Nyer — the legendary ancestors of the Laotians — are kept in a temple and brought out ceremoniously on the occasion of Pimai, the Laotian New Year, which falls in April. Young men put on the masks and dance for the prosperity of the Laotians. According to legend, at the beginning of time, a huge vine linked the earth to the heavens. The vine prevented the sun from lighting and warming the earth, and people could not cultivate rice to feed themselves. Pou Nyer and Nyar Nyer, an old couple, volunteered to cut the vine. Knowing that they would be killed by the falling vine, they asked that their descendants not forget them. This is why in Luang Prabang, before eating a meal, the elder members of the family say, "*Ma Nyer! Kin Nyer!*" (Come, great-grandparents! Eat, great-grandparents!) This is done in memory of these legendary ancestors.

INSIDE THE LAOTIAN KITCHEN

Padek (fermented fish paste) is the basic ingredient of Laotian cuisine. In the past, every self-respecting household would make its own *padek*. Nowadays, people prefer to buy *padek* from the market, or simply replace it with either *nam par* (fish sauce) or *kuer* (salt). To make *padek*, cleaned fish is tightly packed with salt in a stone jar and left to ferment for at least one year. The brown liquid (*nam padek*) is used as a condiment. The salted fish can be steamed in banana leaves (*mawk padek*) or simply fried with onion and garlic (*juern padek*). *Nam par* is fish sauce obtained from letting fish ferment in brine.

ESSENTIAL COOKING TECHNIQUES

Most food is boiled (*tom*), cooked in hot embers (*jee*), grilled (*ping*), steamed plain (*nueng*) or steamed in banana leaves (*mawk*).

ESSENTIAL KITCHEN IMPLEMENTS

The *kheang* (a 10-centimeter-thick chopping board made from the cross-section of a tree) is one of the most indispensable utensils in a Laotian kitchen, since most ingredients are either chopped or minced. A variety of knives are used to chop meat or finely mince vegetables and herbs. Take note that knives are never found on the meal tray.

The *khok* (mortar) and *sark* (pestle) are used for pounding, a frequent operation. Earthenware or aluminum pots called *maw* are used for boiling. The *maw kaeng* is a pot used for making soup. It is the pot which a *huad* (a plaited bamboo container used to hold rice or other items) is placed on. A *maw kharng* (wok or frying pan) is also essential. Bowls (*thuai*) are used when mixing ingredients. They are also used to contain sauces and measure ingredients. For big bowls of soup, a *thuai kaeng* is used. The *jong* is a ladle fashioned out of a coconut shell. It usually has a beautifully carved wooden handle. For scooping drinking water out of a water jar, a deeper *jong* called a *kabuai* is used. The *antong* or *kasong* is a strainer made of thin woven strips of bamboo. It is used to hold *padek* when you only need to add the sauce to your dish. The solid bits, such as the bones, remain in the strainer. The *antong* or *kasong* can also be used to filter any liquid, including coconut milk.

CLOCKWISE (from above) Four newly ordained monks carrying bowls carefully wrapped to resemble the Naga. The bowls are traditionally presented to them by their families; Monks returning from collecting alms in the morning, Vientiane; and Hanging rice baskets, Lao Textile Museum.

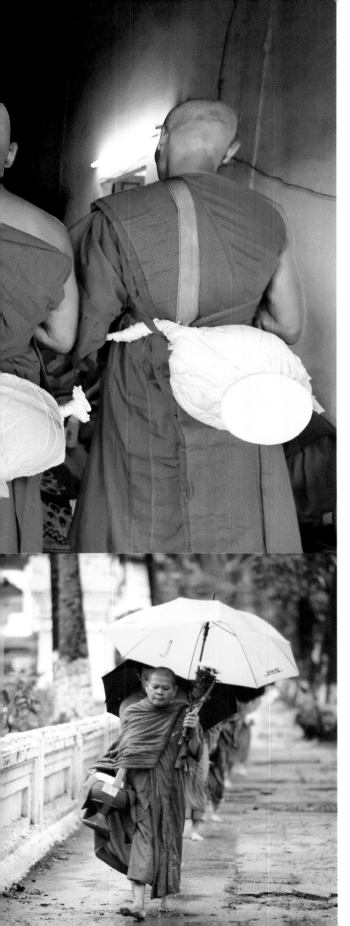

Taboos on eating

There are a few taboos on eating in Lao PDR. If you eat while lying down, the common belief is that you will become a snake. The person who does not shut the lid of the rice box after eating from it faces the prospect of having a marriage which ends in divorce. One should never empty a rice box; always leave a small ball of rice to attract more! Young people must not eat chicken gizzard or liver because if they do, they will become stupid and fail at school. Young people should not eat snakefish guts, which is considered a delicacy, either. If they do, they will feel cold and may even die. If someone has to leave for a long trip during the meal, the tray should be moved a little from its former place so that the person who has left will have a safe trip.

These bits of popular wisdom may have been created to teach children how to behave at the meal tray. Or they may be tricks adults have developed to save the choicest pieces of food for themselves. Perhaps they are mere superstitions. Whichever the case, children usually leave the best pieces of food for their parents and grandparents. In turn, parents and grandparents return those best pieces to the children.

According to the Laotian calendar, each year is marked by the Heed Sipsong (Twelve Festivals) and Khong Sipsee (Fourteen Traditions). Some of the festivals are related to the life of Buddha; the traditions are events that stand out as milestones in the life of a Laotian. During these festivals and events, be they festive or sad, eating is an important part of the ceremony and cooking is a vital activity. If you hear big knives making chop-chopping sounds as you walk past a house, it means that preparations for some event are afoot. The kitchen — which is sometimes extended outdoors to accommodate the unusually large number of people and extra stoves — is usually busy and noisy, punctuated by the banging of utensils against one another, loud conversations and joyous laughter.

In the case of a death, the body of the deceased is kept in an elaborate catafalque in the house for up to one week before it is taken to the *vat* (temple) for cremation. Every day the family has to feed the monks who come to pray, as well as the relatives and friends who will visit. The kitchen is busy all day and all night until the third day after the cremation. Throughout this time, visitors are served *khaow peeak* (rice gruel) and *tam mak som* (pounded sour salad).

On festive occasions such as a *baci* ceremony (a mixture of Brahman and animist rituals of spirit calling, which is conducted in important events like births and weddings), a Buddhist offering, or a house-blessing ceremony, the extended kitchen will also resound with noise and laughter. Female relatives, friends and neighbors

THIS PAGE Women wrapping
rice desserts.

OPPOSITE Small round
eggplants commonly used in
Laotian cuisine.

will come to the house to offer their help, each naturally doing her part of the work without anyone giving orders to anyone else. When the menu has been decided upon and all the items needed are bought from the market, teams are organized according to their various specialties. Some will chop the meat while others scale fish, wash vegetables or mince herbs. Everybody knows what herb goes into which dish and no mistake is ever made. When mealtime comes, all the dishes seem to appear on the tables or trays as if by magic. And there will always be enough for the wave upon wave of guests expected.

On holy days (the eighth and fifteenth days of the waxing moon, and the eighth and fourteenth days of the waning moon) or at religious festivals, each family brings one or several dishes to the *vat* of its area or village. Here, again, women play the main role, placing the dishes in small bowls and the bowls on round trays. Each tray has nine bowls containing nine dishes, plus a box of glutinous rice, a jug of water and a glass. However, the trays can be presented to the monks only by men.

Each senior monk is offered a tray and several novices are expected to share a tray. After the monks have eaten and chanted their blessings, the bowls are refilled and all the laypeople present sit around the trays to eat together. On the anniversary of the death of a parent or grandparent, children bring a tray with nine bowls containing the favorite dishes of the deceased to the temple. The whole tray, including the bowls, spoon, water jug, glass, napkin and rice box, is offered to a monk. After eating the food, the monk will say a prayer to transfer the food and merits to the departed.

During the three-month rainy-season retreat (roughly July through September), there are no Buddhist festivals. No weddings are held. There are no celebrations. This is the period of the Buddhist Lent, a time for more intense religious life, prayer and meditation among monks as well as laypeople. Only two ceremonies are held during Lent. Both are offerings to the dead. One of them is *Hor Khaow Padap Din* (to wrap rice and place it on the ground), which is held mid-Lent. Food wrapped in banana leaves is left on the temple grounds. It is believed that in the darkness of the night, the spirits of the dead come and enjoy the food on this one day when the guardian of the Other World allows them to come out and receive food offerings from the living. Fifteen days later, on *Hor Khaow Salak* (to wrap rice and make a draw) day, each member of the clergy draws a basket from the many containing dried food and amenities that have been delivered to the temple. Each basket bears the name of a deceased and the names of the members of their family who have made the offering. The monk or novice who gets a basket will pray in order to transfer the offerings to the dead.

Nuance and subtlety

Laotian dishes are never too hot, salty, sweet or sour. Any excess is considered in bad taste. Everything lies in nuance and subtlety. Like lunch and dinner, breakfast is meant to be a full meal, although fewer dishes are served. And *jaew* is an important part of every meal. It is a gravy that, in the case of modest families, is sometimes considered a dish in itself. You dip your ball of glutinous rice in it. It gives a tasty flavor to the rice. *Jaew bong*, a specialty of Luang Prabang, is made of grilled dried chili pounded with garlic, shallots, *nam par* (fish sauce), sugar and buffalo skin. Other popular gravies are *jaew mark den* (tomato), *jaew mark phet dip* (green chili), *jaew het* (mushroom), *jaew kheeng* (ginger) and *jaew kapih* (shrimp paste). *Jaew* can be stored for several days. *Jaew bong* can even be kept in a glass container for several months. There are always a few kinds of *jaew* sitting in the Laotian kitchen, ready for hungry children back from school who usually snack on balls of glutinous rice dipped in them.

In cities and modern homes, people use gas stoves and have Western-style kitchens. In the countryside, however, the kitchen is usually kept separate from the living quarters. At the heart of the traditional Laotian kitchen is a clay platform which serves as a hearth. One or several stoves (or braziers) are placed on the platform. The stove can either be specially built for charcoal fires or just a simple iron tripod. Above the stoves, bamboo utensils such as rice boxes and meal trays are hung from the ceiling and left to smoke — this kills the wood worms and gives the utensils a nice brown hue. Men are not supposed to enter the kitchen, which is the kingdom of women. When cooking at the stove, the cook is seated on a wooden or rattan stool. She carries out all other operations seated on a straw mat. On holy days the elder woman of the family places flowers at a corner of the hearth as well as on the lid of the stone jar used to store rice grains. Every time she removes some rice grains for her cooking, she must immediately return three handfuls of what she has taken to the jar and say, "When we eat you, don't let your quantity diminish, when we take you from this jar, don't let your quantity decrease." By doing so, the family hopes to always have enough rice to eat.

THIS PAGE (top) Rice vendors are a common sight in markets. The most popular kind of rice in Lao PDR is a glutinous one called khaow kai noi (meaning "chick rice"); (above) Barbecued meat often sold at local markets.

OPPOSITE The clay hearth found in most traditional Laotian kitchens.

Tam mak som

Pounded sour salad

This snack is popular among women and young girls, although men are allowed to eat it too. It can be enjoyed at mealtime or any other time of the day and is available at just about every street corner in Lao PDR. You can choose to use cucumber, yard-long beans or green bananas as a base, but green papaya (tam mak houng) is the most popular.

Young people, boys and girls alike, like it hot. Sometimes, when several teenagers prepare a tam mak som, they might decide to add up their ages and use that many chilies in the dish. The hotter it is, the funnier they find it. Of course, the resulting fieriness often brings tears to their eyes!

Mark uek

Chef's note:
Mark uek are sour, hairy orange or yellow eggplants slightly smaller than a golf ball. Use a vegetable peeler to remove the hairy fuzz on them.

Serves 8

5 red chilies, chopped
4 cloves garlic, chopped
2 tablespoons *nam padek* (fermented fish paste sauce)
4 *mark uek* (see Chef's note on this page), quartered

5 medium tomatoes, quartered
2 limes, juiced
2 green papayas, peeled and shredded
nam par (fish sauce)
lime juice to taste

1. Pound the chilies and garlic, then add *nam padek*, *mark uek*, tomatoes and lime juice. Pound and mix with a spoon.

2. Add the papaya, pound and mix. Add *nam par* and more lime juice if needed. Serve with fresh salad or water convolvulus.

Larp

Larp is one of the national dishes of Lao PDR. Its name means "luck," which explains why this dish is served on all festive occasions. Eating larp, *it is believed, will bring you good luck. There are many variations on this dish. Either raw, partly cooked or cooked chopped meat (or fish) is seasoned with herbs, lemon juice, pounded roasted rice grains and fermented fish sauce. These days,* larp *is sold at roadside stalls and can be eaten every day. It is usually served with fresh or steamed vegetables.*

Serves 8

1 kilogram chopped beef (boiled to
    preferred doneness)
500 grams boiled offal, sliced
1 tablespoon finely chopped *galangal*
    (blue ginger)
1 tablespoon *nam padek* (fermented fish
    paste sauce)
5 small shallots, peeled and finely chopped
2 cloves garlic, peeled and finely chopped
2 tablespoons lime juice
2 tablespoons ground roasted rice grains
1 teaspoon chili powder
nam par (fish sauce) to taste
extra lime juice

For the garnish
a handful of mint leaves
a handful of coriander, chopped
1 tablespoon sliced red chilies

For the accompanying vegetables
cucumber, sliced
round eggplants (served raw)
khom kadaw (young leaves or
    flowers of the neem tree)
phak khaothong (chameleon leaf)

1. Mix the chopped meat and offal with the *galangal*, *nam padek*, shallots, garlic, lime juice, ground roasted rice grains and chili powder. Add *nam par* and more lime juice if needed.

2. Garnish with mint, coriander and fresh chilies. Serve with accompanying vegetables.

Chef's note:
Ground roasted rice grains are made by first dry roasting them until brown in a pan. Place them in a mortar and grind them until they look like coarse sand (or you may use a coffee grinder).

If *khom kadaw* and *phak khaothong* are not available, rocket or radicchio leaves are possible substitutes.

Khaow poun nam kathih

Spicy rice noodles in coconut gravy

This dish is also central to all occasions in Lao PDR whether festive or sad. It used to be served only at the wealthiest tables, but khaow poun *is now sold at street stalls and served with many kinds of gravies. The special day for eating* khaow poun *is the last day of the That Luang (National Grand Stupa) festival in Vientiane (which falls on the fifteenth day of the waxing moon of the twelfth lunar month, usually around November). After the morning alms-giving ritual which involves several thousand worshippers, including the country's most prominent leaders, every family sits down to a meal of* khaow poun *at the hundreds of stalls scattered along the That Luang Esplanade.*

Serves 8

2 kilograms ready-cooked *khaow poun*
  (rice noodles)

For the gravy
1 chicken
3 stalks lemongrass, bruised
10 slices *galangal* (blue ginger)
nam padek (fermented fish paste sauce)
  or *nam par* (fish sauce) to taste
salt to taste
500 grams *pa nang* (a variety of catfish)
5 shallots, peeled and chopped
2 cloves garlic, crushed
1 teaspoon chili powder
5 red chilies, grilled
1.5 liters *kathih* (coconut milk)
20 kaffir lime leaves

For the accompanying vegetables
200 grams bean sprouts
200 grams mint leaves, chopped
200 grams banana blossom, sliced
200 grams yard-long beans, sliced into
  small rounds
200 grams water convolvulus, cut into
  5-centimeter lengths and blanched
200 grams cabbage, shredded

For the garnish
10 spring onions, finely sliced

1. Place chicken in a large pot with lemongrass and *galangal*. Add *nam padek* and salt to taste. Cover with water and simmer for an hour. Remove the chicken. Strain the broth and set aside. Separate the meat from the chicken carcass and mince it.

2. Boil the fish in a separate pot with water and separate the flesh from the bones. Pound or mix the chicken and fish together. Add to the broth.

3. Pound the shallots, garlic and chili powder together to create a paste. Cook the paste slowly in a frying pan with the grilled chilies and *kathih*. Stir constantly to get a fragrant, oily liquid paste with a beautiful orange and red hue.

4. Bring the pot of broth to a boil. Add the fragrant, oily liquid paste and allow the broth to simmer. Add kaffir lime leaves. Season with *nam padek*, *nam par* or salt if needed.

5. To serve, place some *khaow poun* in a bowl. Top with vegetables before pouring some gravy over it. Finally, garnish with spring onions.

Chef's note:
If fresh *khaow poun* is not available, dried rice noodles or vermicelli can be used.

Mawk kai

Chicken steamed in banana leaf

Banana leaves

Mawk *refers to the technique of steaming a dish wrapped in banana leaves. A mawk dish can be made using anything from fresh or fermented fish to pork brains. It is an easy dish to make. For* mawk kai, *pieces of boneless chicken meat and giblets are rubbed with salt, then wrapped with pounded shallots, lemongrass, chili, chopped spring onions and crushed kaffir lime leaves. The mouth-watering aroma of the condiments is encased within the banana leaf, which also adds its own fragrance as the dish is cooked.*

Serves 8

1 chicken (about 1.5 kilograms)
5 stalks lemongrass, sliced
8 shallots, peeled and chopped
5 dried chilies, deseeded, soaked in
   water and drained

3 tablespoons *nam par* (fish sauce)
salt to taste
10 spring onions, chopped
10 kaffir lime leaves

1. Debone chicken and then chop the meat into bite-size cubes. Rub chicken cubes with salt and set aside.

2. Pound lemongrass, shallots and dried chilies to form a fine paste (alternatively, use a food processor). Add *nam par*, salt, chopped spring onions, kaffir lime leaves and chicken pieces to the paste. Mix well.

3. Divide chicken mixture into eight portions and wrap them in banana leaves or aluminum foil. Steam the packages for 45 minutes to 1 hour before serving.

Kaeng nor mai

Bamboo shoot soup

Bamboo shoots can easily be found wherever there is a bamboo grove. And bamboo groves are found in or near every village across Lao PDR. Kaeng nor mai is cooked with crushed yanang (Tiliacora triandra) leaves, which help temper the bitterness of bamboo shoots and give the soup a greenish color.

Serves 8

100 grams *yanang* leaves
1 kilogram fresh bamboo shoots, cleaned
   and cut into 5-centimeter lengths
100 grams *khaow puey* (roasted steamed
   glutinous rice)
10 slices *galangal* (blue ginger)
3 stalks lemongrass, sliced
5 shallots, peeled and chopped

2 cloves garlic, peeled and chopped
6 red chilies, sliced
padek (fermented fish paste) to taste
300 grams pumpkin, peeled and cubed
200 grams reconstituted cloud ear fungus
   (see Chef's note on this page)

1. Crumble *yanang* leaves in 500 milliliters of water. The water should turn dark green. Bring water to a boil. Add bamboo shoots and *khaow puey*.

2. Pound the *galangal*, lemongrass, shallots, garlic and chilies in a mortar and pestle. Add *padek* and pound some more. Add this paste into the boiling liquid along with the pumpkin and cloud ear fungus. After the broth has reduced and thickened, serve in a large bowl.

Chef's note:
Cloud ear fungus is most commonly sold dried. Reconstituted cloud ear fungus is simply dried fungus that has been soaked in water and drained.

Phan sin choum

Beef wrapped in lettuce leaf

Phan (meaning "wrapped") dishes are often served when family members or friends get together. Diners essentially prepare their own meal. Thin slices of meat (or fish) are cooked in a pot of boiling broth, which is placed over a flame at the table. When the fish or meat is cooked to the diner's preferred doneness, it is wrapped in a salad leaf or cabbage leaf, with rice noodles, onions, garlic, ginger, galangal (blue ginger), lemongrass, sliced star fruit or green mango, tomato (for a hint of a sourness), sliced unripe bananas (to add some bitterness), grilled peanuts and herbs like mint, coriander and dill (which is paired only with fish). The leaf is carefully rolled and folded to encase all these ingredients so as to ensure that nothing falls out when the vegetable packet is dipped in the gravy and eaten. When a diner's mouth is filled with phan, *the rest of the people at the table will tease him by asking him questions. Usually, he is not able to respond, leading everyone to burst into laughter.*

Lettuce leaves

Serves 8

1 kilogram lean beef, thinly sliced

For the broth
2 liters coconut water (also referred to as coconut juice)
4 tablespoons *nam par* (fish sauce)
1/2 shallot, peeled and sliced

For the gravy
nam padek (fermented fish paste sauce) to taste
10 red chilies, sliced
1 small pineapple, peeled and cubed
250 grams tamarind pulp, seeds removed
100 grams sugar

For the accompaniments
1 kilogram lettuce leaves
1.5 kilograms *khaow poun* (rice noodles)
500 grams cabbage, shredded
10 onions, peeled and sliced
5 heads garlic, peeled and minced
1 whole ginger, peeled and shredded
1 whole *galangal* (blue ginger), peeled and shredded
10 stalks lemongrass, thinly sliced
3 star fruits, thinly sliced
15 small tomatoes, quartered and thinly sliced
2 unripe bananas, peeled, halved and sliced
100 grams roasted peanuts
100 grams mint leaves
200 grams coriander leaves

1. You will need a setup similar to that of a fondue pot. To make broth, combine the ingredients in a pot and bring to a boil. Keep it boiling at the table.

2. To make gravy, combine all the ingredients and bring to a boil, creating a liquid paste. Set aside.

3. To eat this dish, put a slice of meat in the boiling broth until it is cooked to your preferred doneness. Remove and place it on a lettuce leaf with some *khaow poun* and a little of each of the other accompanying ingredients. Roll it into a tight packet and dip it into the gravy just before taking a bite of it.

Oh larm

Stew

Oh larm *is a specialty of Luang Prabang, the former royal capital of Lao PDR. This dish is enjoyed just as much at the royal palace as it is in the most modest of bamboo huts. Chicken, beef or water buffalo is usually used, but deer, wild boar or wild rooster make superb delicacies as well. If you are not from Luang Prabang, do not try to serve someone from there* oh larm *which you have made. He or she will snub it.*

Serves 8

1 kilogram beef or buffalo meat,
   cubed and seared
100 grams crisp-fried buffalo skin
5 stalks lemongrass, bruised and
   lightly roasted
10 shallots, peeled and lightly roasted
300 grams yard-long beans, cut in
   2-centimeter lengths
200 grams *mark khuer* (round eggplant,
   usually green)
200 grams *mark khaeng* (pea eggplant)
6 red chilies
100 grams reconstituted cloud ear fungus
   (see Chef's note on page 99)
1 piece *sakharn* wood (a big vine from the
   pepper family), cut into 12 small pieces

100 grams *khaow buer* (see Chef's note
   on this page)
salt to taste
padek (fermented fish paste)
500 grams *phak tamnin* (*Melothria
   heterophylla*)
100 grams *phak bualapha* (wild basil)
100 grams *phak see* (dill), chopped
200 grams spring onions, sliced into
   2-centimeter lengths
100 grams *phak ee too* (sweet basil)

For the garnish
finely chopped spring onions

Chef's note:
Khaow buer is glutinous
or normal rice that has
been soaked in water
and then pounded.

1. Cover the meat and buffalo skin with water. Bring to a boil. Add lemongrass, shallots, yard-long beans, *mark khuer*, *mark khaeng*, chilies, cloud ear fungus, *sakharn* wood, *khaow buer*, and salt to taste. Stir to obtain an unctuous broth.

2. Bring to a boil before adding *padek* using a fine-meshed strainer. Finally, add *phak tamnin*,

phak bualapha, *phak see* and spring onions. Keep cooking over a medium flame until the meat is tender. Add the *phak ee too* leaves and remove the pot from the heat. Serve in a large bowl and garnish with finely chopped spring onions.

Sangkhanya mak ueh

Coconut custard steamed in pumpkin

Sangkhanya *is a custard made with sugar and coconut milk. It can also be served over glutinous (sticky) rice wrapped in banana leaves (*khaow sangkhanya*) or steamed in a coconut shell (*sangkhanya mak phao*). This is a great treat. It used to be served at children's birthday parties before European-style cakes became popular in Lao PDR.*

Pumpkins

Serves 6 - 8

1 medium pumpkin (20-centimeters wide)
10 eggs
200 grams sugar
250 milliliters coconut milk
a pinch of salt

Chef's note:
It is easier to check the doneness of the custard if you halve the pumpkin vertically and fill the two halves with the coconut-egg mixture before steaming them.

1. Cut off the top of the pumpkin and deseed. Retain the pumpkin top, which will serve as a lid.

2. Beat the eggs with sugar, coconut milk and salt. Pour this mixture into the pumpkin, cover with the pumpkin top and steam for 1 hour or until the custard is firm.

3. Serve in wedges.

Malaysia

Introduction by Julie Wong
Recipes by Redzuawan "Chef Wan" Ismail

What makes Malaysian food fabulous is also what makes the nation great: its ethnic, cultural and religious tolerance. This climate of tolerance has allowed the major races to continue practicing their own cultural, religious and culinary preferences. As a result, what you find in Malaysia are three distinct, dominant cuisines: Malay, Chinese and Indian. There is no "Malaysian cuisine" as a single entity; what is referred to is an amalgam of cuisines.

Malay cuisine

The best of Malay cuisine is based on aromatic herbs, leaves and ginger, enlivened with a pungent spice paste. The icons of Malaysian food all have strong Malay influence and the recipes included in this chapter reflect this. *Nasi lemak* (a coconut rice dish) is the unofficial national dish; *satay* (skewered meat) is as famous in Malaysia as it is in its country of origin (Indonesia); most Southeast Asian countries have a *laksa* (a spicy, soupy noodle dish) of their own and Malaysia has not one, but a dozen different *laksas*, with nearly every one of its 13 states having a distinctive variant of the dish.

And it is in its *laksa*, *kerabu* (salad) and *nasi ulam* (rice topped with local herbs) that one gets the full spectrum of the indigenous aromatics such as torch ginger flower, polygonum, lemongrass, *galangal* (blue ginger), turmeric, turmeric leaf, curry leaf, *ulam raja* (cosmos), *selom* and *kalamansi* lime — all of them very strongly flavored. When used together, the Malaysian "bouquet garni" is an explosive potpourri of scents and sensations, especially when you add to the equation pungent dried shrimp paste (*belacan*) and bird's-eye chilies, not to mention the fermented durian condiment known as *tempoyak*. Like Indian food, the aroma of the dish is a large part of the seduction of Malay food.

Bunga kantan, *torch ginger flowers*, are one of the key ingredients that give Malaysian cuisine its distinctive flavor.

The various herbs and types of ginger are also taken for their health-promoting qualities and as digestives, expelling flatulence and keeping the body warm. *Kunyit* (yellow ginger or turmeric) has a festive connotation and is used to flavor and color rice for weddings and celebrations, such as in *nasi kuning* and the glutinous *nasi kunyit*. In the animist Malay world of old, it is believed that the *kunyit* can ward off evil and protect people from harm.

Chicken is the favorite meat, being cheap and tasty, followed by fish and beef. The buffalo is a significant animal in rural Malaysia, especially among the farming community. Besides providing beef, it is a workhorse as well as a sacrificial "cow." On the morning of Hari Raya Haji, an Islamic celebration to mark the end of the haj pilgrimage season, a buffalo is slaughtered and its meat distributed to the poor.

Malay food is hot and spicy, but it is much more than that. Although the Malays — and Malaysians in general — love hot and sour dishes, they also adore mild, coconut cream-enriched dishes (which they describe as being *lemak*) and colorful sweetcakes made of rice flour and scented with pandan leaf.

Most of all, Malaysians love their *sambal belacan*, a condiment of fresh red chilies and toasted *belacan* (dried shrimp paste) pounded in a mortar and pestle, and finished with a squeeze of *kasturi* (*kalamansi*) lime juice. Some Malaysians add shallots or garlic to it, or a pinch of sugar, and yet others like to sauté their *sambal* with a little oil for a more aromatic and mellow flavor. A richer version is made by adding dried shrimps.

Sambal belacan is eaten with almost everything, from salted fish and smoked beef to boiled vegetables. It is an essential condiment at the table of the rich and the poor, and is also a base ingredient added to a whole host of dishes from *nasi lemak* to *kerabu* salads, stir-fried vegetables and fried rice. It has found its way to the Chinese kitchen, and many popular Malaysian Chinese dishes — from Hokkien fried noodles to curry *laksa* and *lor mee* (noodles served in a dark, starchy gravy) — are served with a spoonful of *sambal belacan*. Indeed, *sambal belacan* is what fires Malaysian gastronomy.

Besides boiling rice, one of the first kitchen tasks that a daughter would be asked to help with is the pounding of *sambal*. While one would not mind using the electric blender to grind curry paste, when it comes to making *sambal*, only the mortar and pestle will do. The stone crushes the chilies and seeds, releasing oil and flavor; the uneven pounding also gives *sambal* a more interesting texture. And some cooks swear that the *sambal* will not taste right if you scoop it out of the mortar with a spoon instead of the fingers! Today, however, it is no longer considered a virtue for a young woman to learn how to cook; excelling in academia and securing a good job is more important.

THIS PAGE A variety of delectable skewered food sold by a satay celup vendor in Malacca. The skewers are dipped into a hotpot of spicy peanut sauce before they are served.

OPPOSITE The secret to making a frothy cup of teh tarik is to "pull" the condensed milk-sweetened Ceylonese tea to incorporate air into it and create bubbles.

Chinese cuisine

The Chinese love eating and have developed a culture of dining out, so Chinese food tends to be more visible because there are more Chinese restaurants and food stalls in the country, especially in the towns and cities. Although Malaysian Chinese food bears many similarities to the food of China, it has its own unique nuances which can be attributed to a Malaysianization of Chinese food. Chinese cuisine has been more adaptable because the Taoist and Buddhist Chinese have fewer food taboos. Malays are Muslims and Islam forbids the eating of pork and other non-halal foods, creating an attitude of cautiousness toward culinary appropriation or fusion among practitioners, while many Hindu Indians are vegetarians.

Borrowing flavorings from Malay and Indian cuisines, popular Malaysian Chinese cuisine has evolved from often bland and salty fare to something more robust and spicy. The impetus for change comes from the reality that many Chinese make a living selling food and therefore need to make their goods more palatable to the spice-loving Malays and Indians.

Malaysian Chinese food is a mixture of the regional cuisines of the Hokkiens, Cantonese, Teochews, Hakkas and, to a lesser extent, Foochows and Hainanese. Fine-dining Chinese restaurants usually serve Hong Kong-style Cantonese food such as dim sum and banquet dishes.

The Chinese flavors that stand out include ginger, garlic, soy sauce, oyster sauce, bean paste, sesame oil, rice wine, spring onion and coriander. Popular Chinese dishes include *popiah* (fresh spring roll), *char kway teow* (fried rice noodles), Hokkien prawn *mee* (a noodle dish), *lorbak* (seasoned meat rolls), *bak kut teh* (pork in an herbal tea stock) and a vast variety of dim sum offerings.

Although many Chinese are Taoist and practice ancestor worship, a large number have converted to Buddhism and Christianity. The new generations of Taoists have taken a pragmatic approach and although food is still specially prepared for the altar during major festivals such as Chinese New Year, fruit and store-bought rice cakes suffice during the rest of the year.

THIS PAGE Kuala Lumpur street food.

OPPOSITE (top right) Fried fritters are commonly sold at street-side hawker stalls in Malaysia.

INSIDE THE MALAYSIAN KITCHEN

While all of Southeast Asia turns to the tropical garden and rainforest for food seasonings and flavorings, and makes use of essentially the same herbs, roots and spices, the preference for certain flavorings and the extent to which they are used differentiate the various cuisines. What provides Malaysian food with its most poignant flavorings is the torch ginger flower, lemongrass, coconut milk and grated coconut, ginger, *galangal* (blue ginger), turmeric root and leaves, a host of aromatic leaves such as polygonum, pandan leaf, curry leaf and kaffir lime leaf, seed spices such as coriander, cumin and fennel, chili and *belacan* (dried shrimp paste), as well as a wide array of soybean-based sauces and sesame oil. The ingredients are usually used in combination to produce complex-tasting gravy.

ESSENTIAL COOKING TECHNIQUES

One needs no complicated techniques to learn in order to cook great Malaysian food. Precision is not required in the cold and hot kitchens, but having patience helps during the long hours of stewing a *rendang* or while making leaf casings for *ketupat*. The cooking techniques used are universal: deep-frying, stir-frying, boiling, steaming, grilling, stewing, braising. The most important skill to acquire in a Chinese kitchen is the control of fire. It is essential to imbuing food with an elusive seared flavor known as the "breath of the wok." Curries are made in two ways: in the first method, the spice paste, meat, liquid and other aromatic ingredients are boiled together in the pot; in the second, the spice paste is fried in oil until it is aromatic before the meat and liquid are added. The latter, referred to as the *tumis* method, generally produces a more aromatic curry. One needs to watch the fire when cooking creamy curries because too high a heat and rapid boiling can cause the coconut milk to curdle.

ESSENTIAL KITCHEN IMPLEMENTS

The top three implements to have in a Malaysian kitchen would be a well-seasoned *kuali* (wok) for frying and steaming, a *periuk* (pot) for boiling rice and soups, and simmering curries, and the *batu lesong* (mortar and pestle), which is used to pound the various spice pastes. A coconut grater is essential if you do not have access to pre-packaged coconut milk. Clay pots are also much valued. Indian cooks swear that curries cooked in a clay pot are imbued with a certain earthiness and warmth, while the Chinese appreciate the clay pot's superior ability to retain heat. Meat requiring long stewing cooks faster in a clay pot.

Indian cuisine

Indian food in Malaysia comes from southern India, reflecting the strong Tamil influence. The curries are richly spicy and in hot hues of red, orange and yellow, introducing exotic spices such as cumin, fennel, cloves, coriander, cardamoms, fenugreek, curry leaves and mustard seeds to the Malaysian pantry. The other Indian ethnic groups living in Malaysia are the Sikhs and Ceylonese (Sri Lankans), who add *chapatti* (a whole wheat flatbread) and *sambol* (pungent condiments), among others, to the repertoire. Indian Muslim food is hugely popular, thanks to the business savvy of the *Mamaks* (an affectionate term meaning "uncle" that Malaysians use to refer to Indian Muslim stallholders) who have opened up restaurants and stalls selling *roti canai* (flatbread cooked on a heavily greased griddle) and *teh tarik* (pulled tea) everywhere. The icons of Malaysian Indian food are dishes such as *roti canai* and *dal* curry, fish-head curry, *korma* curry, Indian *rojak* (a spicy, salad like dish filled with cuttlefish, hard-boiled eggs, deep-fried fritters and tofu, as well as vegetables), *Mamak mee goreng* (fried noodles), *biryani* rice and, most of all, *nasi kandar* and banana leaf rice, both of which are fast-food concepts similar to the *nasi campur* of the Malays and the economy rice of the Chinese, where rice is sold with a selection of pre-cooked dishes. Vegetarian fare with its lentils and yogurt is also usually available at Indian food stalls.

Peranakan cuisine

As mentioned, the uniqueness of Malaysian cuisine lies in the culinary autonomy of the various ethnic groups. There is, however, one exception to the rule of culinary autonomy: the food of the Peranakans, an ethnic subgroup with its own distinct culture, patois and cuisine. The term Peranakan generally refers to the Hokkien-speaking Chinese who settled in Malaya up until the nineteenth century, married the local Malays and practiced a localized way of life. The food of the *baba-Nyonyas* (as the Peranakan men and women are called) is today regarded as one of the earliest examples of fusion food as it marries the culinary traditions of Malay, Chinese, Indian and, to some degree, Thai food. Although the Nyonyas speak a Malay patois and wear the Malay *sarong* and *kebaya*, they embrace Chinese religions, customs and festivals, and include pork dishes in their diet. Nyonya cuisine is ultra rich and spicy, using many of the local herbs and coconut milk favored by the Malays. The most famous contributions of Nyonyas to Malaysian gastronomy include dishes such as *pie tee* (top hats), *kerabu*, *kari kapitan* (captain's chicken curry), *asam* (tamarind) prawns, *jiu hu char* (stir-fried shredded cuttlefish with yam bean) and a plethora of sweetcakes.

In many ways, Nyonya cuisine embodies the combined core values of the various Malaysian cuisines. Perhaps if history had taken a different path, and the cuisines of the ethnic groups living in Malaysia were well assimilated into the local culture, it would resemble Peranakan food.

Indigenous cuisines

The indigenous people living in the interior also have a food based on a reliance on what can be gathered from the natural environment and the forest, but this basic fare remains very much on the gastronomic fringe, found only in homes rather than in restaurants. Small river fish, algae, fowl and forest ferns, shoots and leaves feature a lot in the *orang asli* diet. Food is cooked simply using implements fashioned from nature — rice, fish and chicken are often stuffed into a stump of bamboo or wrapped in leaves, and heated over an open wood fire. Seasoning is minimal. Aside from salt, sugar and pepper, an acidulating agent such as a sour fruit is desirable. Sauces, even simple ones, are rare and food is left to flavor in its own juices.

In a typical Iban longhouse in Sarawak, rice and dishes such as *manok pansoh* (chicken in bamboo) is cooked the way it has been done for centuries, stuffed inside a length of bamboo sealed with leaves. Life is simple and food fulfills its purpose of sustaining life. Ingredients for the pot are harvested from the rainforest and rivers whenever possible; many locals also engage in backyard cultivation of vegetables and the rearing of chickens. Meat is a treat and fish is available only when a catch is netted. However, the use of the wok has reached the interior and food is cooked by frying, boiling and steaming.

In the longhouse where up to 30 families may live under one roof, the family works, eats, sleeps and cooks in the same space. In the morning, foam or straw mattresses are rolled up and put away, and the "bedroom" becomes the living or dining room. Food is eaten with the various dishes laid out in plates and bowls on the floor, and family members gather around, sitting cross-legged or with legs folded under and tucked away. Food is taken with the hand or a spoon.

One of Sarawak's best-loved dishes is *umai*, a salad of raw fish or prawn tossed in lime juice, shallots and chilies. The dish is credited to the Melanau tribe, who are skilled fishermen.

THIS PAGE (above) Coconut fronds are used to create these woven casings which are initially filled with uncooked rice. When these are boiled, the rice grains expand and become compressed. This transforms them into the festive ketupat *rice that accompanies* satay *and other rich and spicy dishes such as beef* rendang.

OPPOSITE Noodle vendors always have a pot of boiling water ready for scalding noodles, and cooking meat and vegetables.

Regional cuisines

One may argue that Malaysia has no regional cuisines, because the landscape, vegetation and climate (which usually give rise to regional variations) are the same throughout the country. But just as Malaysians like to identify themselves as coming from a certain state (of which there are 13, nine of them with royal houses, each headed by a Sultan) and speak different regional dialects, one can still find culinary differences between states.

The northern states of Peninsular Malaysia share a border with Thailand and have landscapes dominated by rice fields. The Thai influence is strong in the local cuisines and rice dishes reign supreme, especially in Kelantan, where they come in colorful hues: indigo-colored *nasi kerabu*, brown-speckled *nasi dagang* [a kind of glutinous (sticky) rice] and saffron-colored *nasi kunyit* (turmeric rice).

Still within the northern ambit is the island of Penang, considered a food paradise. From *asam laksa*, fruit *rojak* and *ais kacang* (a shaved ice dessert) to prawn noodles, curry *mee*, *lor mee* and *char kway teow*, the Penang hawkers do it supremely well. Penang is a Hokkien and Peranakan stronghold, and the food reflects that. The island is also renowned for Indian-Muslim (locally referred to as *Mamak*) food such as *nasi kandar*, *Mamak mee goreng* and Indian *rojak*.

Perak is famous for its tin mines, *rendang tok*, silky *kway teow* rice noodles and bean sprouts. Cantonese food predominates in the state capital of Ipoh. There is also a sizable Hakka population and Hakka food such as *yong tau foo* and Hakka noodles can be found in the state.

The food in the central region around the capital city of Kuala Lumpur is very much a hodgepodge of the food of the various Malaysian states because the area is populated by out-of-towners who have come to work in the city. Through the years the exodus has spilled over to the neighboring state of Selangor.

Minangkabau cuisine has its home in Negri Sembilan, while Malacca is famous for its Peranakan and Portuguese-Eurasian food. The south's most famous dish is *laksa* Johor, a sour and hot noodle dish with a thick, fish-based gravy. Dutch and Javanese influence can be seen in the local Malay cuisine while Teochew specialties dominate the southern Chinese foodscape.

Malay food reigns supreme in the Malay-dominated east coast states and seafood abounds. The east coast beguiles with its *laksam* (a pale, almost white, *laksa* dish of homemade rice sheets in a fish and coconut milk gravy), *keropok lekor* (a fish-based fried snack), *nasi dagang*, *ikan bakar* (grilled fish) and various fish curries.

Yard-long beans are used in a variety of stir-fries and curries in Malay, Chinese and Indian homes across the country.

Sabah is famous for its fresh seafood such as king prawns and lobsters, cooked in the localized Chinese styles popular in the seafood restaurants. And Sarawak has its *laksa* and *umai*. The indigenous influence is strong in east Malaysia, which has over 30 ethnic groups living in the state and having dishes that use ingredients from the rainforest. The people eat a greater variety of ginger, bamboo shoots and ferns, as well as *butod*, a creamy grub. *Sago*-based foods can be found across the two states, being a major producer of *sago*.

Kenduris and the Malaysian open house

Reflecting the generosity of Malaysians, the open house concept of entertaining is very popular, especially on festive occasions and in celebrations. During the holy Muslim celebration of Hari Raya, the doors of Malay homes are open to guests who may drop by throughout the day. Guests help themselves to the pre-prepared food and drinks laid out buffet style. A typical Malay festive spread will include a beef or chicken *rendang*, or both, spicy *serunding* meat floss, *masak merah* (a mildly spiced dish with a tomato-based sauce), a curried mixed vegetable dish of *sayur lodeh*, fried rice vermicelli, *biryani* rice, palm leaf-wrapped *ketupat* (compressed rice parcels), a cold drink made from rose syrup, and various colorful cakes and festive cookies. This *kampung* (village) way of entertaining has been taken up by the other races, as well as the corporate world.

In the *kampung*, food for festivals and weddings is prepared the *gotong royong* way in which just about the entire village turns up to help. At a wedding I attended on the northern island of Langkawi, a 6-meter-long makeshift wooden platform was erected for preparing food. On it a dozen women sat cross-legged, peeling, chopping and cutting vegetables, herbs, ginger and chilies. The cooking tasks were divided between the genders, the men handling the chopping of meat and slaughtering of animals, as well as the physically demanding work of stirring gigantic cauldrons of curries. Earlier in the day, a water buffalo was slaughtered according to Muslim rites by the village headman, and every part of the animal was used for the feast. The cooking squad was well organized — everyone knew their individual roles, having taken part frequently in such cooking sessions. Chances are, you are likely to encounter the same squad of cooks and helpers at the village's next *kenduri* (feast).

Statistics in this Introduction are based on the 2000 Malaysian census.

Beef putri manis

I first learned to make this dish when I was twelve or thirteen. Since I was the eldest of seven children, I was responsible for helping my mother prepare all the snacks, desserts and dishes that she would sell for a living. Even as a young boy, I would help her make hundreds of ondeh-ondehs [coconut-coated glutinous (sticky) rice balls] or curry puffs — every day, all week, all year round. Most of my time was spent cooking by my mother's side. On weekends I would help women living in our neighborhood with their catering businesses. They would pay me to grind their chili paste for nasi lemak.

So, by the time I was fourteen or fifteen years old, I had become famous for my cooking skills and was a popular chef for hire at Malay wedding banquets. This beef putri manis was my signature dish (the name of the dish literally means "sweet princess beef"). I would prepare it for the bride and bridegroom's table since they are traditionally considered king and queen for the day and are treated like royalty. They are usually served more elaborate dishes than the ones offered to their guests.

Serves 6

3 tablespoons ghee (clarified butter)
10 shallots, peeled and sliced
3 curry leaves
250 milliliters coconut milk
60 milliliters tamarind juice made
   with 2 tablespoons tamarind pulp
   and 60 milliliters water
500 grams rib eye steak, thinly sliced
sugar and salt to taste

For the ground paste
10 shallots, peeled and finely chopped
6 cloves garlic, peeled and finely
   chopped
1-centimeter piece of ginger,
   peeled and finely chopped

1 tablespoon ground fennel seed
1 tablespoon ground cumin
2 tablespoons ground coriander seed
15 dried chilies, soaked in hot water for 10
   minutes, drained and puréed

For the garnish
2 tomatoes, halved
2 potatoes, peeled, sliced and fried
1 large onion, peeled and sliced
   into rings
a handful of coriander leaves,
   coarsely shredded

1. Combine the ingredients for the ground paste in a blender and process until smooth.

2. Heat ghee in a wok and fry shallots and curry leaves until browned and fragrant. Add the ground paste and stir over a low fire until a layer of oil develops. Pour in the coconut milk and tamarind juice. Simmer until the sauce thickens before adding the beef. Fry lightly for 5 minutes. Add sugar and salt to taste.

3. Plate and garnish with tomatoes, potatoes, onion rings and coriander leaves.

Sup ekor
Oxtail soup

This is my version of the soup my paternal grandfather taught my father to make and which he used to cook at weddings. Over the years my father (who was probably influenced by his mother's culinary preferences) made the spice element in this dish much more powerful. In the old days they also did not use tomato paste. That is something I have added to the recipe.

My dad was often given the job of preparing the meat needed at wedding banquets held in our community. He would use the meat scraps to make this soup, which would serve as a quick lunch for the people helping out at the event. I used to watch him make it. He would throw potatoes into his cauldron and they would always fall apart after all that slow cooking. Gradually, I came to realize that they thickened the soup.

In Malaysia sup ekor is a street food which is most frequently enjoyed late at night. At home it is more commonly eaten on Sundays because it takes quite a long time to prepare. I have memories of it being a weekend treat. When I was a child, beef was not an ingredient we had ready access to. It was only on special occasions like weddings that we got to enjoy beef dishes.

Serves 6

500 grams oxtail sections
10 shallots, peeled
4 cloves garlic, peeled
2 stalks lemongrass, thinly sliced
1-centimeter piece ginger, peeled
125 milliliters vegetable oil
1 onion, peeled and diced
4 cardamom pods
1-centimeter-long cinnamon stick
6 cloves
2 star anise

2 tablespoons ground coriander seed
1 tablespoon ground cumin
1 tablespoon ground fennel
2 tablespoons tomato paste
1 beef bouillon cube
1 carrot, peeled and diced
2 stalks celery, diced
300 grams potatoes, peeled and cut into
    large chunks
salt and freshly ground black pepper
    to taste

1. Season oxtail with salt and pepper, dust with flour and sear in hot oil for a few minutes. Remove and set aside.

2. Pound shallots, garlic, lemongrass and ginger with a mortar and pestle into a fine paste (or blend in a food processor).

3. Heat oil in a pressure cooker pan and fry the paste. Add the onion, cardamom pods, cinnamon, cloves, star anise, coriander seed, cumin, fennel and tomato paste, and continue to fry for a few more minutes until fragrant. Add the oxtail, beef bouillon cube, 1 liter of water or beef stock, carrot, celery and potatoes. Cover the pressure cooker and let the ingredients cook for 25 minutes. Release the pressure gradually and remove the lid. Season with salt and pepper.

4. Serve with chopped celery leaves, spring onions and fried shallots.

Dalca kambing
Mutton dalca

Dalca is served at every banquet and Malay wedding. I learned how to make it by watching other chefs prepare it countless times at numerous banquets. Some would just have dal *in their* dalca, *but I like mine with loads of vegetables. The Indian-style* dalca *is usually very thick and contains few vegetables. The Malay version tends to have a lot more vegetables and is not cooked until everything becomes mushy.*

Leftovers are often served with roti canai *(an Indian flatbread) the following day. Day-old* dalca *usually tastes better anyway.*

Serves 6

200 grams yellow split peas
 (either *channa* or *toor dal*)
10 shallots, peeled
2 cloves garlic, peeled
1-centimeter piece ginger, peeled
55 grams ghee (clarified butter)
3 cardamom pods
3 cloves
5-centimeter-long cinnamon stick
2 star anise
4 curry leaf sprigs
6 tablespoons beef curry powder mixed
 with enough water to form a paste
1 kilogram mutton ribs chopped into
 bite-size pieces
1 liter coconut milk

2 potatoes, peeled and quartered
1 large carrot, peeled and cut into
 6 pieces
1 eggplant cut into 6 pieces
6 lady's fingers (okra)
2 green chilies, halved
1 red chili, halved
100 grams long beans, cut into
 3-centimeter lengths
2 tomatoes, sliced or quartered
4 tablespoons tamarind juice made
 with 1 tablespoon tamarind pulp
 and 3 tablespoons water
salt to taste

For the garnish
6 shallots, peeled, sliced and fried

1. Soak yellow split peas in water overnight or for at least 30 minutes. Boil until soft and set aside.

2. Pound the shallots, garlic cloves and ginger into a paste.

3. Heat the ghee and fry the paste with the cardamom pods, cloves, cinnamon stick, star anise and curry leaf sprigs. Add the beef curry paste and fry until fragrant. Add the mutton. Stir

and simmer until tender. Add the coconut milk and simmer for another 10 minutes before adding the split peas and hard vegetables. Allow to cook for another 5 minutes before adding the rest of the vegetables.

4. Finally, add the tamarind juice. When done, the split peas should retain their shape. Do not cook them until they get mashed up. Season with salt and garnish with fried shallots just before serving.

Lady's fingers (okra)

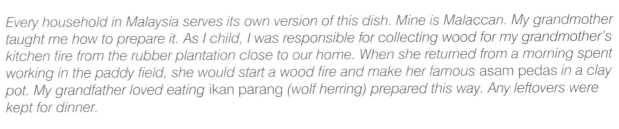

Gulai asam pedas

Hot and sour fish

Every household in Malaysia serves its own version of this dish. Mine is Malaccan. My grandmother taught me how to prepare it. As I child, I was responsible for collecting wood for my grandmother's kitchen fire from the rubber plantation close to our home. When she returned from a morning spent working in the paddy field, she would start a wood fire and make her famous asam pedas *in a clay pot. My grandfather loved eating* ikan parang *(wolf herring) prepared this way. Any leftovers were kept for dinner.*

This dish has become very much part of the Malaysian meal. The Nyonyas have also created their own version of this dish. These days, even Chinese restaurants serve steamed fish with an asam pedas *sauce.*

Serves 6

4 tablespoons chili *boh* (chili paste)
1/2 tablespoon shrimp paste
1-centimeter piece turmeric
8 shallots, peeled
3 cloves garlic, peeled
60 milliliters vegetable oil
500 grams *ikan parang* (wolf herring) cut
　into three portions

125 milliliters tamarind juice made with
　3 tablespoons tamarind pulp and
　125 milliliters water
1 bunch *laksa* leaves (polygonum)
6 lady's fingers (okra)
salt and sugar to taste

Chef's note:
To make chili *boh*, soak 30 dried chilies in hot water for 10 minutes. Drain and purée them in a food processor.

1. Using a mortar and pestle, combine the chili *boh*, shrimp paste, turmeric, shallots and garlic into a paste.

2. Heat the oil and fry the paste until it becomes fragrant. Add the fish and fry for a minute or two before adding the tamarind juice, 750 milliliters of water, *laksa* leaves and lady's fingers. Simmer for 10 minutes. Season with salt and sugar, and serve with rice.

Kerabu udang dan soohoon
Prawn and glass noodle kerabu

This is a dish my Nyonya maternal grandmother used to make. For as long as I can remember, it was served at every birthday celebration because noodles signify longevity. As a young boy, I would squat in front of my grandmother and watch her while she prepared this dish using a batu giling (flat granite grinding stone). Nenek (grandmother) would always say "hor miah" (good life or good blessing in Hokkien, a Chinese dialect). She refused to use a blender, believing that nothing compares to grinding the paste by hand.

Serves 6

300 grams prawns
50 grams glass noodles
4 red chilies
4 bird's-eye chilies
3 large tomatoes
2 cloves garlic
60 grams dried shrimp soaked in
   hot water and drained
4 tablespoons palm sugar

2 limes
3 tablespoons fish sauce
2 kaffir lime leaves, shredded
6 shallots, peeled and thinly sliced
a handful of coriander leaves and
   chives, chopped
25 grams fried shallots
2 fried tofu squares, cubed

1. Cook and shell prawns. Blanch glass noodles in hot water and strain.

2. Pound the red chilies, bird's-eye chilies, tomatoes, garlic, dried shrimp and palm sugar into a paste. Juice the limes. Combine the lime juice, fish sauce and kaffir lime leaves with the paste.

3. Toss in the rest of the ingredients and mix well before serving immediately.

Prawns

Sambal sotong

Spicy squid

When I was growing up, my family was very poor. We would always have sambal ikan bilis *(anchovies) or* sambal *sardine. But once or twice a month, when my father got paid, we would have* sambal sotong. *The wait for my mother to finish cooking the dish always felt so long. Once she placed her* sambal sotong *on the dining table it would be gone in mere minutes because there were seven of us. Very often, she would find us licking the plate!*

Serves 6

8 shallots, peeled
1 clove garlic, peeled
1 large onion, peeled
1 tablespoon shrimp paste
20 dried chilies, soaked in hot water
    and drained
60 milliliters vegetable oil
125 milliliters tamarind juice made from
    2 tablespoons tamarind pulp and
    125 milliliters water

3 tablespoons sugar
2 teaspoons salt
125 milliliters coconut milk
500 grams squid, cleaned and cut into
    small rings

1. Grind shallots, garlic, onion, shrimp paste and dried chilies into a paste.

2. Heat oil and fry paste on low heat for 10 minutes, until the oil begins to float to the surface. Add the tamarind juice, 125 milliliters of water, sugar and salt. Boil until the *sambal* thickens. Add the coconut milk and squid. Simmer for another 3 minutes before serving with *nasi lemak* (refer to *nasi lemak* recipe on page 126).

Acar mentah

Raw salad

This simple dish is eaten either as a salad or as a side dish. Its sour notes pair well with nasi minyak or nasi biryani. You will find it served at every kenduri (banquet), be it one to mark a birth, wedding or death. Just as the Indians serve their curries with chutneys, so the Malays serve theirs with acars. The clean, uncomplicated combination of tart vinegar, salt and sweet pineapple or cucumber offers balance when served alongside richer dishes.

Serves 6

4 tablespoons dried shrimp, soaked in
   hot water and drained
4 red chilies
1 tomato, quartered
1 teaspoon shrimp paste, dry roasted in
   a hot pan until it releases an aroma
1/2 a ripe pineapple, skin and eyes
   removed

1 teaspoon cider vinegar
3 tablespoons sugar
salt to taste
1 cucumber, peeled, deseeded and
   sliced thinly
2 tomatoes, sliced
1 large red onion, sliced

1. Grind dried shrimps, red chilies, tomatoes and shrimp paste into a fine paste. Set aside.

2. Cut the pineapple into eight lengths. Discard the center pulp and slice thinly. Set aside.

3. Mix the paste with the cider vinegar, sugar and salt. Add the pineapple, cucumber, tomatoes and onion to the paste. Mix well and serve immediately.

Pineapples

Nasi lemak

Rice cooked in coconut milk

When I was a child, I was a nasi lemak seller. I would get up at four or five in the morning to help my mother wrap portions of nasi lemak in banana leaves before stationing myself at the gates of my school where I would sell them. My schoolmates would have the nasi lemak for breakfast or save it for recess time. This is an exact reproduction of my mother's recipe.

I remember spending every night soaking dried chilies in recycled milk-powder bottles before grinding them in a batu giling (flat granite grinding stone) for my mother's sambal. Her recipe is special because she boils down her sambal, making it sweet. It would take two whole hours for me to do this! By the time I was done, my hands would feel like they were on fire. I had to cool them down by covering them with grated coconut before wrapping them in plastic bags until one day they no longer burned because I had grown accustomed to it.

Today, nasi lemak is served with all kinds of dishes including beef rendang, fried chicken, sambal ikan bilis (spicy anchovies), sambal sotong (spicy squid) or sambal udang (spicy prawns). Every Malaysian probably has it for breakfast at least once or twice a week.

Serves 6

675 grams fragrant long-grain rice,
  washed and drained
1.125 liters coconut milk
1-centimeter piece of ginger,
  thinly sliced
3 pandan (screw pine) leaves, torn
  and tied into a knot
1 teaspoon salt

Side dishes
85 grams peanuts, deep-fried until
  golden brown
50 grams dried anchovies, deep-fried
  until crispy
3 hard-boiled eggs, peeled and halved
sambal sotong (refer to the *sambal
  sotong* recipe on page 123)

1. Place the rice, coconut milk, ginger, pandan leaves and salt in a heavy-bottomed pot. Simmer until all of the liquid has been absorbed. Stir and reduce the heat to a low fire. Cover the pot and leave the rice to cook for 7 to 10 minutes before serving. Alternatively, you may use a rice cooker.

2. The rice can be garnished with lettuce, tomatoes and cucumber, and served with fried peanuts, deep-fried dried anchovies, hard-boiled eggs and *sambal sotong*.

Myanmar

Introduction and Recipes

by Ma Thanegi

Myanmar lies between India, China, Lao PDR and Thailand, but its cuisine is not influenced by any of its neighbors. Most dishes do not contain strong spices and are rarely steamed. Coconut cream is used only in desserts, and green chilies usually in relishes or fish dishes. Meals are constructed around steamed rice, which is usually served with a soup, curry, a stir-fry or salad, and a sour and salty relish to be eaten with fresh, pickled or blanched vegetables. The dishes must complement one another in texture, taste and aroma (plain soups are paired with rich curries, stronger soups are placed alongside milder-tasting dishes), so how a menu is planned is of utmost importance. Curries in Myanmar are mild because gravy bases are made up of little more than onions, some garlic and a little ginger sautéed until fragrant in peanut oil with a hint of turmeric and a handful of pounded red chilies (usually added for color). Most snacks consist of rice cakes, noodles or deep-fried fritters and are commonly sold at street stalls, but some are prepared collectively by the community in honor of annual celebrations.

For the price of a pot of tea, customers often spend half a day sitting in one of Yangon's many teahouses, making deals or discussing poetry.

INSIDE THE MYANMAR KITCHEN

Shallots, garlic, ginger and chili form the backbone of curry dishes and are required in large amounts. Also, fresh coriander is a must. To flavor dishes, *ngar ngan pyar yay* (fish sauce), which has a strong taste and aroma, is used. *Nga pi* (shrimp paste) is another essential ingredient that often features in relishes. *Lahpet* (pickled tea leaves), pounded and steeped in oil, is always on hand as it is eaten as a snack, usually with nuts, beans, sesame and fried garlic.

ESSENTIAL COOKING TECHNIQUES

The *hsi thut* method consists in sautéing the pounded shallots, garlic and ginger in oil first before adding the meat. This gives the curry a beguiling fragrance.

The *lone che'* method calls for everything to be seared together. All the ingredients apart from the quick-to-cook ones (such as shrimp and soft vegetables or leaves) are mixed together in a pot, which is then placed on the stove and topped with a dash of water. The remaining ingredients are added later.

ESSENTIAL KITCHEN IMPLEMENTS

The Myanmar kitchen is simply equipped. Most dishes can be prepared without the use of specially purchased equipment. The items most prized in the kitchen, however, are the *sint ni don*, a round chopping block cut from the trunk of the tamarind tree; *sint ohs*, small glazed earthenware pots for holding salt, turmeric powder and paprika; and *ya win ohs*, glazed Martaban jars which have bottoms buried in the ground, and which are used to hold water, rice, oil and shrimp paste to last a year.

Myriad cuisines

Comprising seven major races and nearly 130 smaller ethnic groups, Myanmar has a diverse cuisine. The Rakhine in the west use so much chili that unwary dinner guests might think that their tongues have caught fire. In contrast, the Chin in the northwest have a cuisine that is extremely light and highly dependent on the fresh vegetables and roots they gather from the forests. The Shan, who live in the northeast, season their oil-free curries with herbs; the Kachin in the north love steamed vegetables and chopped pork wrapped in banana leaves. The tender meat of the *nanauk*, a placid buffalolike animal that roams wild in the jungles, is prized by both the Chin and the Kachin. The Kayin in the southeast make hearty vegetable stews rich with nutty jackfruit seeds and chunks of bamboo shoot. The Kayah, who live just north of them, love beans, which they cultivate themselves, and the rich pork curry they make using homegrown pigs. The Mon, on the southern coast, eat a variety of seafood unfamiliar to the rest of the country. To adequately describe the myriad cuisines of Myanmar would require several volumes. For the purposes of this book, we have chosen to focus on the food of the Burmese who make up the majority of Myanmar's population.

Most Burmese are Buddhists. However, their taste preferences vary depending on where they live. A meal eaten in the delta would be different from one served in central or upper Myanmar (also referred to as the upcountry regions). The southerners in the delta cook with less oil and eat more fresh greens. They enjoy a great variety of salt-water fish which the people in upper Myanmar consider too strong-smelling. Upcountry dwellers, on the other hand, fill their meals with various beans that abound in their dry fields, cooking them with lashings of oil produced from their own wooden grinders. They prefer freshwater fish and river prawns, but have also developed delicious dishes featuring salted fish and dried shrimp.

There are few hard and fast rules in preparing Burmese food. Each family develops its own specialties and preferred ratio of ingredients. Even towns situated close to one another have quite different cuisines. One town may be famous for a noodle dish worth traveling for, while a neighboring town would boast another culinary triumph. In Myanmar, people are willing to travel great distances just to visit a favorite restaurant, even if it is two towns away.

For the Burmese, dining out often means dinner at a Chinese or Indian restaurant, but at lunchtime traditional Burmese eateries do a flourishing business. At home the family nibbles on snacks throughout the day since vendors constantly walk around neighborhoods hawking their wares. From dawn to way past midnight, the eating goes on. In cities every high-rise apartment will have a string hanging out of a window and reaching down to street level for vendors to attach their bags of snacks. Apartment dwellers merely need to haul their orders up ten stories or so at any time of night or day. Salads are considered snacks, as well as substantial, one-dish meals. They usually consist of vegetables, rice or noodles, and fish cakes, boiled tripe or chopped fritters, all tossed in a dressing of onion oil, tamarind paste and roasted chickpea powder.

Food and auspiciousness

Life in Myanmar centers around two things, food and the concept of *mingalar*, or auspiciousness. A home is thought to be full of *mingalar* if its shrine sparkles with fresh flowers and has three glasses of water and the first three scoops of rice cooked for the morning meal laid out in clean plates. Each symbolizes gratitude toward Buddha, His teachings and His Order. People are considered to have *mingalar* when they behave with dignity. A man is full of *mingalar* when he gets up early, a woman has *mingalar* when her appearance is neat, and children earn *mingalar* when they show respect for their elders.

The New Year in April is heralded with an auspicious display of flowers for Thagyarmin, King of the Celestials, who is believed to make a four-day visit during the Water Festival preceding the New Year to check if little children have been behaving themselves. The Water Festival not only cools everyone down (it occurs at the peak of summer) but supposedly cleanses them of ill fortune so that they might greet the New Year with a fresh start. It is a time of year when people share joy, friendship and food. Communities and organizations will prepare free snacks for passersby and families send desserts to friends. A glass noodle soup called *kyar zan chet* that is considered full of *mingalar* is often served on such special occasions.

OPPOSITE (clockwise from top left) In small monasteries like Maha Htu Payon, a family can earn merit, as our country contributor and her sister did, by preparing the monks' morning meal; In a large monastery like Kya Khat Waing monastery in Bago, feeding between six hundred to a thousand monks every day is a major undertaking and even junior monks have to lend a hand.

THIS PAGE Tomatoes are widely used in Myanmar cooking. They are used to thicken gravies and are served in salads and soups, as well as in the hot and sour relishes that are never absent from a Myanmar table.

OPPOSITE (top) Boiled beans are a popular breakfast food. They are usually fried with rice or eaten with Indian-style naan; (bottom) Betel leaves are filled with slivers of betel nut, shredded glacé coconut, a bit of tobacco leaf, cloves and a sprinkling of anise seed before they are folded into neat triangles and chewed for hours on end.

Every day many households also offer food to monks out on their morning collection of alms. However, a family is especially filled with *mingalar* when it hosts a feast for monks in a ritual known as *soon kyway*, which may be to celebrate a new year, birth or marriage; to sanctify a novitiation of sons (the first social rites of a Buddhist boy's passage into puberty); to bless a new house; or to commemorate a dead person. According to Buddhist philosophy, monks should be detached from worldly desires and must eat without sensual enjoyment, but this does not prevent hosts from offering as generous a meal as they can possibly prepare. *Soon kyway* celebrations are held before noon because monks and nuns cannot eat solids after this time up until the dawn of the next day. Novitiations called *shin pyu mingalar* are especially auspicious, marking the time when boys enter the monastery and get initiated as novices, even if only for a few days or weeks. It is a great prestige for parents to have their sons do this. Daughters have their ears bored at the same time in a ritual called *nar tha mingalar* or the auspicious decorating of her ears.

In towns these feasts are usually held at monasteries because they have big halls that are ideal venues for such occasions. The hosts go from table to table thanking guests for their presence, always exchanging a few words on happy subjects. The food is usually prepared by monastery volunteers who will shop and cook for the specified number of guests. The monks are served first or separately. Guests come and go in groups, and often stay to chat until late into the afternoon. In the smaller villages where the monastery might not have enough space to accommodate large groups, temporary halls called *mandat* which are made of bamboo are built for guests to sit in and chat while nibbling on *lahpet* (pickled tea) after the meal. Another hall is built for use as a dining area. At such country festivities the most prestigious fare the host can offer is glossy red pork curry in pieces "as big as a fist."

Feasts for the spirits

In contrast, feasts thrown for the *nat* or spirits are more about securing worldly fortune rather than earning honorable *mingalar*. Since Buddhism does not offer believers a savior who will come to their rescue as such and salvation depends much on the individual's correct thought and deed, people who want instant assistance sometimes turn to the *nat*, who, if it pleases their willful minds, may deign to reward devotees with more profits or a swifter advancement in their careers. Some spirit devotees do not eat pork, as two of the more powerful *nat*, the Taungpyone brothers, were sons of a shipwrecked Muslim sailor (followers of the Muslim faith do not eat pork). Although the Taungpyone brothers themselves are Buddhist and not restricted from consuming pork, their devotees insist on abstaining from dishes containing it. It is mostly the people who live out in the

countryside and who make a living off the land who worship the *nat*. They believe that ideal weather and seasons of good crops rest on the will of these beings. For the farmers, it seems to be the only plausible explanation for the sudden, dramatic climatic changes they sometimes experience. However, they also usually adore pork, so very diplomatically they choose to make other *nat* (from the pantheon of 37 available) their main patrons rather than worship the Taungpyone brothers.

The people living out in the country are considered the soul of Myanmar. Not only do they make up 90 percent of the population; they also cultivate the rice that the rest of the nation eats. And because the farmers plow their fields with the aid of their bulls, both man and animal are considered benefactors. Many Buddhists don't eat beef because of this. The farmer's work is usually done by October each year, which coincides with the end of the three-month-long Buddhist Lent and the close of the monsoon season. Having time, money and good weather all on hand, they are able to truly enjoy the annual pagoda festivals. These festivals are country fairs filled with traveling shops grouped inside bamboo pavilions. Street vendors simply set up their stoves by the road to cook their fritters and rice cakes. Noodles such as *monhinga* are sold from a stand that has a stove and soup pot at one end and bowls, noodles and condiments at the other. The two ends are connected at the top by a pole, which the vendor then balances on his shoulders when he needs to move from place to place.

The lunar month of Tabodwe

In the lunar month of Tabodwe, villages and communities hold a unique annual celebration which involves cooking the glutinous (sticky) rice dish, *hta ma nai*, in large pans using wooden oars to stir and mash the soft-cooked rice. Such community affairs, usually held on monastery grounds or in someone's backyard, offer the errant young men who had stolen chicken and gourd for midnight suppers, the opportunity to make it up to their elders by tirelessly chopping firewood for the stove, all the while still eying the hen coop in anticipation of another raid. It also gives young lovers a chance to interact. At other times of the year, young sweethearts don't have many opportunities to spend time together alone, since her fierce mother and hot-tempered brothers would most likely be watching them closely. During a community effort like this, the young man is often forgiven for murmuring sweet nothings as he walks past his girlfriend who might be demurely slicing coconuts. His apparent eagerness to serve the community will sit well with his sweetheart's parents. A willingness to help others is an admired trait in men, and for women it is neatness at work. In the past, prospective mothers-in-law would often watch closely as a bride-to-be pounded chilies, checking to see if she was neat and whether the chilies splattered or stayed inside the mortar.

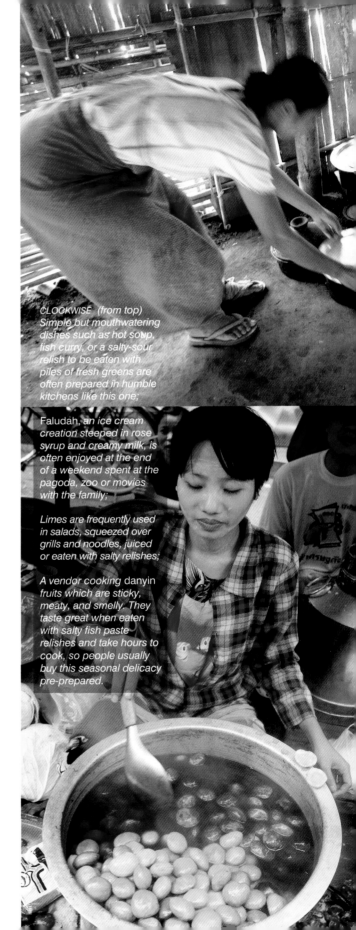

CLOCKWISE (from top) Simple but mouthwatering dishes such as hot soup, fish curry, or a salty-sour relish to be eaten with piles of fresh greens are often prepared in humble kitchens like this one;

Faludah, an ice cream creation steeped in rose syrup and creamy milk, is often enjoyed at the end of a weekend spent at the pagoda, zoo or movies with the family;

Limes are frequently used in salads, squeezed over grills and noodles, juiced or eaten with salty relishes;

A vendor cooking danyin fruits which are sticky, meaty, and smelly. They taste great when eaten with salty fish paste relishes and take hours to cook, so people usually buy this seasonal delicacy pre-prepared.

At mealtimes, particular respect is given to elders. No one may touch a dish before the oldest person has been served. If he or she has somehow been delayed, a spoonful of soup or curry is placed on the rice on his or her plate to symbolize that the eldest has been served. The younger members may then begin their meal. To chat while eating rice is considered highly disrespectful of the staple and to sing or hum at the dinner table is thought to be scandalous — so scandalous that it is believed that the offender will be cursed with having to marry a person many decades older than him- or herself! If rice is spilled onto the floor and one is so careless as to step on it without begging for pardon, it is said that the rice ghost will toss you out of your bed with a nightmare.

However, food isn't important only on formal occasions. At all levels of Myanmar society, it is believed that you remember loved ones most when you eat good food. Thus, it is not unusual for a family to send a dish of curry to relatives, close friends or good neighbors. Sharing food is part of the culture. Farm girls sitting by paddy fields or co-workers eating in the canteen would invite their companions to have a taste of whatever they have in their lunchboxes. Friends who drop in on one's home unannounced are happily welcomed to join in at family meals. Preparing more than the necessary amount of food is the norm, especially when one is entertaining. To be *ei wuk kyay*, which means offering good hospitality, is the credo Myanmar hosts live by. They are not convinced that they've done their jobs as hosts until they are absolutely certain that their guests cannot eat another morsel.

Of all the foods enjoyed in Myanmar, the one dish enjoyed by almost all races is pickled tea leaf or *lahpet*. It is so loved and revered that it is always served to honored guests. It is said that Alaung Sithu, a king of the twelfth century Bagan Kingdom, received it as a gift from celestials nearly over a thousand years ago. At *nat* ceremonies, *lahpet* is also an essential part of the rituals. Farmers agree to their children's engagement by exchanging *lahpet* and betel. Invitations to the subsequent wedding are delivered with a packet of pickled tea. And since a signed document is not required to formalize a marriage, a couple may also legalize their marriage by announcing the union, and serving green tea and *lahpet* to friends and neighbors. In the past, opposing sides of a court case could settle matters with finality only by sharing a dish of pickled tea in the presence of the presiding judge and witnesses. The way this unique snack and honored dish is made and eaten can be likened to the simplicity of life in Myanmar, where one aspires to live in harmony, to share what one has and to behave with dignity and graciousness toward friends and strangers alike.

Kyar zan chet
Glass noodle soup

Kyar zan (glass noodles) are made of mung beans and look like strands of glass when cooked. This dish is considered auspicious because its name corresponds roughly to the term kyar-kyar san, meaning "live long in luxury," and it is often served to the hundreds of guests invited to traditional a-hlu feasts. Usually accompanied by nga hpai thoke (fish cake salad), it makes for a light but satisfying meal.

This is a dish of delicate flavors with a diverse combination of textures. It can also be served as the soup course in a meal of rice and curries.

Kyar zan (glass noodles)

Serves 6 as a main course with nga hpai thoke (fish cake salad)

20 grams dried *hmo chauk* (cloud ear fungus)
20 grams *pan chauk* (dried lily flowers)
12 quail eggs, boiled and peeled
30 fish balls, fried or boiled
1 sheet dried tofu, soaked in water until soft, cut into strips
salt or fish sauce, and pepper to taste
200 grams fine glass noodles, soaked in water for 1 hour, cut into short strands

For the soup stock
1 kilogram chicken bones
1 teaspoon salt
2 tablespoons fish or shrimp sauce
2 slices ginger
50 grams onions
50 grams garlic

For the chicken
500 grams chicken meat, deboned
1/4 teaspoon salt
1/4 teaspoon turmeric powder
20 grams garlic
30 grams onions
4 tablespoons oil
1 teaspoon sweet paprika

For the garnish
lime wedges
30 grams coriander, chopped
nga yoke thee hmont (roasted dried red chili powder)

Chef's note:
To make roasted dried red chili powder (nga yoke thee hmont), pan-fry 50 grams dried red chilies quickly on low heat. Remove stems, and seeds if preferred, and pound roughly. Store in an airtight jar. This step can be done one day ahead.

Fish balls can be made by pounding 200 grams fish paste with 1/8 teaspoon salt until the paste becomes firm enough to be shaped into balls.

1. Start by making the soup stock by adding the chicken bones, salt, fish or shrimp sauce, ginger, onions, and garlic in 2.5 liters of water. Simmer for about 3 hours, topping up with additional water as the liquid reduces. Sieve and chill to remove fat. This can be done a day ahead.

2. Soak *hmo chauk* in warm water, once reconstituted, cut into 3-centimeter squares, removing the hard parts. Drain well and set aside.

3. Wash *pan chauk* well. Tie a knot in each and boil for 5 minutes in a lot of water to remove the smell which can be strong. Drain, squeeze dry and set aside.

4. Prepare the chicken:
a) Cut chicken meat into small cubes and rub with salt and half the turmeric powder.
b) Pound the garlic and onion into a paste.
c) Heat the oil in a pan, add remaining turmeric.
d) Add the garlic-onion paste, and fry until fragrant.
e) Add the sweet paprika.
f) After a few seconds, add the chicken with 50 milliliters water and cook, stirring a few times. Remove from heat when chicken is seared.

5. Bring soup stock to a boil; add the prepared chicken, *hmo chauk, pan chauk,* quail eggs and fish balls, then simmer gently for 5 minutes. Lastly, add the tofu strips. Season with salt or fish sauce and pepper to taste. Remove pot from heat.

6. To serve, place a portion of glass noodles in a bowl and pour the boiling hot soup stock over it. Fine glass noodles cannot be boiled. However, if you are using a firmer version, add the noodles to the soup just before removing the pot from the heat. Set out fish sauce, pepper, lime wedges, coriander and the *nga yoke thee hmont* for guests to add to their noodles.

Nga hpai thoke
Fish cake salad

Salads are an essential part of Myanmar cuisine and are often eaten as snacks. The basic flavorings consist of roasted chickpea powder, onion oil, deep-fried onion slices, fish sauce and lime juice or tamarind paste. This fish cake salad is traditionally served with kyar zan chet (glass noodle soup).

Serves 6 as a side dish

For the fish cake
500 grams fish paste, preferably of *nga hpai* (featherback fish)
1/4 teaspoon salt
Oil to deep-fry fish cakes

70 grams onions
200 grams fresh cabbage, julienned
2 tablespoons *pei hmont a kyet* (roasted chickpea powder)

1 tablespoon fish or shrimp sauce
1 tablespoon shallot oil
2 tablespoons fried shallot slices
lime juice to taste
salt to taste
10 grams coriander or to taste
4 green chilies

1. To make fish cakes, pound fish paste with salt until the paste hardens. Form into flat, round cakes. Deep-fry in hot oil until golden. Cut horizontally into half and then slice thinly.

2. Peel onions and slice thinly. Soak in water.

3. Just before serving, drain the onion slices and squeeze dry. Mix with the fish cake slices and all other ingredients, apart from the coriander, which should be chopped and used as a garnish. Slice green chilies and place them at the table for guests to add to taste.

Chef's note:
To make roasted chickpea powder (*pei hmont a kyet*), pan-fry chickpea powder (also known as *channa dal* or split pea flour) on very low heat until fragrant. It should begin to turn slightly darker. Take care not to let it burn. Cool and store in an airtight jar.

To make fried shallot slices and shallot oil (*kyet thun ni kyaw* and *kyet thun ni hsi chet*), peel and slice 50 grams of shallots. Put the shallot slices with 125 milliliters of peanut oil in a pan on medium heat and fry until golden brown and crisp (about 5 minutes). Do not let them turn dark brown. Remove pan from heat and immediately drain the shallot slices on absorbent paper. Store the cooled oil and fried shallots separately in airtight jars.

Hta ma nai

Glutinous rice with sesame

Celebrating each harvest remains a community effort. Everyone chips in to the cost of the celebrations and many will also offer a lending hand. Central to the revelry is the tradition of cooking many pans of hta ma nai. Invariably, a kitchen is set up on monastery grounds and the cooking continues well past midnight. When every pan is done, most of the helpers head home for a few hours of sleep, usually leaving the grandfathers in the community in charge of keeping the monastery dogs away from the pans of cooling rice. Early in the morning, the young women bathe and put on their finest clothes before delivering packets of the glutinous (sticky) rice wrapped in banana leaves to every household.

This snack may seem a little bland at first, but its appeal lies in the subtle fragrance of ginger, the nuttiness of sesame seeds and peanuts, and the mild sweetness of coconut it brings together in each mouthful.

Serves 6 as a snack with green tea

1 1/2 tablespoons peeled and
   pounded ginger
200 grams glutinous rice, washed
   and drained
1/2 teaspoon salt
200 grams roasted peanuts, skinned
   and crushed into halves
150 grams roasted sesame seeds

For the coconut slices
150 grams fresh coconut flesh (ideally
   extracted in wide bands)
250 milliliters peanut oil

1. Prepare the coconut slices:
a) Cut the coconut flesh into thin strips. The lengths can vary but should be about 3-centimeters long.
b) Heat the peanut oil in a cast-iron or non-stick wok and fry the coconut strips for 10 to 15 minutes on medium heat until golden brown at the edges. Drain and set aside.

2. Remove half the oil from the cast-iron or non-stick wok, then fry the pounded ginger in the remaining oil for half a minute on medium heat. Add the glutinous rice and fry for another half minute, stirring a few times. Add 650 milliliters of water and the salt. Bring to a boil, stirring frequently. After 20 minutes, when the mixture has thickened and the glutinous rice has softened, take the pan off the heat and mash the glutinous rice between two wooden spatulas (this should take 5 minutes).

3. Return the pan to the heat and cook for another 10 minutes, stirring constantly. Be sure to stir hard with a wooden spatula until the mixture becomes dryer and some oil appears at the bottom of the pan. Stir in the peanuts, the sesame seeds and the fried coconut slices. Continue cooking and stirring for another 5 minutes. Remove pan from fire. Serve with green tea.

Chef's note:
To get sections of coconut flesh, crack a coconut open by hitting it sharply with the blunt side of a cleaver (be sure to have a bowl beneath it to contain the water that will leak from it). If the water tastes musty, do not use the coconut. Wrap one coconut half in a towel. Lay it with its cut side down and hit it hard with a hammer to break it into pieces. Unwrap and remove coconut flesh by inserting a flexible thin blade between the shell and the flesh. For this recipe there is no need to cut away the dark skin.

Whet thani chet

Glossy red pork

The high points of every family's social life revolve around soon kyway *ceremonies, special occasions that commemorate weddings, birthdays and other milestones in life. Following the traditional Buddhist rituals, a breakfast or lunch is served to the presiding monks. Guests, often numbering in the hundreds, are also presented with a feast. The whole village, as well as friends from other villages, is invited and expected to attend. To refuse an invitation for whatever reason is considered bad manners.*

While families in the cities might prefer to have their food catered, in the villages the meal is invariably cooked in the backyard by young volunteers under the supervision of an old hand. This gives the young ones a chance to stray away from their parents' watchful eyes and flirt discreetly. On such occasions, being able to serve this glossy red pork in meltingly tender pieces "as big as a fist" is considered highly prestigious.

Serves 6 as part of a multicourse meal

1.2 kilograms pork rump, with rind and
   some fat
2 tablespoons thick, dark soy sauce
1 teaspoon salt
4 slices ginger

150 grams garlic
3 tablespoons peanut oil
3 tablespoons sugar
salt to taste
12 small shallots or pearl onions, peeled

1. Wash, drain and cut the pork into approximately 7-centimeter cubes. Rub well with dark soy sauce and salt. Pound the ginger slices and garlic together, and rub into the pork. Let the mixture stand for half an hour.

2. Heat the oil in a deep pan and add the sugar, cooking until it takes on a dark caramel hue. Quickly add the pork cubes and stir until the meat is seared. If the caramel and garlic stick to the spatula, scrape them back into the pan. Add just enough water to cover and simmer for 2 hours or until the meat and rind are tender, and only a little water remains. Add salt to taste and stir in the peeled whole shallots. Cook until the oil sizzles loudly and the shallots turn translucent. The gravy can be further reduced (until almost dry) if desired.

Karla thar chet
Country-style chicken curry

This is a typical dish enjoyed in the villages. When country lads or karla thar *are called upon to stay up late to keep a lookout for fires during the dry hot summers, they often plan for a supper of stolen chicken and calabash gourd to be washed down with palm wine. By sunrise the following day, they would have snuck off to "visit" other villages until the furor over the thefts has died down. The victims usually do not take legal action, because the thieves are likely to be their own sons or sons of neighbors — in which case they are considered* yut swe yut myo, *those related not by blood but belonging to the same village or town. Within these communities, the idea of the extended family is taken very seriously. Legally obtained chicken, however, tastes almost as good.*

Naturally, this light, soupy dish is cooked quickly. The onions and garlic can be chopped or crushed if you don't wish to pound them. Karla thar chet *is a very versatile dish which you may choose to make as spicy or soupy as you wish.*

Serves 6 as part of a multicourse meal

1 free-range chicken
1/4 teaspoon turmeric powder
1/2 teaspoon salt
2 tablespoons fish or shrimp sauce
5 dried red chilies
100 grams onions, pounded
6 cloves garlic, pounded

1 stalk lemongrass, bruised
3 slices ginger
2 tablespoons oil
300 grams calabash gourd, peeled and
    cut into 3-centimeter cubes
salt to taste
10 grams coriander, chopped

1. Cut chicken into medium pieces, bones and all. Rub with turmeric powder, salt and fish or shrimp sauce. Set aside.

2. Soak dried red chilies in water for 15 minutes, squeeze out water and pound after removing stem and seeds.

3. Mix everything apart from the gourd and coriander in a large pot. Place pot over the fire and cook for a few minutes, stirring often. When the oil sizzles, add just enough water to cover the ingredients. Cover and cook until the chicken is almost tender and just half the liquid remains.

4. Add the cubed gourd, stir and simmer until the white part of the gourd turns almost transparent. Add salt to taste.

5. Stir in coriander and remove pot from the heat, but keep the lid on. The heat of the soupy dish will continue to cook the gourd. Some cooks prefer to add the gourd at the very beginning so that it disintegrates into the gravy, making it sweeter.

6. The amount of liquid the curry should have varies according to individual taste. Remove ginger slices and lemongrass before serving. Serve very hot with plain rice and *nga pi daung* (grilled shrimp paste relish), see recipe below.

Nga pi daung Grilled shrimp paste relish

This is the easiest relish to make. Nga pi or shrimp paste is an acquired taste. For those who like it, its aroma is an appetizer in itself. However, some neighbors would disagree. To keep them from pounding on your door, wrap the shrimp paste in aluminum foil before grilling it. The rind of the lime, cut into small pieces, goes well with the nga pi daung *when nestled together in a mouthful of rice.*

Serves 6 as a relish

100 grams *nga pi* (shrimp paste)
6 cloves garlic, peeled
4 green chilies

1 tablespoon peanut oil
1 lime

1. Flatten the shrimp paste on a wooden spatula and grill it over an open fire, keeping the spatula far away enough so that the shrimp paste cooks without burning.

2. Pound the garlic and green chilies together, then pound in the shrimp paste.

3. Again, flatten the shrimp paste mixture thinly on a wooden spatula and grill lightly. Mound on a small plate and drizzle with oil and a squeeze of lime juice. Serve lime rind cut in small pieces separately.

Kayan chin thee nga pi chet
Tomato and shrimp paste relish

No meal in Myanmar is complete without a spicy, sour and salty relish eaten with raw, blanched or pickled vegetables. In the south, relishes are often made with salted whole fish that have been allowed to decay a little, but the less pungent recipe below is favored in the central and up-country regions.

A complete meal in Myanmar should have meat, fish or chicken curry and a soup, as well as side dishes. However, a hearty, delicious meal can also be created with just rice, a good relish and piles of greens. Often a poor family's meal is only that. The clear soup that goes best with sour-salty relishes is made using a grilled fish or a few roughly pounded dried shrimps combined with edible leaves freshly plucked from the vines climbing over the fence.

Serves 6 as part of a multicourse meal

3 dried red chilies
50 grams *ma jii thee chauk* (dried ripe
   tamarind)
3 tablespoons oil
1/4 teaspoon turmeric powder
50 grams onions, peeled, chopped
   and pounded
6 cloves garlic, peeled, chopped
   and pounded

1/2 tablespoon shrimp paste, dissolved
   in a little water
500 grams tomatoes, finely chopped
2 tablespoons dried shrimp, pounded
1 tablespoon fish or shrimp sauce
5 green chilies, deseeded and
   chopped roughly
salt to taste (or more fish sauce)
10 grams coriander, chopped

1. Soak dried red chilies in water for 15 minutes, squeeze out water and pound chilies after removing stem and seeds.

2. Soak *ma jii thee chauk* in 100 milliliters water for 15 minutes, kneading well to separate pulp and pods. Sieve and set aside.

3. Heat oil in a pan and add the turmeric powder. Add the pounded onions, garlic and dried chilies, fry until fragrant. Stir in the dissolved shrimp paste and cook until its raw smell is gone. Add the tomatoes, cook for 2 minutes more. Next, add the

ma jii thee chauk. Stir in the pounded dried shrimp, fish or shrimp sauce and green chilies. Cook, stirring often, until oil sizzles and the tomatoes are very soft. Add salt or fish sauce to taste, stir in coriander and remove pan from heat.

4. Raw carrots, radishes, unpeeled small green mangoes, tiny eggplants, limes, boiled bamboo shoots, blanched cauliflower, water spinach, lady's fingers (okra), string beans and pea tendrils cut into bite-size pieces can be served with this tomato and shrimp paste relish.

Lahpet

Pickled tea leaves

In Myanmar no meal offered to monks or guests is complete without lahpet. *It is considered a dish that one serves to the honored and therefore plays an important role at key events such as weddings and spirit-worshiping ceremonies. It has a savory taste much like a stronger version of pesto and is a little earthy without being overpoweringly so.*

Freshly plucked tea leaves from the Shan State are steamed and then packed into jars and buried in the ground for six months. The resulting wilted leaves are washed and squeezed dry, pounded with garlic and salt, and then steeped in the best peanut oil. The paste is sold ready-to-eat as a snack or after-meal savory, but never as an appetizer. You'll find it served, however, as an appetizer at restaurants in Myanmar because tourists and expatriates seem to prefer it at the beginning of the meal.

Serves 6 as an after-meal or midday snack

150 grams *lahpet* (pickled tea leaves)
  steeped in 2 tablespoons peanut
  or sesame oil
50 grams roasted peanuts
50 grams fried chickpeas

50 grams deep-fried slices of garlic
50 grams roasted sesame seeds
50 grams dried shrimp
50 grams toasted pumpkin seeds
50 grams deep-fried butter beans

1. To serve *lahpet* formally, the pickled tea leaves and accompaniments listed above are placed at the table in a lacquer box. Some containers have compartments to separate each ingredient. Guests are invited to spoon a little of each ingredient that appeals to them into their own dishes.

2. More informally, everything is mixed together in a salad called *lahpet thoke,* which also contains shredded cabbage, bits of raw garlic, chopped green chilies, sliced tomatoes and hard-boiled eggs. This is then drizzled with some fish sauce and lime juice.

Shwe yin aye

Golden heart cooler

Shwe yin aye *in a street market*

Summers in Myanmar are scorching and the Myanmar New Year falls right in the middle of it, in April. Fortunately, five days of the riotous Water Festival precede it. People splash each other with water out of bowls, buckets and even hoses to cool down and cleanse everyone of the past year's bad luck. Sweets and snacks are prepared by communities, organizations and families, and are given out to passersby or packed in stacked, multitiered tiffin carriers and sent to friends and neighbors.

One of the most popular dishes is a sweet that is aptly called golden heart cooler, an icy concoction filled with coconut cream, strips of colorful jelly, sago pearls and chewy glutinous (sticky) rice set against the tenderness of soaked white bread, a later addition that started to appear in this traditional dish only during the colonial era.

Serves 6 as dessert or snack

For the sugar syrup
400 grams sugar

For the jelly
1 packet plain agar-agar powder (usually 12 grams or 3 3/4 teaspoons)
sugar as required in the packet instructions (usually 250 grams)
red and yellow food coloring
a few drops rose essence

For the sago
100 grams small *sago* pearls
50 grams sugar

For the glutinous rice
300 grams glutinous rice

2 liters coconut cream
6 slices white bread, cut into thick strips
crushed ice

Chef's note:
If using fresh coconuts, finely grate the flesh of five. Place a handful of the grated coconut in a piece of muslin. Squeeze out the milk and repeat until completely dry. Repeat with the remaining grated coconut. Next, mix the squeezed coconut flakes with 1 liter warm water. Stir well and repeat the squeezing process again. If you have a blender, it is much easier to mix the squeezed coconut flakes with water in it.

1. Make the sugar syrup by boiling 250 milliliters of water and stirring in the sugar until it completely dissolves. Cool and set aside. This step can be done a day ahead.

2. Make the jelly with the packet of agar-agar powder, following the packet instructions and using the required amount of sugar. (This usually calls for the agar-agar powder to be dissolved in 1 liter of water before the sugar is added. Next, the mixture should be stirred and brought to a boil over low heat.) Remove the pan from the fire and

color half of the agar-agar liquid red. Color the remaining liquid yellow. Add a few drops of rose essence to both. Pour into square or rectangular molds and cool to set. Cut the agar-agar into long strips, storing the two colors separately.

Alternatively, use two sachets (approximately 20 grams or about 6 1/2 teaspoons) of plain gelatin in place of the packet of agar-agar powder, but use only half of the amount of water required in the instructions (a half quantity of water is usually 500 milliliters).

3. To prepare the *sago* pearls, boil 1.2 liters of water and stir in the *sago* pearls. Keep stirring until the white centers in the pearls disappear. Drain and stir in sugar. Allow to cool. If you like, add a few drops of food coloring to the *sago*.

4. Wash, drain and cook the glutinous rice with 560 milliliters of water in an uncovered pot on high heat until it bubbles and the water thickens. Cook for another minute, then lower heat to medium. Stir once and simmer for 3 minutes until the surface is almost dry and holes appear. Adjust heat to the lowest setting and cover tightly, or place two layers of paper towels between the pot and the lid, and cook for 10 minutes. Turn off the heat but do not remove the pot from the heat source, and allow the pot to stand for a further 10 minutes with the lid on.

5. To serve, place 250 milliliters coconut cream, sugar syrup to taste, some strips of bread, 4 tablespoons of *sago*, 3 tablespoons of glutinous rice and a generous portion of the jelly strips in each bowl. Top with crushed ice.

Monhinga

Fish soup and rice noodles

Monhinga is Myanmar's national noodle dish. Although it is a street food that you'll find at any bazaar, families and friends enjoy preparing large batches of it at home so that everyone in the household may indulge in multiple helpings throughout the day. Every available person is roped in to help out with the whole process, from boning the fish to pounding the onions. The shared work makes it taste even more delicious!

The thick fish broth is heavily laced with fish sauce, lemongrass and pepper. Crunchy rings of banana stem, chewy fish cake, smooth thin rice noodles and crispy fritters offer a delightful contrast of textures. Some cooks prefer to add more pepper, and omit the roasted chickpea and rice powders included in the recipe below so that the soup remains clear. However, the addition of fried hilsa roe to either version is considered the ultimate in luxury.

Calabash gourd

Chef's note:
Japanese somen noodles are perfect for *monhinga*. Rice vermicelli is not suitable, because it has a crunch to it.

If banana stem (*nga pyaw oo*) is unavailable, dried lotus root is an acceptable substitute. The banana tree stem contributes more to the texture than to the taste of the dish.

To make roasted rice powder (*hsan hmont a kyet*), pan-fry dry rice grains until light brown, taking care not to burn them. Finely grind or pound.

To fry hilsa roe, prick the sacs all over with a fork. Rub gently with a little salt and turmeric powder. Place the two sacs in a pan with 50 milliliters water and 2 tablespoons oil. Cook uncovered over medium heat. Turn gently once when half the liquid has evaporated. Flip them one more time after the oil sizzles and one side has turned golden brown.

Serves 6 as a complete meal

20-centimeter-long *nga pyaw oo* (banana stem)
salt to taste
2 tablespoons *pei hmont a kyet* (roasted chickpea powder), see Chef's note on page 140
3 tablespoons *hsan hmont a kyet* (roasted rice powder)
10 small shallots, peeled
1 hard-boiled egg, peeled and sliced
20 grams garlic, peeled
1/2 teaspoon ground black pepper
6 servings thin, soft rice noodles
shallot oil (see Chef's note on page 140)
fried shallot slices (see Chef's note on page 140)

For the broth
500 grams whole catfish, gutted and washed
300 grams hilsa steaks (if hilsa is not available use more catfish)
extra fish bones (optional)
4 cloves garlic, peeled and crushed
4 thin slices ginger
3 stalks lemongrass, bruised

2 tablespoons *ngar ngan pyar yay* (fish sauce)
1/2 teaspoon salt
1/8 teaspoon turmeric powder

For flavoring the cooked fish
50 grams onions, peeled
6 cloves garlic, peeled
1 stalk lemongrass, thinly sliced
1 slice ginger
4 dried red chilies
5 tablespoons oil
1/4 teaspoon turmeric powder
2 tablespoons *ngar ngan pyar yay* (fish sauce)

For the garnish
100 grams fish cake, fried and sliced
boo thee kyaw (calabash gourd fritters)
1 whole hilsa roe, which comes in a pair of sacs (optional)
coriander, chopped
3 hard-boiled eggs, unpeeled
lime wedges
roasted dried red chili powder

1. To make the broth, place fish and extra fish bones (if using) in a pot. Add just enough water to cover the fish and bones. Bring to a boil with garlic, ginger, lemongrass, *ngar ngan pyar yay*, salt and turmeric powder. Remove the fish when it is just cooked and retain the broth.

2. Flake the fish into 2-centimeter pieces, taking care to remove all the bones, especially from the hilsa.

3. Pound the fish bones (or put it in the blender with some water). Return the bones to the pot with the broth, adding more water to finally get about 3 liters of soup. Boil for another 15 minutes. Strain the soup to make sure that all the bones have been removed.

4. To flavor the cooked fish:
a) Pound the onions, garlic, lemongrass and ginger.
b) Soak dried red chilies in water for 15 minutes. Squeeze out water and pound the chilies after removing stem and seeds.
c) Heat oil with the turmeric and fry the pounded onions, garlic, lemongrass and ginger for 1 minute. Stir to prevent sticking. Add the pounded chilies and cook for a few more seconds until fragrant. Add the flaked fish and *ngar ngan pyar yay*. Cook until the oil sizzles, stirring gently. Set aside.

5. To assemble the *monhinga*:
a) Peel away the tough outer layers of the *nga pyaw oo*. When only two outer layers and the soft core remain, slice into 1-centimeter-thick rounds. Soak in water for an hour and discard the stringy sap.
b) Bring the fish broth to a boil in a large pot, adding salt to taste.
c) Dissolve the *pei hmont a kyet* and *hsan hmont a kyet* in 100 milliliters of water. Stir the mixture into the boiling broth until it thickens.
d) Stir in the cooked fish, *nga pyaw oo*, shallots and sliced hard-boiled egg. Simmer until about 2.5 liters of stock remain. Add salt or fish sauce to taste.
e) While the broth boils, pound garlic with black pepper. Just before removing the pot from the heat, stir in the pounded garlic and pepper.
f) To serve, place some rice noodles in a bowl. Drizzle with 1 teaspoon of shallot oil and top with a few slices of fried shallot. Ladle in a generous amount of the fish soup. Garnish with a few slices of fried fish cake, bite-size pieces of *boo thee kyaw*, hilsa roe, coriander, and half a hard-boiled egg (cut the unpeeled egg in half with a knife and scoop the egg white and yolk out with a metal spoon).

6. Set out dishes of more coriander, lime wedges, fish sauce and roasted dried red chili powder for guests to add according to taste.

Boo thee kyaw Calabash gourd fritters

Here, the fresh taste of calabash gourd is enhanced by a crunchy batter. It is one of the most popular accompaniments to monhinga *and is also a snack that is enjoyed with a tomato-chili-vinegar dip. On misty, chilly mornings,* boo thee kyaw *huts located near lakes and parks are popular stops among joggers.*

Serves 6 when eaten with monhinga

300 grams calabash gourd
150 grams rice flour
1 tablespoon glutinous rice flour
1 teaspoon salt
1/2 teaspoon baking soda
180 milliliters water
1/2 tablespoon ginger juice
oil for deep-frying

1. Peel calabash gourd and cut into 8-centimeter-long batons roughly 1.5-centimeters thick.

2. Mix dry ingredients thoroughly and slowly stir in the water and ginger juice until the thick batter is smooth. Set aside for an hour.

3. Fill a pan with enough oil to deep-fry the gourd batons and heat. Dip each baton into the batter to coat completely and slide it carefully into the oil. Do not overcrowd the pan. Fry until red, then drain on absorbent paper. The batter will be hard and crunchy. Serve within half an hour. Using a pair of scissors, snip the *boo thee kyaw* directly over the *monhinga*.

Philippines

Introduction and Recipe adaptations

by Michaela Fenix

The earliest account of local Filipino cuisine can be found in the sixteenth-century chronicles of Antonio Pigafetta, a Venetian nobleman who accompanied the Portuguese maritime explorer Ferdinand Magellan on his landmark journey to the Spice Islands (in the process of getting there, Magellan also became the first explorer to circumnavigate the globe). The account describes a feast hosted by an island king. In his diary, Pigafetta recounts the dishes of pork with gravy, roasted fish with freshly cut ginger, rice and the local wine. Although some Malay dishes such as *satay*, the sour broth of *sinigang* (called *singgang* in Malaysia) and rice cakes have remained on the Filipino menu, the menu itself has since evolved to include dishes adapted from the cuisines of the Spanish, who ruled over the country for 300 years, and of the Chinese, who first arrived as traders although some eventually settled in the country.

In tune with the region

In many ways, Filipino cuisine is very different from the other cuisines of Southeast Asia because the Philippines was colonized by the Spanish. Only a few provinces in the southern islands have cooking styles that share similarities with the culinary traditions of Malaysia and Indonesia. This is because these provinces have predominantly Muslim populations. The ancestors of the people living here were converted by Arab missionaries who had arrived before the Spanish. Even so, there are notable differences in some of their cooking. While the *satay* served in this region also features small slices of chicken and beef skewered on coconut midrib, the sauce is red and soupy — quite unlike the brownish, thick sauce Malaysian and Indonesian *satay* is served with. This is because the Filipino sauce contains tomatoes, one of the ingredients introduced by the Spanish.

Lechon *(a whole roasted pig) is the centerpiece of most feasts.*

The Philippines has a predominantly Christian population. Cultures and religions, however, have still clashed, even to this day. Yet, in places like the southernmost Tawi-Tawi Islands, parties will inevitably have both Christian and Muslim tables (followers of Islam adhere to strict dietary restrictions; they are forbidden to eat pork or drink alcohol). In the spirit of tolerance, it is acceptable for the Christian table to be served roasted pig (*lechon*) as a main dish. On the other hand, Christians who were born in and live on these islands have made Muslim cooking their own, recalling each dish with gusto and eating every item with equal relish.

A representative dish

Adobo, which has a Spanish name and contains some ingredients closely associated with Chinese cuisine, can be said to best describe the mix that is Filipino. It is also the one dish that comes to mind when Filipinos are asked to describe the quintessential cooking of their country. Although *adobo* is always stewed, many versions of this dish exist. The differences lie in the ingredients and flavorings used and the colors of the resulting dishes. The version cooked in most places incorporates vinegar, soy sauce, garlic, whole peppercorns and bay leaves. The last three ingredients are often sold pre-packaged at wet markets.

Adobo can be made using pork, chicken or beef; or a combination of two or all of these meats. Certain vegetables, such as *kangkong* (water convolvulus), can be used. Soy sauce is added not only for its salty flavor but for the color it gives the dish. In some regions, annatto seeds are used to give it a more reddish hue. Fish sauce is used in another version called white *adobo* because the finished dish should not be brown or red. In the Bicol region where cooks are renowned for adding coconut milk to many of their dishes, they put coconut milk in their *adobo*. There are also many variations on how the dish is cooked. Some cooks like their *adobo* dry, others make theirs even drier by frying the meat whole or shredding it into flakes after it has been stewed. Some prefer to have their *adobo* with a lot of sauce, either soupy or thickened, and with crushed chicken liver.

Adobo originally presented a way of preserving food in an era when there was no refrigeration. The fat expressed from pork *adobo* ensured that it was of even better quality when the dish was eaten days later. And because *adobo* keeps well, it is a picnic favorite. The proper way to create a picnic packet called *binalot* is to take a banana leaf and place a mound of rice in the middle of it. Top it with *adobo* pieces and some sauce, if any, before wrapping it.

THIS PAGE Alimango (mangrove crabs) steaming in a kawali (a wok with one handle) placed on a traditional wood-fire stove crafted out of stone.

OPPOSITE (top right) Activity in the kitchen is centered on the open hearth.

INSIDE THE FILIPINO KITCHEN

The Filipino pantry must contain garlic, onions, tomatoes and ginger. Flavors come from salt and pepper, *patis* (fish sauce), *toyo* (soy sauce) and *suka* (vinegar). It is also important to have some *siling haba* or *siling pangsigang* (green finger chili) handy for some major dishes that require a mildly hot touch.

ESSENTIAL COOKING TECHNIQUES

Roasting or charcoal broiling (*inihaw*), boiling and stewing are among the very basic techniques used. Fresh ingredients such as seafood are usually prepared using the first two techniques so that their natural flavors are preserved.

Guisa, or sautéing, is a technique acquired from the Chinese and Spanish. The trinity of crushed garlic, chopped onions and tomatoes sautéed in oil often marks the very first step of cooking for many Filipino dishes, most especially vegetables which all have *guisado* appended to their names.

Rice is not only a staple in the Philippines but a basic ingredient found in many dishes. It is used to make native cakes. It is fermented to sate the hankering for something sour to accompany certain dishes. It is harvested as immature grains, then toasted and mixed into a thick chocolate drink.

Rice fields have been the source of riches for many families who own land. Some of them remind themselves of this gift at Christmas, the major Christian feast celebrating the birth of Jesus Christ, by eating a simply cooked rice gruel called *pospas* before savoring the rich food laid out at the table. One of the Christmas dishes is likely to be *arroz Valenciana*, which is similar to the Spanish *paella* except that it uses tomato sauce instead of saffron to give color to the rice. It is usually served to the landowner as well as his family and guests in the upstairs parlor; another version called *bringhe* is served to the tenants, who dine downstairs. There is a class distinction between the rice dishes because *bringhe* uses indigenous ingredients rather than items such as tomatoes and *chorizos* (sausages) which were introduced by the Spanish. For *bringhe*, glutinous (sticky) rice is first cooked with coconut milk and then colored and flavored with turmeric. The resulting rice dish looks yellowish green.

ESSENTIAL KITCHEN IMPLEMENTS

While most homes now have the modern kitchen conveniences, some cooks still slow cook their stews and tenderize meat in what is called the "dirty kitchen." This is an area sometimes separate from the house which has stoves that use either charcoal or gas. This is also where the coconut grater (*kudkuran*) is kept.

The *kawali*, a wok with one handle, is used for sautéing and frying. Heavy, thick-bottomed *calderos* (soup pots) are used for tenderizing meat and preparing soups. Clay pots (*palayok*) were once used for preparing stews, especially those containing vinegar because the acids react in metal containers. In spite of this, most people today use pots made of aluminum and other heavier metals. If clay pots are still employed, they are usually the glazed ones used in Chinese cookery.

The mortar and pestle, made of marble or wood, are necessary for crushing ginger and peppercorns, and extracting juice from shrimp heads. Wooden chopping boards (*tadtaran*) are still used. They are usually made from the cut trunk of the *santol* tree. A metal turner called *sianse* is used when a cook sautés food or wants to create a caramelized sugar glaze on Christmas hams. In a method called *plantsa* (ironing), the *sianse* is heated before it is pressed onto the sugar.

THIS PAGE In the southernmost
Tawi-Tawi Island, women grate some
coconuts to be used in many dishes
and especially in the Muslim spice
mix called pamapa itum.

OPPOSITE (left) Wood-fire is still
the preferred fuel for slow cooking
because it imparts a certain smoky
aroma that is important in traditional
food; (right) A great variety of seaweed
can be found in the waters around
the Philippine archipelago. This rich
source of iodine is usually served as a
side dish to seafood.

Notes on noodles

During Christmas or any other feast, the other dish that is frequently served is *pancit*, the generic name for noodle dishes. In particular, noodles are expected at birthday celebrations because Filipinos believe that they symbolize long life (but only if they are not cut into pieces). Yet, *pancit* can also be found at wakes because it can easily be prepared in vast quantities and the bereaved are expected to feed everyone who attends.

Pancit has Chinese origins, but it has been adapted to include local preferences for specific ingredients and flavors. This has resulted in as many variations of *pancit* as there are towns in the country. The names of these dishes are sometimes based on the town where the version was first created, some on the color of noodles and still others on the kind of noodle used. But the noodle names will always be Chinese or at least sound very similar to its Chinese original. Some examples include *miki*, *miswa*, *bihon* and *sotanghon*. *Sotanghon* (glass noodles) is made of mung beans. In the past, it was served on important occasions because it used to be imported and therefore cost more. Like all the other noodles, the transparent, thin *sotanghon* can be served in a soup or stir-fried, but the dish will always include shredded chicken and the cloud ear fungus locally known as *tengang daga* (rat's ear).

Rice cake seasons

The Day of the Dead falls on the second day of November, a holiday. On this day, families flock to the cemeteries to clean gravestones, light candles and pray for those who have passed on. Traditionally, they also prepare a rice cake made of glutinous rice combined with coconut milk and sugar. No one can explain why this is so, but the tradition is considered a proper offering for the dead because it contains the most important staple, rice. The rice cake is shared with neighbors and friends. Usually, a small porcelain plate, called a *platito*, is greased with a bit of coconut oil before a piece of cake is placed on it. This method ensures that the cake will not stick to the plate. This gift of rice cake is always presented with a reminder to return the *platito*.

What one calls this rice cake heavily depends on which part of the country one comes from. It is called *bibingka malagkit*, *biko* or *sinukmani*. It is doubly confusing because a pancake lookalike once served only during Christmas is also called *bibingka*. Those who attend the nine dawn Masses held before the actual celebrations on Christmas Day are treated to this seasonal *bibingka*, which is made of rice which has been ground into flour. It is cooked and sold at stalls near the church. This *bibingka* is enjoyed with hot ginger tea which heats up the body and protects it from the bracing cold morning air.

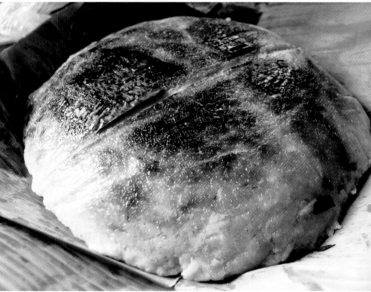

THIS PAGE (top) Bibingka (the local pancake) is cooked using charcoal heat positioned below and above the pan; (above) In Arayat, a town in Pampanga province, bringhi (or bringhe) is served inverted, thus exposing the toasted underside.

OPPOSITE Countless versions of lumpia (spring roll) exist. This one consists of a vegetable mix encased in fresh wrappers.

The national hero Jose Rizal immortalized the *tinola* in his novel, *Noli me Tangere*. The dish was described by one of the characters, a Franciscan friar, as a stew of chicken with squash. In many parts of the Philippines, *tinola* consists of chicken boiled with pieces of green papaya and chili leaves. Readers of the *Noli* are bound to remember the point in the novel when the friar, Father Damaso, was given a portion that "turned out to be composed of a lot of squash and broth with barely a chicken neck and wing, while his fellow guests were eating chicken legs and chicken breasts."

Again, great confusion can arise from dish names because in another part of the country, *tinola* is a sour fish soup. In other areas that same soup is called *sinigang*. To one of the country's eminent food writers, the late Doreen Gamboa Fernandez, *sinigang* is the "dish most representative of Filipino taste… the lightly boiled, the slightly soured." Like *adobo*, many versions of *sinigang* exist. It may contain fish, shrimp, pork or beef and some vegetables. The type of souring agent used — it is usually a fruit — depends on where it is cooked. In the northern Philippines a more sour *sinigang* is preferred. In the center, where *sinigang* is called *tinola*, the soup is preferably milder.

Sinigang is similar to Thai *tom yam* and the Malay *singgang*, but is not as spicy. Both contain chili, but the milder *siling haba* or green finger chili, kept whole rather than sliced, is used in preparing *sinigang*. In her book *Philippine Food and Life*, Gilda Cordero Fernando wrote of the lakeshore town of Angono in Rizal, where a party by the lake is always called *panigang*. The word actually refers to food that is cooked like *sinigang* and the main ingredient is the *kanduli* (a cousin to the catfish) caught in traps along the lake. Perhaps this was the case in the past, but lakeshore parties are still called *panigang* even if the food cooked is no longer *sinigang*. *Panigang* gives people an excuse to get together and sing along to guitar music or to recite flowery verses extracted from traditional poems.

Cookies are a big part of Filipino cuisine. Several small bakeries not only produce breads suited to local tastes but also make cookies that have become part of their town's specialties — something for visitors to take with them as souvenirs. One such bakery is Panaderia de Molo in Iloilo. It has been producing special cookies such as whirlpools of crisp *hojaldres* for more than a century.

Unsold bread and cakes are resurrected as toasted wonders, which in turn become another set of cookies. *Machacao*, toasted dried bread dipped in carabao

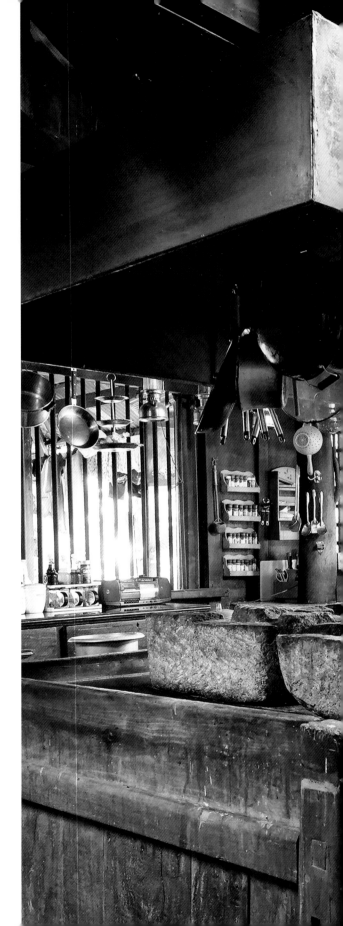

A traditional kitchen in the central plains of Luzon island (Pampanga province) which has stone stoves located on its wooden platform.

milk, is fed to fattened male chickens (*capon*) before they are slaughtered because in the past, cooks believed that the *capon* would acquire the same milky flavor.

Cookies are also part of certain rites. One of these is the *pan San Nicolas*, a sort of shortbread that has images of saints stamped on it. These were once baked only during the feast of San Nicolas de Tolentino in September, blessed at the church and then given to children, especially those who were sick. In a town in the province of Leyte where *roscas* (butter cookies) and their saltier counterparts, *de caña*, are baked, a bride is required to feed cookies to the farm animals. If the newlyweds exchange their wedding vows in the city, these cookies are fed to children instead.

Sweet ending

A peek at the dessert section of any Filipino cookbook will reveal sweets with mostly Spanish names. These are adaptations of Spanish desserts which are mostly made of egg yolks. One of these sweets is *leche flan*, a rich egg and milk custard eaten as it is or used to top *halo-halo*. *Halo-halo*, which means "mix of many elements," consists of sweetened beans, fruits and jams mixed together (hence the name) before they are served with shaved ice and milk.

In Quiapo, once the genteel part of Manila, the same ingredients are served separately as part of small charity tables, called *caridad*, which are placed outside houses on *Lunes Santo* or Holy Monday during the Lenten Holy Week, the Christian period of atonement and mourning. The *caridad* serves as a spot for those who take part in a procession during the early afternoon to replenish their energy by stopping for some food. Cora Alvina, whose family used to live in Quiapo, describes that procession in her essay ("*Caridad* begins at home" in *Slow Food: Philippine Culinary Traditions*). "The *hijos de Nazarenos* [are] reinforced by *pasos*, or women and children clad in violet robes, their faces veiled, their heads crowned with wreaths of *makabuhay* [a vine] are joined by other Catholic faithful. The procession is a show of faith by so many humans, for the compassion of the Señor, as the Black Nazarene is fondly and respectfully called by the Quiapo folk."

Fruits and root crops are also served sweetened. These may be enjoyed as a dessert or a snack taken in-between meals called *merienda*. In Infanta, a town in Quezon province, serving sweetened yams called *binagka*t is considered an excuse to get together. All one has to say is "*Ta'y magbinagkat!*" — let's eat the dish and party.

Community effort

For fiestas or banquets the menu is almost predictable. Many of the dishes have some element of Spanish influence. This even extends to their names — *menudo* (pork and liver stew), *estofado* (braised pork with *saba* bananas and bread), *mechado* (beef larded with pork fat in the middle and cooked with tomato sauce), *asado* (braised whole piece of pork cooked in soy sauce), *embutido* (meat loaf). Notice how each name ends with "do." This is why fiesta menus are nicknamed "do-do-do."

Like *pancit*, fiesta dishes are designed to feed many. To create volume, supplementary ingredients such as potatoes or bananas, as well as liters of sauce usually made with tomato and soy sauce are added. The array of food presented at the festive table usually reflects the great community effort that went into getting it there. Days ahead, a whole army of helpers would have turned up to slice and chop ingredients. Huge chunks of meat would have been precooked — sautéed in garlic and onions with some salt — using a method called *sankutsa* in order to prevent spoilage, since it would have been difficult to otherwise store such vast quantities of meat. This way, there is no need for refrigeration, even if the main cooking is scheduled for the next day.

It is common for hosts to wrap some of the food for departing guests to take with them. And because running out of food at a fiesta is unthinkable, households always prepare far more food than they need. Thus, there are always leftovers. The day after the fiesta, these are often savored at a riverside or beach picnic. In the Angono town of Rizal province these leftovers are wrapped in banana leaves and are called *minaluto*.

THIS PAGE *(clockwise from top left) Fruits common throughout the region —* durian, kamias *(bilimbi or* belimbing) *and mangoes.*

OPPOSITE *Dishes rest on a window sill in a northern Luzon kitchen (Vigan, Ilocos Sur province).*

Bringhe

Coconut glutinous rice with chicken

Most often served at Christmas time, bringhe *or* bringhi *is said to be the local version of* arroz Valenciana, *the rice dish from the Spanish city of Valencia. It uses turmeric and, in the old days, a kind of bark to create its distinctive greenish-yellow coloring. Fish sauce is added to accentuate the savory flavors in the dish. However, some will argue that* bringhe *already existed in the Philippines long before the Spaniards came and that the two dishes simply share some similarities. This is conceivable because many Filipino dishes with Spanish names actually contain local ingredients and use local cooking techniques. In his book* Why We Eat What We Eat, *the renowned food writer Raymond Sokolov goes as far as to argue that the "Spanish cloak of words [disguised] the blatant originality of Filipino food."*

The banana leaves used here prevent the rice from sticking to the pan and give the dish a special aroma. Aluminum foil can be used instead.

Different types of rice and beans sold in markets

Serves 10 - 15

1 kilogram *malagkit* (glutinous rice)
3 mature coconuts or 1.2 liters
   coconut milk
60 milliliters cooking oil
1 tablespoon minced garlic
250 grams onions, peeled and chopped
1 kilogram chicken, dressed, cleaned
   and cut into about 10 pieces
60 milliliters *patis* (fish sauce)
60 milliliters *dilaw* (turmeric juice)

6 banana leaves, cut into
   25-centimeter squares and
   wilted over fire to strengthen
patis (fish sauce) to taste
1 medium green bell pepper, roasted,
   peeled, and cut into cubes

For the garnish
3 hard-boiled eggs, peeled and sliced
   lengthwise into 6 wedges

Chef's note
To prepare *dilaw* (turmeric juice), peel and then pound a piece of turmeric (roughly 5-centimeters long). Add 4 tablespoons of water, then strain.

(Adapted from a recipe in *Philippine Food and Life* by Gilda Cordero Fernando)

1. Clean the *malagkit* by washing and draining the grains thrice. Set aside.

2. If using coconuts, grate them. Add 900 milliliters of hot water to them and squeeze out the milk a little at a time. Strain and set aside.

3. Heat oil in a saucepan. Sauté the garlic and onions over high heat. Add the chicken pieces and cook until chicken is slightly browned. Add *patis*, *dilaw* and 120 milliliters of water. Add the *malagkit*, stir and cook for about 10 minutes. Gradually add the coconut milk, stirring constantly. Bring to a boil, then lower the heat. Continue cooking until almost all the liquid has evaporated. Adjust seasoning

by adding fish sauce according to taste. Add the green bell pepper cubes. Stir.

4. Line a *kawali* (a wok with one handle) with three squares of banana leaf. Transfer the mixture to the wok. Cover with the remaining banana leaves. Cover the wok with a lid and cook over a low flame until the rice is done. A clear sign of doneness is when a steady stream of steam appears on the sides of the wok.

5. Place cooked rice dish on a platter (if you wish, retain the banana leaf at the bottom so that the rice does not stick to the plate). Just before serving, garnish with sliced hard-boiled eggs.

Pancit sotanghon

Sautéed glass noodles

Kalamansi, *a lime indigenous to the Philippines*

Most pancit *(noodle dishes) are prepared using steps similar to the ones outlined in this recipe. First, the accompaniments are sautéed using a method called* guisa, *a basic cooking technique acquired from the Spanish. Adding the broth helps keep the noodles moist and flavors the dish.*

Pancit sotanghon can be made into soup by just adding more water (about four times more than the quantity used for making noodles). In the past, sotanghon *soup was called* langlang *in some parts of the Philippines and was a Christmas dish. The difference is that for* langlang, *the broth used is usually richer due to the inclusion of ham and chicken bones.*

Unlike the Chinese who slurp their noodles to prevent the strands from being broken, Filipinos have been taught that slurping any food or making any noise while eating is not de rigueur. Noodles are not twirled around a fork like the Italians do, but are eaten with a spoon and fork. Although pancit *is served at birthdays because the long noodles convey a wish for the celebrator to enjoy a long life, the first thing that diners will do is to cut the noodles to make it easier for them to spoon the* pancit. *An exception to the rule is* pancit Malabon, *which is the specialty of the seaside town Malabon. In the past,* pancit Malabon *was eaten from a small bowl called a* mangkok *(the word itself is of Chinese origin). Long chopsticks called* sipit *or a pincer were the utensils used.*

Pancit can be served as part of a multicourse menu or by itself, especially during merienda *(snack time). Some* pancit *are served paired with a specific accompaniment.* Pancit Malabon *is properly served with a butter cookie called a* camachile, *which is shaped like the fruit it is named after. But for many Filipinos,* pancit *is best eaten with sliced white sandwich bread.*

(Adapted from recipes by
Myrna Segismundo and
Glenda Barretto)

Serves 4 - 6

250 grams *sotanghon* (glass noodles)
1/2 teaspoon annatto (*achiote* or
  achuete) seeds
3 tablespoons oil
1 tablespoon garlic, peeled and minced
1 white onion, peeled and minced
100 grams lean pork, diced or boneless
  chicken breast, sliced
100 grams small shrimps, peeled
  and diced
100 grams chicken livers, coarsely
  chopped
1 carrot, peeled and cut into matchstick-
  size pieces

200 grams *habichuelas* (green beans),
  thinly sliced or *chicharo* (snow peas),
  trimmed
200 grams cabbage, shredded
240 milliliters chicken stock or broth
patis (fish sauce) to taste
freshly ground white pepper
6 dried *tengang daga* (cloud ear fungus),
  soaked in water and cut into strips

For the garnish
1 stalk spring onion, minced

1. Bring 480 milliliters of water to a boil. Place *sotanghon* into the boiling water. Cook until it softens and then drain. Set aside.

2. Mix annatto seeds with 2 tablespoons water. Stir until color appears, then strain. Reserve annatto water and discard seeds.

3. Heat oil in a pan, then sauté garlic and onions over medium heat. Add pork or chicken, shrimps and chicken livers. Toss in the carrots, *habichuelas* or *chicharo* and cabbage. Stir-fry. Add the chicken

stock or broth and the annatto water. Simmer the stock for another 3 to 5 minutes or until the vegetables are tender but still firm. Season with *patis* and white pepper. Add the *sotanghon* and *tengang daga*. Mix well and continue to simmer for another 10 minutes.

4. Place the *pancit sotanghon* on a serving dish, then garnish with spring onions. Serve with sliced *kalamansi* and fish sauce for added flavoring.

Menudo

Pork and liver stew

After the revolution against Spain, the former cooks of Spanish friars were hired by rich families. They were trained in the Spanish culinary arts, which included mastering the ability to cook with wines, and knew how to substitute local ingredients for Spanish ones. These culinary masters were called kusinero de campanilla. Kusinero *is the local word for cook;* de campanilla *the Spanish phrase for a professional. They prepared big banquets, where* menudo *would be one of the featured dishes, and could tell just from smelling the dish which seasonings were still needed to enhance its flavors.*

The tradition of the kusinero de campanilla *lives on, but very few cooks are now hired to create whole banquets for families. They have been superseded by catering businesses where the cooks are faceless suppliers and the shared community involvement in preparing ingredients has been pared down.*

This dish is a mainstay of fiesta cooking. Just imagine how many kilograms of pork, pieces of garlic, onions and tomatoes, and liters of tomato and soy sauces go into creating enough menudo *to feed the hundreds of guests one expects to welcome to one's home on a town feast day! In the Philippines, everyone — be they strangers or friends — is welcomed to a fiesta.*

Serves 4 - 6

2 tablespoons oil
2 teaspoons garlic, peeled and minced
1 medium white onion, peeled and minced
1 medium tomato, minced
2 tablespoons tomato sauce
1 tablespoon soy sauce

500 grams *pigue* (pork rump), cut into 1.5-centimeter cubes
1 potato, peeled and cubed
250 grams pork liver, cubed
1 red bell pepper, seeded and cubed
120 grams green peas, cooked
salt and pepper to taste

(Adapted from a recipe by Myrna Segismundo)

1. Heat oil in a pot. Sauté garlic, onion and tomato over medium heat. Add tomato sauce, soy sauce and pork. Stir-fry until pork is lightly browned. Add just enough water to cover the meat and bring to a boil. Lower the heat, cover the pot and simmer until the meat is partly cooked.

2. Add potatoes and continue simmering until the potatoes are cooked. Add the liver, bell pepper and green peas. Simmer until all the meat and vegetables are done. Season with salt and pepper.

Adobong baboy at manok

Pork and chicken adobo

This version of adobo uses pork and chicken, and includes annatto seeds for color. More often than not, only one kind of meat is used in adobo to shorten the cooking time. Adobo improves with time, so it is best savored a day or two after it is cooked. When prepared in a large batch (as is the case with this recipe), it makes a fabulous dish to have on standby. Some cooks pour the resulting sauce over rice to both soften and flavor it. Others enjoy adobo with ripe bananas, making sure that each bite includes some adobo, a slice of banana and a little rice.

Serves 12 - 15

6 cloves garlic, peeled and crushed
120 milliliters white vinegar
60 milliliters soy sauce
1/2 tablespoon black peppercorns, cracked
1 bay leaf (*laurel* leaf)

1.5 kilograms *liempo* (pork belly) with skin on, cut into 5-centimeter cubes
1 kilogram chicken, cut into stewing pieces
2 tablespoons annatto (*achiote* or *achuete*) seeds

(Adapted from Myrna Segismundo's recipe in *Philippine Cuisine: Home-cooked Recipes Wherever You May Be*)

1. Combine garlic, vinegar, soy sauce, pepper and bay leaf in a wok or pot. Add *liempo*, chicken and just enough water to cover the meat. Simmer over medium heat until chicken is cooked. Remove chicken from mixture, set aside, and continue simmering the rest until the pork is tender. At that point, oil will be expressed from the pork fat. Remove about 2/3 of the fat and discard.

2. Soak the annatto seeds in 120 milliliters water for 5 minutes. Strain and reserve liquid (annatto water). Discard the seeds.

3. Increase the heat under the wok or pot to high. Fry the pork pieces in the remaining fat until they are golden brown. Return the chicken to the wok or pot. Add the annatto water and stir to mix well. Reduce the fire to medium heat. Gently toss cooked meat. Some of the meat will stick to the pot, so scrape the sides to ensure that they are incorporated into the mixture (the secret of a good *adobo*). Remove the bay leaf and serve warm.

Sinigang na bangus

Milkfish in sour broth

The classic version of this sour soup is prepared using the national fish bangus *(milkfish). It is important to note that there is also a proper way to cut the fish. The trick is to start near the base of the head, where its back begins. Create a diagonal cut which stretches toward the belly. The other pieces should also be cut at that same angle.*

However, sinigang *can also be made using other fish (sometimes just the head is used), prawns, shrimp, shellfish or a combination of all of these. Pork and beef are also sometimes used. In this case, a variety of yam that thickens the broth is added.*

There are many souring agents to choose from. Each one gives the broth a different flavor. Sometimes, tomatoes with a bit of kalamansi *are used to create a milder* sinigang *called* tinola. *In the north a more tart broth is preferred. On the island of Palawan, grated green mangoes are used to sour* sinigang.

While this recipe employs the traditional method of extracting juice from green tamarinds, powdered tamarind can also be used.

Green tamarind

Serves 4 - 6

1 kilogram *bangus* (milkfish), fish weighing 500 grams each are ideal
150 grams green tamarind
1.8 liters rice wash (liquid saved from washing rice before it is cooked)
100 grams onion, peeled and diced
200 grams tomatoes, skinned and sliced
200 grams *sitaw* (yard-long beans), washed and cut into 2.5-centimeter pieces

1 white radish, peeled, and sliced into five diagonal 1.5-centimeter pieces
1 eggplant, washed and cut crosswise into 2.5-centimeter-thick circles
1 *siling haba* (green finger chili)
250 grams *kangkong* (water convolvulus), washed, leaves separated, then upper stalks cut into 5-centimeter pieces
patis (fish sauce) to taste

1. Clean *bangus*. Remove scales, then slice each *bangus* diagonally into 3 to 4 pieces.

2. Boil tamarind in 480 milliliters of water until tender. Mash and pass through a strainer. Set juice aside and discard solids.

3. In a soup pot, boil the rice wash, onions and tomatoes. Add the fish and tamarind juice and let it return to a boil. Add the *sitaw* and white radish. Next, add the *siling haba* and the *kangkong*. Simmer over low heat until fish and vegetables are done. Add *patis* to taste. Serve immediately.

(Adapted from recipes by Myrna Segismundo and Glenda Barretto)

Pan San Nicolas

Saint Nicholas cookies

This recipe is a modern version of a traditional one which used araro *(arrowroot) flour and the San Nicolas (Saint Nicholas) de Tolentino wooden mold carved in the saint's likeness. It is also called* saniculas *or* tinapay San Nicolas. Pan *is Spanish for bread and* tinapay *is its Filipino equivalent.*

These characteristically leaf-shaped cookies used to be baked only on the tenth of September to mark the feast of San Nicolas de Tolentino. Now, they are sold throughout the year at bakeries in the towns of Pampanga province where the cookies originated.

The coconut milk makes the cookies truly native, giving this version of shortbread a decidedly Filipino flavor.

Makes 20 pieces

1 mature coconut or 120 milliliters
   coconut cream
3 tablespoons butter
240 grams sugar
4 egg yolks

360 grams flour
360 grams cornstarch
1 tablespoon baking powder
a few anise seeds
60 milliliters milk

1. Pre-heat oven to 350 degrees Fahrenheit (175 degrees Celsius) and grease a baking sheet.

2. If using coconut, grate it and then squeeze to extract cream. Strain and set aside.

3. Cream butter in a mixing bowl. Gradually add the sugar. In another bowl, beat egg yolks and then incorporate into the butter-sugar mixture.

4. Sift the dry ingredients — flour, cornstarch, baking powder and anise seeds — together. Add half of the dry ingredients to the butter mixture. Add the coconut cream gradually. Add the

remaining half of the dry ingredients. Mix well to create a dough.

5. Knead the dough on a floured tabletop. Roll it out thinly to a thickness of 5 millimeters using a rolling pin that has been dusted with flour. Using a rectangular cookie cutter roughly measuring 10-by-6 centimeters, cut out cookies or press into a wooden San Nicolas mold. Place the cookies on a greased baking sheet and then brush each one with milk.

6. Bake for 10 minutes.

(Adapted from a recipe
by Nora Daza)

Leche flan

Crème caramel

This is the dessert most commonly served at the end of a Filipino meal at a restaurant. The recipe here is less dense because it uses whole eggs rather than just egg yolks. But even leche flans that use only egg yolks are not as rich as their Spanish cousin, the tocino del cielo *(heaven's bacon), which traditionally contains just egg yolks and sugar.*

A water bath, also known as a baño maria in Spanish or a bain-marie in French, is needed to steam-bake this dessert. The traditional container used to prepare this dish in is the llanera, *an oval tin pan. It is also used in other recipes either as a cooking vessel or as a container.*

Serves 4

455 grams sugar
370 milliliters evaporated milk
4 eggs

1 teaspoon *dayap* (lime) zest or
pure vanilla extract

1. Heat a heavy-bottomed pan and caramelize 115 grams of sugar over medium heat. Immediately pour the sugar into a 15-by-10 centimeter baking pan or a *llanera* (oval tin pan) that is 5-centimeters deep. Be sure to coat the entire base of the pan with the caramelized sugar. Allow to cool.

2. Scald the evaporated milk in a double boiler for 10 minutes.

3. Beat the eggs. Add the rest of the sugar (340 grams), scalded milk and *dayap* zest or vanilla extract. Pour into the pan.

4. Place the pan in a large pot or wok. Fill the large pot or wok with enough water to reach halfway below the rim of the pan. Steam-bake for about 1 hour or until egg mixture is set. Remove the pan and cool.

5. Slide a knife along the sides of the pan to loosen the flan. Place a serving platter on top of the pan and invert to allow flan and caramelized sugar to slide out. Remove the pan and serve the flan chilled.

(Adapted from recipes written by Myrna Segismundo and Nora Daza)

Biko

Sweet rice cake

This is the simplest biko recipe. This dish has several names and variations. Some Filipinos like serving it topped with solidified cream called latik. Latik is made by boiling coconut cream until the oil separates from the browned creamy bits. Others prefer not to add anise seeds and use kalamansi zest instead. A bit of crushed ginger can also be added to the rice and removed just before the biko is served.

Rice cakes like biko are usually served during merienda, the traditional mid-morning and mid-afternoon snack. This is because native cakes made of rice, corn or the root crops that abound in the country are too heavy to be eaten as part of a complete meal. Merienda can be called break time in today's working world or recess, as it is referred to in schools. But in the past, the role of merienda was described more poetically as panawid gutom — something to bridge hunger. This is why merienda portions are generally smaller. Nonetheless, pretty much anything can be considered merienda food. It can be as light as a cookie or as heavy as rice and a viand. You may choose to serve freshly prepared food or leftovers. The dish may be sweet, salty or sour. And it can be served hot or cold.

Serves 8 - 10

1 kilogram *malagkit* (glutinous rice)
4 mature coconuts or 1 liter coconut milk
750 grams dark-brown sugar
1/2 teaspoon salt
1/2 teaspoon anise seeds

(Adapted from a recipe by Nora Daza in *A Culinary Life*)

1. Wash and drain the *malagkit* three times. Add 1.2 liters of water and bring to a boil. Simmer until most of the water has been absorbed and the rice is done. Set aside.

2. If using coconuts, grate them. Add a little hot water, then squeeze the milk out by hand. Strain and set aside.

3. In a heavy-bottomed pot, combine the coconut milk, sugar, salt and anise seeds. Mix well and boil until the mixture thickens. Lower heat and add the cooked *malagkit*. Blend well by stirring continuously until the mixture thickens and is difficult to handle, about 30 minutes.

4. Remove from the fire and spread out on a tray or platter so that the *biko* conforms to the shape of the container. Cut into squares and serve on a small plate or banana leaf.

Singapore

Introduction and Recipes

by Christopher Tan

L et's begin with the facts, as they lay the dry, but firm, foundation for the story. Singapore's original inhabitants were indigenous peoples from the Malay Peninsula, joined by migrants from southern China as early as the thirteenth century. In 1819 the British established a trading post on the island, which later became a crown colony and then an entrepot town. The next phase of Singapore's economic flowering as a port city began in the post-World War II era, when it officially became an independent nation in 1959. On its 660 square kilometers live around 4.3 million people, of whom just over 80 percent are residents. Of these, around 75 percent are of Chinese heritage, 14 percent of Malay heritage, 9 percent of (mostly southern) Indian heritage, and a small but potent seasoning of other cultures, including Arabs, Punjabis, Javanese, Jewish and European peoples. All the major world religions are represented in the population. Official discourse is conducted in four main languages, English, Mandarin, Malay and Tamil, and colloquial communication also includes dialects of these.

Those are the facts. Here is some of the story, drawn from past and present:

With a whispered "Amen," a little Nyonya girl finishes her prayers at Sunday afternoon Mass, then eagerly trots across the road with her family to the Hainanese bakery, a local institution, for her favorite toasted buns smeared with butter and sweet, sticky coconut egg jam.

***

A young Indian couple, dripping gold and scented flowers, shyly feed each other sweetmeats, dripping syrup and silver leaf. They look into each other's eyes, finding a moment of quiet as the room around them whirls with noise and good wishes. They have just been married.

An eye-catching array of Chinese red dates, gingkgo nuts, cloud ear fungus and other dried goods.

Six ears strain to hear the clacking of bamboo sticks, as three sisters wait at the window for the *tok-tok* noodle man to pass their house. When he arrives, they run out to the cart, breathlessly reciting their orders: one *tar mee pok* (flat egg noodles) with chili! One *kway teow* (flat rice noodles) soup! One *tar mee kia* (dry thin egg noodles) with fish balls!

***

As the hour of prayer draws near, a Malay mother browses street food stalls, assembling the meal that her family will break their daily Ramadan fast with. She buys fat, glossy dates, fried chicken, *biryani* rice speckled with raisins, lightly cooked vegetables. Satisfied and laden with bags, she heads home as the sun sinks toward the horizon.

***

During Chinese New Year, a small boy, tongue hanging out of his mouth, gingerly brushes egg over coconut-*sago* cookies he has just helped his grandmother cut out. He sprinkles sesame seeds over them, trying to cover each flower shape and star shape as neatly as possible. Later on, he will take maybe, oh, three seconds to eat each cookie.

***

An old man at a cart prepares *kuih tu tu*, steamed sugar-stuffed cakes. He greets his regular customers, "Hello sir," "Thank you *brudder* [brother]," as he carefully smooths tapioca flour into a fluted mold, tops it with a pinch of palm sugar and then more flour, and upends it onto a cloth-lined hollow in a steamer tray. He scoops up a finished *kuih* onto a square of pandan leaf and puts it in a waiting bag, with its fellows. He repeats this ritual, always with the same unhurried care, almost a hundred times a day.

***

On the eve of Diwali, the Hindu festival of lights, a young Indian mother makes a chocolate cake for her Chinese neighbors, with a smile and a murmured blessing.

THIS PAGE Little India's vegetable stalls open from early until late.

OPPOSITE Mrs. Lim, the inventor of the famous Singapore chili crab at her son Roland's restaurant.

A many-colored weave

Those are only small glimpses of the bigger tableau. But you get the picture: Singapore's food culture is not singular, monocultural or monohistorical — it is plural, polyglot. It resists simple definition. It is a confluence of what anthropologists call foodways, the traditions and protocols of kitchens and dining tables.

Stir-frying is an art that depends on searing heat and a deft wrist.

The cooking of Singapore's original native Malay population would have been contiguous with that of Malay communities in the region: Peninsular Malaysia, Indonesia, Sumatra and so on. Its legacy lives on today mainly in the private homes of Malay families, in the shape of tamarind-soured seafood curries, beef, mutton and poultry curries rich with coconut milk, simply cooked vegetables, *ulam* (assortments of herbs and greens), and *sambals* (spicy relishes). Rice is the main staple, and fresh herbs and spices ever present as seasonings. Countless variations of *kuih* (cakes and desserts), many of Indonesian origin and elaboration, are spun out of a simple palette of coconut, palm sugar, *sago* pearls, pandan leaves, sweet potatoes, *cassava* and glutinous rice. While small family establishments do cook from this repertoire, the Muslim restaurant scene is dominated by *nasi padang* (Padang-style rice and cooked food) and *rijsttafel* establishments, which reflect Indonesian roots rather than specifically Singaporean Malay elements.

Immigrants from further afield overlaid this Malay foundation with subcuisines from southern China, namely Hokkien, Teochew (Chiu Chow), Hakka, Foochow and Cantonese. Each dialect group has its own particularities in the kitchen. Hokkiens use different pickled and preserved items, take special care in slicing ingredients, season with a light hand and are famous for noodle dishes; Teochews are experts at steaming, love seafood and make paramount rice congee; Hakkas make much use of pork and preserved vegetables, season robustly but appetizingly, and have created some very unusual dishes, such as "thunder tea rice," rice mixed with stir-fried vegetables, peanuts and a watery purée of fresh herbs and tea leaves; Foochows are famous for their soups, pressed glutinous rice flour cakes fried like noodles, shellfish dishes, pork-stuffed fish balls, and stews made with red-fermented rice wine lees; and the Cantonese brew potent slow-simmered soups, leave few animals or animal parts uneaten, and emphasize the freshest ingredients as a foundation, precisely cut and cooked to bring out rather than transform their essential character.

Special mention must also be made of the Chinese from Hainan Island, who on coming to Singapore established themselves as cooks of singular distinction for European expatriate and Peranakan families. Many Hainanese later went on to found independent bakeries, coffee shops and restaurants, the latter often serving Asianized versions of the Western dishes that their chefs learned from their former bosses; few are still around, but those that are, like Shashlyk — which serves "Russian" food — have iconic status.

INSIDE THE SINGAPOREAN KITCHEN

As Singaporean food encompasses several different cuisines, you'll need a well-stocked pantry to cook your way across its ethnic breadth.

Condiments: light, dark and thick dark soy sauces, fermented salted soybeans (*taucheo*), vinegar, rice wine, sesame oil, oyster sauce.

Pantry staples: *belacan* (fermented shrimp paste), *asam* (tamarind pulp), *hay bee* (dried shrimp), different kinds of *dal* (dried lentils), freshly grated coconut.

Dried spices, whole or ground: red chilies, cinnamon, cloves, coriander seeds, cumin, white and black peppercorns, fennel, star anise, turmeric, cardamom, five-spice powder, candlenuts, blended curry powders.

Fresh spices and herbs: red and green chilies, Chinese celery, chives, coriander leaves, curry leaves, garlic, *galangal* (blue ginger), kaffir lime leaves, lemongrass, pandan leaves, purple shallots, spring onions, turmeric.

ESSENTIAL COOKING TECHNIQUES

All the core Asian cooking techniques such as stir-frying, braising, steaming and deep-frying are called on in the Singaporean kitchen; all involve the precise application and control of heat, a skill that experienced cooks push to its limits. The oldest houses in Singapore all have outside kitchens for preparation and wok cooking, to keep the noise and heat away from living spaces.

Two very important and related techniques are the correct pounding and correct frying of a spice paste (or *rempah*, as the Malays and Nyonyas call it) in ample oil to achieve a fragrant and flavorful base for curries and other dishes. Modern Singaporeans use blenders and non-stick pans, but traditionalists insist on granite pestles and mortars and well-seasoned woks to achieve the correct texture and intensity of flavor.

ESSENTIAL KITCHEN IMPLEMENTS

The two most crucial requirements are a good sturdy wok and a source of heat that can be varied from fierce to gentle. These will allow you to cook everything from stir-fries to curries to braises to deep-fried items. A mortar and pestle or a mini-chopper is essential for grinding spice pastes and *sambals*. As with most other cuisines, a good set of sharp knives and a sturdy chopping board are also basic necessities.

CLOKWISE (from top left)
Murtabak, a stuffed flatbread, is made of dough flipped and stretched until it is thin enough to see through; Dried seafoods are used by Chinese cooks to make stocks and flavor dishes; Succulent links of lup cheong (Chinese pork sausage); and Pop art and vegetables at Little India.

The largest proportion of Singapore's Indian community traces its roots to southern Indian states such as Kerala and Tamil Nadu. However, explore the restaurants, shops and market stalls of Little India — the epicenter of community life since the eighteenth century — and along with Tamil, the lilt of Malayalam, Hindi, Gujarati, Bengali, Sindhi and other languages will show you that many of the mother country's regions are represented here. Most of those restaurants specialize in a particular subcuisine, though the coconut, rice, and pungent, warm *masalas* of southern Indian cuisine hold sway; its other hallmarks include *dosas* (rice and *dal* crepes), *idlis* (steamed rice pancakes), *sambar* (vegetable and toasted coconut curry), *rasam* (hot and tangy vegetable broth), *thorans* (vegetable and coconut stir-fries) and innumerable curries — mostly dry-style — of mixed vegetables, seafood and meat. Regular diners in Little India also know where to find the best Hyderabadi *biryanis*, Punjabi-style *tandoor* cooking, Mumbai *chaats* (snack-salads), Bengali sweetmeats and the like. A popular Indian Muslim street food is the *roti prata* (a distant relative of the Indian *paratha*), a fried flatbread of stretched and folded paper-thin dough.

Some of the communities of foreign expatriates and workers living in Singapore are large and established enough to have given rise to cultural enclaves where the homesick can feast on their mother cuisine. Hence there is also Little Philippines, Little Thailand, Little Myanmar and so on.

Melding pot

The "melting pot" metaphor has often (and imprecisely) been applied to Singapore's food. The image it suggests of a sort of indiscriminately multifarious stew lags far behind the reality, the complex and unpredictable way in which the cuisines of Singapore's different cultures have evolved side by side, shared and swapped influences.

Your order of Hokkien fried noodles, for example, will invariably be accompanied by a tropical *kalamansi* lime (*kalamansi* being a Filipino name) and a spoonful of *sambal goreng*, a Malay fried chili-paste condiment. And although similar dishes do exist in Bengal and elsewhere in India, fish-head curry is often touted as being concocted by Singaporean Indian restaurants for fish-cheek-loving Chinese diners, and is thus a unique local dish — even more so when cooked by the Chinese hawkers who have "re-adapted" it to their own style!

There are also two communities, originally from Malacca but established in Singapore for well over a century, that despite their small size have made lasting contributions to Singaporean food culture.

The Peranakans (also known as the Straits Chinese) are descendants of Chinese immigrants who married Malay or Indonesian spouses, or adopted a mix of traditional Chinese and Malay customs. Their food also intertwines Malay, Chinese and Indonesian elements. Classic Peranakan dishes include *ayam buah keluak* (chicken and black *keluak* nuts in spicy tamarind gravy), *laksa* (rice noodles and seafood in a rich coconut gravy-cum-soup), *babi pongteh* (pork cooked with fermented soybeans, garlic and cinnamon) and *udang pedas nanas* (prawns and pineapple in a thin, sour gravy with aromatic leaves), to name but a very few.

Like their heritage, the Eurasians' cuisine is both broad and intricate, stemming from Portuguese, Dutch, British, Indonesian, Indian, Malay and Chinese roots. Standards include buttery *sugee* (semolina) cake, served at weddings and birthdays, a host of tamarind-braised dishes, *putchree* (a type of spicy relish related to Indian *pacheris*), and curry *debal*, roast chicken, roast pork, onions, cabbage and other ingredients cooked in a fiery brick-red gravy seasoned with dried chilies, mustard and ginger. Different families often cook the same dishes in fiercely individual ways.

Both Peranakan and Eurasian cuisines meld a thoroughly Asian penchant for vigorous spicing with a Chinese/European love for pork and organ meats. Hence the Eurasian *feng*, a curried stew of finely diced heart, lungs and liver, traditionally served at Christmas, and the Nyonya *hati babi bungkus*, meatballs of minced pork and liver heavily spiced with ground coriander, wrapped in caul fat and fried, and served with pickled mustard greens.

These two cuisines are also vivid examples of how every major religion in Singapore has special foods associated with festival seasons. Advent sees Eurasian families pulling out all the stops for grand Christmas dinners. The Peranakans — who sometimes dub themselves "more Chinese than the Chinese," as some of their traditional practices have been forgotten by the pure Chinese, — have a plethora of dishes associated with Chinese New Year, as well as specific foods for offerings, weddings, funerals and so on, all laden with symbolism.

You could, in fact, mark up a year's worth of festivals just by observing the *pasar malams* (night markets) that spring up. At Chinese New Year, the narrow lanes of Chinatown are narrowed further by street stalls selling everything from ornamental bamboo to preserved waxed duck and sticky *nian gao* (glutinous rice flour cakes) for offerings. During Ramadan, lanes around Geylang Serai and Arab Street come alive with stalls selling choice delicacies for Malay families to break their fasting with. Deepavali (Diwali), the Hindu festival of lights, sees *mithai* (sweets) blossom in sugary profusion next to other stalls blaring the latest Bollywood soundtracks.

THIS PAGE Singapore laksa bathes rice noodles in a rich and spicy coconut-milk gravy.

OPPOSITE Freshly-made fish balls are kept in a bath of cool water.

Heart and soul

Hawker centers, open-plan food courts housing many small stalls each specializing in a different dish or style of dish, are the great equalizers of Singaporean culture. Originally conceived as a cleaner and more hygienic setting for street hawkers to be housed in, they have become places where the nation's heart beats, three times (and more) a day.

Everybody, from ministers to taxi-drivers, eats at hawker centers, whether they are after a quick breakfast, light lunch, indulgent tea, family dinner, supper or wee-hours snack. Every suburban area or satellite town has at least one hawker center in its midst. The bigger centers usually house all of Singapore's different ethnic food streams under one roof. The shared orders of groups of diners typically reflect this in microcosm, with Chinese noodles jostling for space next to Indian *thalis* heaped with vegetarian food, and plates of Malay *satay*.

In fact, in culinary terms, hawker stalls and small family restaurants are both the lowest common denominator — not in the sense of moral rank, but egalitarian level — and highest indigenous evolved form of Singaporean cuisine. This latter statement can be qualified if we understand that hawker food has always been fueled by these factors: the hawker's personal heritage and cooking style; the availability of raw ingredients; an adaptive understanding of what the broader public wants to eat; and the lively competitive pressure of compatriots and rivals.

THIS PAGE Lau Pa Sat festival market, a pavilion of filigreed cast iron, was built in 1894, and was restored in the late 1980s and recommissioned as a hawker center.

OPPOSITE (top) Chinese cooked-food hawker stalls typically serve a very wide array of dishes to go with rice; (bottom) Freshly made flour skins make all the difference to a good popiah, like these at Kway Guan Huat in Singapore's Joo Chiat area.

The intensity of this last factor, coupled with the low prices that hawker food must command, sets hawkers in a different arena from higher-tier restaurateurs with more space, time and capital: hawkers hone their craft on the very edge of survival. The very best ones infuse their food with such passion and care that they build up crowds of devotees. Some do well enough to send their children for overseas education! Others have even taken advantage of the Internet and renamed themselves with website addresses.

Food in public life

The postwar era's slow return to the comforts of normal life, combined with a new onus to establish national unity and economic integrity, has had a lasting effect: it is very Singaporean to obsess about your rice bowl at both the abstract level — that is, your financial security — and the literal level, on the table in front of you.

Food is an ever-present backdrop — one could even say underpinning — to Singaporean life. It is a constant topic of conversation (and argument), the center of virtually every celebration, the reason for many a long drive across town. When people say "Oh, we discuss where to have dinner while we're eating lunch," they do so cheerfully, not sheepishly.

Whenever the topic of "Singaporean identity" comes up in the press, you can bet that food will be mentioned. In *Singaporeans Exposed*, a collection of essays on local identity and globalization published by the Singapore International Foundation in 2001, both the personal reflections and professional surveys of what it means to be Singaporean are riddled with food references, from *roti prata* to chicken rice to buying fish.

For most of our life as a country, this ceaseless foodie foment has gone on without much comment. Only within the past 10 years or so, along with the rise of "lifestyle" magazines, books and television programs around the globe, has food become a trendy topic of media coverage in Singapore. Now you can't escape it: virtually every week sees the debut of a new food TV series, food magazine, restaurant guide or local cookbook.

Add food blog, an online diary dedicated to gourmandise, to that list. Singaporeans love to eat, love to cook, love to travel and love to talk about what they eat and cook, and where they go. All these traits have proved to be lusty leaven for the rise of the local food blogosphere. The vividly social way in which food blogging satisfies hunger for information, self-expression and gastronomical experiences seems to have particular appeal for us.

Food and the future

The mid-range to high-end dining scene in Singapore becomes ever more ramified — and some would say stratified — with each passing year. Fueled by visiting foreign chefs and the travels of local chefs, global food and beverage industry trends ripple through local kitchens surprisingly quickly: they are encouraged by events like the World Gourmet Summit and guest-chef promotions organized by hotels, which bring visiting foreign chefs and local talents together for mutual edification.

But we are not just talking the talk. In 2005 in Basel, Switzerland, the Singapore Culinary National Team walked away with the overall champion's crown at the *Salon Culinaire Mondial*, an extremely prestigious international competition held every six years. The young team (and the only one from Asia to compete) pipped nine other countries to the post.

Asian youths beating old-school Continental chefs at their own game; hawkers who own stretch luxury cars; a single dish imprinted with nuances of four countries. In folklore, places where such different worlds touch are known as liminal points, and are regarded with awe and caution. They are junctures where one can take a step and find oneself far beyond known borders.

Intentionally or not, this has become part of the dream of Singapore, a country, itself poor in natural resources, made successful by transforming itself into a strategic crossing point for goods and information. It's not so surprising, then, that this has also become the emergent goal of the food culture it has forged.

THIS PAGE (left) Trays of veggies for sale at a wet market stall; (right) Small bitter gourds.

OPPOSITE To make popiah skins, stretchy blobs of dough are tapped on a griddle to form paper-thin crepes.

Yu sheng

Chinese New Year raw fish salad

In the 1960s a humble southern Chinese dish of raw fish slices was given a gentrified, glamorous makeover by Singapore's "Heavenly Kings," a quartet of Chinese chefs then prominent on the local restaurant scene. Chefs Sin Leong, Lau Yoke Pui, Hooi Kok Wai and Tham Yui Kai elaborated on the original dish's sour-salty-pungent seasonings of lime, coriander leaves, ginger and five-spice by adding a host of candied, preserved and fried ingredients, turning it into a seven-colored celebratory feast to be savored on the seventh day of Chinese New Year. Every ingredient has a symbolic association with good fortune for the new year, and diners use chopsticks to toss the salad together, with vigorous motions representing the heights of success.

During times of economic vigor, extravagant variations of yu sheng *tend to turn up in the posher Chinese restaurants: with lobster sashimi, abalone, gold leaf, sea urchin, caviar and so on. One variant now firmly established is salmon* yu sheng, *surely traceable to Singaporeans' love of Japanese salmon sashimi; in fact, it is becoming more common than* ikan parang yu sheng, *as it requires less tedious preparation.*

Serves 10 as an appetizer

The fresh ingredients
60 grams white or green daikon radish, peeled
60 grams carrot, peeled
50 grams pomelo flesh, crumbled into individual sacs
1 1/2 tablespoons finely julienned young ginger
1 cup loosely packed fresh coriander leaf sprigs
1 red chili, deseeded, cut into fine slivers
4 kaffir lime leaves, with thick veins removed, cut into hair-fine shreds

For the fish
200 grams *ikan parang* (wolf herring) fillet
75 grams prepared jellyfish

The preserved ingredients
25 grams pickled papaya, finely julienned
25 grams drained sweet pickled red ginger, finely julienned
25 grams drained sour pickled white ginger, finely julienned

25 grams drained pickled leek bulb, very thinly sliced
25 grams candied winter melon, finely chopped
30 grams candied dried kumquat or tangerine peel, very thinly slivered

For the condiments
100 milliliters plum sauce, thinned with 50 milliliters water
100 milliliters peanut or vegetable oil
1/2 teaspoon ground cinnamon
1/2 teaspoon ground white pepper
2-3 *kalamansi* limes

The fried and roasted ingredients
35 grams sesame seeds, toasted until golden
60 grams roasted peanuts, ground medium-fine
125 grams *pok chui* (fried dough flakes, also called gold ingots)

1. Slice daikon and carrot into very thin slices, with a mandoline if you have one, then stack the slices and cut into very fine julienne. (Do not grate them since this will make the *yu sheng* mushy.) Transfer to separate bowls of ice water and let stand 20 minutes while you prepare the other ingredients.

2. Slice *ikan parang* very thinly. To help you do this, firm up the fish flesh by partly freezing it. Lay the slices out on a small plate, fanning them out in a decorative rosette pattern. Set aside for a few minutes to let it reach room temperature.

3. Drain the soaked vegetable shreds, then wrap them in a thin cloth and wring it out gently, to extract as much moisture as possible. Arrange them, along with all the other fresh and preserved ingredients in separate mounds on a very large round serving plate.

4. Have the plum sauce, oil, cinnamon, pepper and *kalamansi* halves available in separate individual saucers, and the fried and roasted ingredients ready in separate bowls or plates.

Chef's note:
Prepared (that is, presoaked, and sometimes seasoned) jellyfish is available in vacuum-packed sachets from Chinese grocery stores.

Ikan parang, or wolf herring, has a clean, subtle flavor, but unfortunately also many tiny bones. Traditionally, the fillets are hung up in a well-ventilated area for a while to dry out and firm up the flesh. This makes it easier to slice it very thinly, during which the bones can be picked out or sliced up with the flesh into indiscernible fragments.

Chinese grocery and dried-goods stores should sell all the preserved and dried ingredients. At Chinese New Year, most Singaporean supermarkets and Chinese groceries sell *yu sheng* kits, which contain measured portions of all the preserved, fried and toasted ingredients and condiments.

If you cannot find *pok chui* (fried dough flakes), simply cut wonton skins into strips and deep-fry until golden. Also, make sure your peanuts are fresh — stale, rancid nuts will ruin the entire dish.

Tossing the *yu sheng*

Arm all the diners with long chopsticks. Place the large round plate in the middle of the dining table, and the other plates, bowls and saucers around it. Say "*xin nian kuai le*" (may the new year bring you joy) or "*gong xi fa cai*" (may you be prosperous), or "*wan shi ru yi*" (may life sail smoothly). Squeeze the *kalamansi* in a Chinese spoon, using the *kalamansi* halves to hold the seeds back, and let the juice trickle over the sliced fish. Say "*da ji da li*" (may luck accrue). Place the fish on top of the fresh ingredients. Say "*nian nian you yu*" (may every year overflow with abundance), and "*long ma jing shen*" (may health be good).

Sprinkle the cinnamon and white pepper evenly over everything. Say "*xin xiang shi cheng*" (may you receive your heart's desire), or "*hong yun dang tou*" (may luck grace your doorstep). Pour the oil over everything. Say "*rong hua fu gui*" (may you enjoy prosperity).

Pour the plum sauce over everything. Say "*tian tian mi mi*" (may life be sweet). Sprinkle the peanuts over. Say "*jin yin man wu*" (may you have riches aplenty). Sprinkle the sesame seeds over. Say "*sheng yi xing long*" (may business flourish).

Finally, sprinkle the *pok chui* over. Say "*man di huang jin*" (may you harvest much gold). Say "*zhu da jiao lao dao feng sheng shui qi*" (toss until the winds and waters rise — wind and water being symbolic of good fortune) to exhort everyone to begin tossing the *lo hei*.

Everyone stands up to mix all the ingredients together with their chopsticks. The aim is to lift clumps of ingredients as high as you can above the dish, without making too much of a mess. As they do so, diners may repeat any of the above wishes, or add others, such as "*bu bu gao shen*" (may you have career success), or compose new ones to say.

When everything is well mixed, diners sit down and help themselves.

Popiah

Fresh spring rolls

This dish originates from Xiamen (formerly Amoy) in southern China's Fujian province, the home of many of Singapore's Chinese settlers. Today, Hokkien (as the Fujian are called locally) eateries and hawker stalls in Singapore do a steady trade in popiah, *an "anytime" food as appropriate to breakfast or supper as it is to lunch or dinner.*

The dish has also been adopted by the Peranakans. Generations ago, my Nyonya grand-aunts would scoff at the presence of bangkwang (yam bean or jicama) *in* popiah *filling, their Platonic ideal comprising exclusively bamboo shoots, pork and, perhaps, small prawns. In both homes and hawker stalls, this traditional recipe has over the years given way to a combination of* bangkwang *and a much reduced amount of bamboo shoots. This is probably for reasons of flavor as well as economy and efficiency;* bangkwang *is cheaper, sweeter-tasting and reaches tender palatability in less time than bamboo shoots.*

Though having also largely substituted bangkwang *for bamboo shoots, Hokkien versions of* popiah *filling otherwise hew close to the Amoy original, including carrot, green beans or snow peas in the filling, and ground peanuts and crumbled crisp-fried flatfish among the garnishes.*

Serves 8 - 10 as a main dish

Chef's note:
Most people these days buy *popiah* skins from market stalls; made from a flour, water and salt batter, these are quite thin, slightly chewy, and keep for a couple of days in the refrigerator. Some families — especially Peranakan ones — with the time and inclination make their own skins from a batter of flour, water, eggs and salt; thicker and more moist, they should be eaten the same day they are made. To do this yourself, take any reliable crepe recipe and replace most or all of the eggs with egg whites alone, preferably duck egg whites, as they yield a desirably resilient texture.

500 grams belly pork
250 grams whole fresh prawns
150 milliliters oil
2 cakes *taukwa* (cotton beancurd),
   about 300 grams
1 kilogram *bangkwang* (yam bean, jicama)
700 grams bamboo shoots, well rinsed
60 grams garlic, pounded to a rough paste
4 tablespoons *taucheo* (salted, fermented
   soy beans), pounded to a paste
3 tablespoons sugar, or to taste
1 tablespoon light soy sauce
salt to taste
20-25 *popiah* skins
sweet flour sauce (see Chef's note on
   page 195)

For the garnishes
26-30 lettuce leaves
2 *lup cheong* (Chinese dried sausages),
   steamed until cooked through, sliced

5 eggs, hard-boiled and sliced
1 large cucumber, peeled, deseeded
   and julienned
250 grams bean sprouts, cleaned,
   blanched for 10 seconds, and drained
large handful fresh coriander leaf sprigs

For the chili paste
5 large red chilies, finely chopped
2-5 *chili padi* (bird's-eye chilies),
   chopped (optional)
1/2 teaspoon salt
1/2 teaspoon sugar
1 teaspoon lime juice or white vinegar

For the garlic paste
50 grams garlic
1/4 teaspoon salt

1. Rinse belly pork with boiling water and drain. Combine pork with 1 liter fresh water in a pot, bring to a boil, then reduce heat, partly cover and simmer gently for 40 minutes, or until pork becomes tender. Remove pork, let cool, then slice into thin matchsticks. Set aside the pork stock.

2. Remove prawn heads and shells. Reserve them for later use. Blanch prawn bodies in boiling water until just cooked through. Let cool, then halve lengthwise and devein. Set aside, tightly covered and refrigerated.

3. Heat 1 tablespoon of the oil in a wok over high heat. When very hot, add prawn shells and stir-fry vigorously until shells are bright red-orange, about 1 minute. Pour pork stock into the pan, bring to a boil, and simmer for 15 minutes. Strain, pressing on shells to extract as much flavor as possible. Then set aside.

4. Cut *taukwa* into strips about 4-centimeters long and 4 to 5 millimeters thick. Pat dry with kitchen towels. Heat 2 tablespoons of the oil in a frying pan over medium heat. When very hot, add *taukwa* strips. Fry for 5 to 7 minutes, or until golden brown and slightly shrunken. Set aside.

5. Peel *bangkwang* and cut it into slices about 2-millimeters thick. Stack slices and cut across into matchsticks about 3 to 4 millimeters thick and 5-centimeters long. Drain *bangkwang* in a large sieve, pressing gently to extract excess moisture.

6. Cut bamboo shoots into matchsticks of similar dimensions, or very slightly bigger. Be as meticulous as you can about slicing, because uneven shreds will produce a jarringly rough mouthfeel. On no account use a grater, or the filling will be mushy.

7. Heat remaining oil in a wok over medium-high heat. Add garlic and fry, stirring constantly, for 1 minute or until fragrant. Add *taucheo* and sugar and fry 1 minute more, then add *bangkwang*, bamboo shoots and 300 milliliters of the pork-prawn stock. Bring to a simmer and cook, stirring gently and frequently, for 30 minutes. Add *taukwa* strips and pork, and simmer 30 to 45 minutes more, until vegetables are very tender but not disintegrating. Filling should be very moist but not sodden with gravy. Moisten with more stock if necessary. Season with soy sauce and salt to taste.

8. Make chili paste by pounding or blending all ingredients together until finely ground. Make garlic paste likewise. Spoon into separate bowls and cover with plastic wrap, pressing wrap onto surface of pastes. Refrigerate until serving time.

9. Assembling the *popiah*:
This is basically similar to making a spring roll. However, as the filling is more moist, be careful not to overstuff or the *popiah* might burst. Lay a *popiah* skin on a flat plate. Smear with a little chili paste, a little garlic paste and a little sweet flour sauce. Lay a lettuce leaf on top of the sauces. With a slotted spoon, scoop up some filling and form it into a long mound atop the leaf. Arrange your chosen garnishes over, then roll up, tucking the sides in as you go. Slice into neat sections with a sharp knife, or simply tackle it whole.

Additional Chef's note:
Often misidentified as turnip, *bangkwang* is also known as yam bean, or jicama in the Americas. A top-shaped root with rough brown skin, it is usually sold at wet markets with most of the earth cleaned off.

Sweet flour sauce is a concoction of flour-thickened caramel, sold at Chinese supermarkets and grocery stores. If you can't get it, melt equal volumes of water, dark-brown sugar and honey, and a splash of light soy sauce together over low heat, and let cool before using. Do not substitute *kicap manis* or any sweetened soy sauce, which are too salty and will throw the balance off.

The lettuce leaves used for *popiah* are soft and slightly frilly, with a flavor like a blend of romaine, oak-leaf lettuce and butterhead. Any of these can be used instead.

Or chor ter kar

Pig's trotters braised with black vinegar and ginger

The Chinese consider this dish essential for new mothers during their postbirth confinement period. This form of benign house arrest lasts a month, during which nursing mothers refrain from taking baths or showers, get plenty of rest and eat foods designed to strengthen, energize and detoxify the system — especially this dish! So important is this dish that some local private hospitals include it on their catered food menus. Each of its ingredients has a specific role to play in nourishing the new mother: in Chinese gastronomy, every food has a function and medicinal value over and above its flavor.

Ginger has a warming yang nature, alleviates nausea, cures indigestion, chills and colds, and expels wind. This last attribute is especially pertinent, as giving birth is thought to leave a lot of postpartum "wind" in the mother's body, which if not expelled, cools the body too much and makes it prone to rheumatism and other aches and pains.

Vinegar is also warm, detoxifying, purifies the blood, promotes digestion, alleviates bleeding and strengthens the respiratory system. Brown sugar is a warming energy tonic that promotes circulation, while sesame oil helps to lubricate the system and speeds skin healing. Pig's trotters contain collagen, fat and proteins that promote lactation and temper the heat of the other ingredients, and eggs are generally nourishing.

New mothers aside, this dish has many fans of all ages and both genders. Containing so much vinegar as to be practically a pickle, it keeps very well, as you might expect. If you are new to it, you may find its flavor shockingly concentrated at first, but you will soon warm to it — literally!

Chef's note:
Old ginger, rich in pungent oils under its thick buff skin, must be used for this brew. Young ginger is not potent enough. By the end of the cooking, it acquires an almost candied flavor, while retaining enough heat to make your mouth tingle.

There is no real substitute for black vinegar, which is distilled from glutinous rice, millet or sorghum, and has a musty, sweet flavor somewhat like balsamic vinegar. Some brands commonly available in Singapore are infused with flavorings such as dried orange peel and red dates; these will yield a more complex flavor than plain black vinegar from China.

Other than trotters, pork belly and thick-cut pork ribs are also delicious in *or chor ter kar*.

Serves 6 - 8 as part of a multicourse meal

2 pig's trotters (about 1.5 to 2 kilograms)
100 milliliters sesame oil
1 kilogram old ginger, peeled, slightly bruised, and sliced thickly
750 milliliters black vinegar

425 grams unrefined brown sugar, plus more to taste
4-6 hard-boiled eggs, peeled
salt to taste

1. Use a sharp-bladed knife to scrape off any hair or stubble from the pig's trotters' skin. Wash trotters well and chop into large chunks. You can get your pork butcher to do this for you. Set aside.

2. Heat sesame oil in a wok or frying pan over medium heat. When hot, add ginger and stir-fry for 3 to 5 minutes, or until fragrant. Add vinegar, 1.5 liters of water and sugar to the pan and bring to a boil. Reduce heat slightly and leave it to simmer.

3. Bring another large pot of fresh water to a boil. Add pig's trotters and blanch for 1 minute, then drain. Add trotters to the simmering vinegar. Partly cover and simmer for 2 hours. Add eggs and simmer 30 minutes more, until trotter is meltingly tender and ginger is soft enough to eat. Taste the gravy: the pungent, sweet and sour flavors should be intense but in balance. If necessary, add a touch more sugar or vinegar, as necessary. Add salt if desired — some people prefer not to. Serve with plenty of hot steamed rice.

Nyonya birthday mee

Nyonya birthday noodles

Absolutely essential for a Peranakan birthday celebration: one of the most persistent symbolisms among the Chinese and the Chinese diaspora is that noodles represent long life, and hence must be eaten at birthday, wedding and other life-honoring feasts.

This dish derives from the Hokkien way of frying yellow noodles, though with different — and non-negotiable! — garnishes. A similar dish is made with mee sua, *thin wheat noodles that also feature in two other birthday items. These are* mee sua *in sugared water with hard-boiled eggs — a symbolic concatenation of longevity and birth — and* mee sua *in a savory soup with pork offal.*

Serves 4 - 5 as part of a multicourse meal

175 grams belly pork, in one long strip
300 grams whole fresh prawns
100 milliliters rendered lard
  or vegetable oil
6 cloves garlic, pounded to a paste
1 tablespoon *taucheo* (salted, fermented
  soy beans), pounded to a paste
600 grams yellow noodles
150 grams *kangkong* (water convolvulus),
  thoroughly washed and cut into
  5-centimeter lengths
75 grams bean sprouts, cleaned

1/4 teaspoon salt
1/4 teaspoon ground white pepper
1/2 teaspoon sugar

For the garnishes
1 cucumber, peeled, deseeded
  and julienned
2-3 red chilies, julienned
3 eggs, beaten, fried into a thin omelet
  and shredded
fresh coriander leaves
crispy-fried shallots

1. Rinse belly pork with boiling water and drain. Combine pork with 700 milliliters fresh water in a pot, bring to a boil, then reduce heat. Partly cover and simmer gently for 40 minutes, or until pork is tender and stock has reduced to about 500 milliliters. Remove pork, let cool, then slice thinly.

2. Remove prawn heads and shells, set aside and reserve. Keep prawn flesh in a separate bowl, covered and refrigerated.

3. Heat 1 tablespoon of the lard or oil in a wok over high heat. When very hot, add prawn shells and stir-fry vigorously until shells are bright-red orange, about 1 minute. Pour pork stock into pan, bring to a boil, and simmer for 15 minutes. Strain, pressing on shells to extract as much flavor as possible. You should have about 300 milliliters of pork-prawn stock, dotted with beads of orange-tinted oil from the prawn heads.

4. Heat remaining lard or oil in a wok over high heat. When hot, add garlic and fry 30 to 40 seconds or until fragrant, then add *taucheo* and fry 20 seconds. Add 200 milliliters pork-prawn stock and bring to a boil, then add prawn flesh and pork slices and cook 1 minute, stirring. Add noodles, *kangkong* and bean sprouts and stir-fry vigorously for 2 to 3 minutes. Add a little more stock if noodles look too dry — they should be moistly coated with a little liquid, but not swimming in it. Season with salt, white pepper and sugar and transfer to a serving plate. Arrange the garnishes on top and serve immediately.

Chef's note:
It is preferable to buy whole-bean *taucheo* and pound or mash it yourself. Ready-mashed brands are often too sweet, or lack oomph.

The correct yellow noodles to use for this dish are about the same thickness as spaghetti. They are sold fresh at wet markets and Chinese supermarkets.

Hainanese chicken rice

Among the culinary specialties of China's Hainan Island is Wenchang chicken, poached chicken of a breed treasured for its flavorful meat and fat. In the hands of Singapore's Hainanese immigrants, who quickly established a tribal reputation for being superlative chefs, this dish evolved into "Hainanese chicken rice" — which, amusingly enough, has since been re-exported to Hainan Island as "Singapore chicken rice."

This is one of those fiercely polarizing dishes, the kind that you can start ongoing arguments about by asking a group of people "Where do you think is the best…." In its canonical Singaporean form, it centers on a chicken poached and rested for just long enough to render meat and skin silken, served with rice cooked with chicken stock and a suite of condiments.

At home, Hainanese cooks simply gloss the chicken with sesame oil after poaching. Others plunge it into iced water, which gives the skin a firm and jellylike texture — much loved by the Cantonese — and douse the sliced chicken with a blend of light soy sauce, cooking juices and sesame oil. This has become the predominant hawker presentation, perhaps because it is also more attractive.

In Muslim versions of chicken rice, the ayam *(chicken) is typically roasted, the* nasi *(rice) grains may be seasoned with lemongrass or other spices, and instead of simple sliced cucumber, you may get a spoonful of* achar, *a spicy mixed vegetable pickle.*

Chef's note:
Choose a good free-range chicken, as tasteless battery hens will yield an utterly bland dish. Capons are even better, as they have flavorful meat and ample fat.

The kind of treacly-textured soy sauce served as a garnish is so specific to this dish, it is sometimes called "chicken rice soya sauce." It is not often seen outside Singapore and Malaysia, so you can substitute the thickest, darkest soy sauce you can find.

For a Cantonese-style presentation, plunge the poached chicken into a large bowl of water and ice, breast down. Let it stand for 15 minutes, then transfer to a plate and rub with sesame oil. If possible, hang it up with a meat hook for a while, to help meat relax.

Serves 4

1 large chicken, thoroughly cleaned and giblets removed
3 slices ginger, bruised
3 cloves garlic, bruised
2 tablespoons sesame oil
650 grams long-grain rice, preferably jasmine rice
5 tablespoons finely chopped garlic
4 tablespoons finely chopped ginger
5 shallots, peeled and minced
1 pandan leaf, tied in a knot
1 teaspoon salt, plus more to taste

For the chili sauce
7 large red chilies
3 red *chili padi* (bird's-eye chilies), or more to taste

4 cloves garlic
2 tablespoons freshly squeezed lime juice
1 1/2 tablespoons chopped young ginger
sugar and salt, to taste

For the ginger sauce
5 tablespoons peeled and chopped old ginger
2 tablespoons oil
salt to taste

To serve
thick black soy sauce
fresh coriander leaves
sliced cucumber and tomato
chopped spring onion

1. Cut off and set aside excess skin and fat pads from chicken; do not break skin covering breasts and legs.

2. Bring 2.5 liters of water, ginger and garlic to a rolling boil in a deep pot. Gently submerge chicken in water. Bring to a vigorous simmer and cook, partly covered for 12 minutes. Cover pot tightly, switch off the heat and let stand for another 20 minutes. Carefully lift out chicken from the hot stock. Rub skin with sesame oil and set chicken aside, covered.

3. Wash rice very well until water runs almost clear. Spread rice out on a plate or tray and let stand until dry.

4. Finely chop reserved chicken fat and skin, combine with 100 milliliters water in a non-stick pot and cook over medium-low heat until water has evaporated and fat has fully rendered, 10 to 15 minutes. Strain fat. You will need 100 milliliters of rendered fat. Make up the difference with cooking oil, if necessary.

5. Heat chicken fat in a wok over medium heat. When hot, add garlic, ginger and shallots and fry until fragrant, 1 to 2 minutes. Add rice and stir-fry gently until grains turn slightly opaque, about 2 minutes. Transfer rice to rice cooker, add pandan leaf, salt and 800 milliliters of the chicken stock. Switch on and leave to cook. (Alternatively, combine ingredients in a pot, cover and bring to a boil. Reduce heat to very low and cook 18 to 20 minutes or until rice is done.)

6. Make chili sauce by pulsing all ingredients in a blender until finely ground. Add 50 milliliters hot stock to help blend the ingredients until smooth. Make ginger sauce by blending ingredients to a fine paste with 1 tablespoon hot stock.

7. To serve, fluff cooked rice and adjust salt to your taste. Chop chicken into pieces: to make the breast more tender, flatten it with a cleaver before chopping. Serve with rice, sauces and garnish with coriander leaves, cucumber and tomatoes. Serve any remaining stock as soup, sprinkled with chopped spring onions.

Kuih tart

Pineapple tart

A natural fusion dish if ever there was one, the word "tart" in the name being a dead giveaway. And a very successful fusion it is too, of rich pastry and sweet-tart jam. In Singapore as well as in Malaysia, both Peranakan and Eurasian communities make pineapple tarts, a clue to the recipe's possibly Portuguese origins.

The pastry, discernibly a short-crust variant, was two or three generations ago made with lard, largely now superseded by butter, or — unfortunately — margarine, in the case of commercial producers. Commercial jam is often also a pale and oversweetened shadow of the real thing, which should be fruity and a rich amber.

Kuih tarts are classically made in a few different shapes. The basic "open" tarts have a raised rim decorated by pinching it with tweezers (bronze in my grandmothers' time, nowadays stainless steel or plastic), and a central pillow of jam, sometimes decorated with thin twiddles of pastry. "Closed" tarts are round or oval balls left plain, or adorned with little scissor-snipped V-shapes to mimic the hide of a pineapple, and a clove stuck in for a stalk. Sausage-roll shapes, plain or attractively corrugated, are more recent inventions.

Kuih tarts are an essential part of the lazy Susan of snacks and tidbits that all Chinese families have on hand to offer visiting relatives at Chinese New Year, so much so that comparing the merits of the tarts you ate at, say, Third Aunt's house with those at Second Cousin's house may engender long discussions!

Makes around 100 tarts

For the pineapple jam
1.5 kilograms peeled, cored pineapple, or canned pineapple in unsweetened pineapple juice
2 cinnamon sticks
6 "petals" star anise
6 cloves
800 grams sugar
200 milliliters fresh or bottled pineapple juice

For the tart pastry
400 grams plain flour, sifted
2 tablespoons caster sugar
2/3 teaspoon fine salt
250 grams cold unsalted butter, cubed
3 large egg yolks
1 1/2 teaspoons natural vanilla extract

Chef's note:
For a browner finish, brush tarts with an eggwash made of 1 egg beaten with 2 tablespoons water. To avoid damaging your design, it is best to brush open tart rims or closed tart surfaces with eggwash and let them dry for a few minutes, before pinching or snipping.

1. Make the pineapple jam ahead of time. If using fresh pineapple, save all the juice that escapes the peeling and coring. If using canned, do not discard juice. Pulse pineapple and juice in a food processor until fruit is very finely chopped.

Combine pineapple, all spices and 500 grams sugar in a large, wide, heavy-based pot, preferably non-stick. Stir well over medium heat until sugar dissolves. Taste pineapple mixture. If necessary, add a little more sugar or pineapple juice to achieve a sweet-fruity flavor balance. Bring to a boil, reduce heat to medium-low and cook, stirring very frequently, until jam is reduced to an amber-colored jam, 90 minutes to 2 hours and 30 minutes. Once most of the free liquid has evaporated, stir constantly and watch it like a hawk, to prevent it scorching. Jam is done when it has become a glossy paste about the texture of marmalade, able to hold a loose shape. Scrape into a bowl and let cool completely — it will get much stiffer as it cools. Stored in spotlessly clean airtight jars or plastic containers in the refrigerator, and touched only with clean utensils, pineapple jam will keep up to a year or more.

2. To make the pastry, whisk flour, sugar and salt together in a large mixing bowl until well blended. Add butter cubes to flour and toss well. Rub butter into flour with your fingertips or a pastry blender, until mixture resembles fine bread crumbs. Whisk egg yolks, vanilla and 50 milliliters of cold water (or more if necessary) together and drizzle evenly over flour mixture. Stir with a fork or butter knife to bring dough together into a ball. Knead dough very lightly for 5 seconds, then divide into 4 portions. Wrap in plastic wrap and chill for at least 1 hour.

3. Shape tarts:
a) *For open tarts*: With dampened fingertips, roll teaspoonfuls of jam into small balls. Roll out pastry dough about 5 to 6 millimeters thick. Use a pineapple tart cutter — press outer piece down first to cut through dough, then press inner piece down to make central dent in tart. Lift off cutter, tart will come with it. Gently ease tart off cutter. Pat jam ball into central dent. Pinch rim of tart decoratively with pincers. Place tarts on baking sheet. Decorate jam center with thin strips of dough. Brush tart rims with eggwash, if desired.

b) *For closed tarts*: Roll teaspoonfuls of jam into small balls. With lightly floured hands, pinch off a piece of dough the size of a large walnut. Press it into an irregular round about 3 to 4 millimeters thick. Place a jam ball in center of round, then bring up sides to enclose jam completely. Pinch seams well to seal, twisting off excess dough. Place on baking sheet, brush with eggwash if desired, and stick a clove in the top to make a stalk.

c) Alternatively, for an old-fashioned pineapple-shaped tart, make closed tarts oval-shaped (like an olive). If desired, brush with eggwash and set aside for a few minutes to dry slightly. Then, with small, sharp scissors, snip rows of 'V' shapes in pastry, being careful not to cut through to the jam. Stick a clove in one end to make a stalk.

4. Place tarts on baking sheet and bake at 325 degrees Fahrenheit (165 degrees Celsius) for 15 to 18 minutes if open shaped tarts and 20 to 25 minutes if closed and old-fashioned shaped tarts, or until pastry is pale gold. Cool on a rack.

5. Finished tarts will keep, refrigerated in an airtight container, for at least a week. Pastry will be crisp for one to two days after baking, but will soften and become more melt-in-your-mouth as tarts stand.

Curry puffs

The short-crust or puff pastry is recognizably European, the filling definitely Asian. In Indonesia and Macau they are called pastel, a Portuguese derivation; in Sri Lanka, patties, a Dutch one. Served at colonial teatime in India, they seem to be cousins of samosas *and Arabic* sambusaks.

Wherever they came from, curry puffs are an inescapable part of Singaporean cuisine. Decades ago, itinerant hawkers bearing baskets laden with them would cycle round neighborhoods, prompting hungry kids and adults to dig for loose change and get a kari pap *for tea. Every hawker center has at least one stall selling them. And no party, potluck, buffet spread or home economics textbook was — is! — ever complete without curry puffs.*

In Singapore the classic Indian curry puff encloses curried diced potato in a crisply deep-fried half-moon shell. Premium versions contain bits of mutton or chicken; super-premium ones have chunks of hard-boiled egg. Old-fashioned Muslim curry puffs are slightly different, flat, triangular and made with flaky puff pastry, baked instead of fried. Chinese hawkers, never one to miss a trick, have developed the shell curry puffs, which have spiral-ridged crusts of layered pastry, similar to a crust used in certain dim sum items. (And, oddly enough, in terms of shaping technique, almost identical to sfogliatelle, *a traditional Neapolitan pastry.) Getting rarer these days is a decent sardine curry puff, stuffed with canned sardines given verve with chili, onions and sliced hard-boiled egg.*

Makes about 22 - 26 puffs

For the pastry
450 grams plain flour
1/8 teaspoon ground turmeric
1/2 teaspoon fine salt
200 grams cold butter, or vegetable
  shortening, cubed

For the filling
4 tablespoons meat curry powder
125 milliliters oil
2 medium onions, finely chopped
4 cloves garlic, crushed

1 tablespoon finely minced ginger
3 cardamom pods
30 curry leaves
200 grams coarsely minced chicken,
  mutton or beef
300 grams potatoes, peeled and cut
  into 1-centimeter dice
150 milliliters coconut milk
salt to taste

oil for deep-frying

1. Make pastry: Sift flour, turmeric and salt into a mixing bowl. Add butter or shortening and rub it in with your fingertips until mixture has the consistency of bread crumbs. Sprinkle over 75 milliliters of cold water (or more if necessary) as you stir the dough with a knife — add only just enough water to bring together a slightly crumbly dough. Knead dough briefly to even out texture, then shape it into a flat disk, wrap in plastic wrap and chill for 30 minutes.

2. Make filling:

a) Mix curry powder with just enough water (approximately 3 tablespoons) to make a thick but flowing paste. Set aside.

b) Heat oil in a wok over medium-high heat. When very hot, add onions, garlic and ginger to wok and stir-fry until softened and lightly browned, 5 to 6 minutes. Add cardamom pods, curry leaves and curry paste, reduce heat slightly and fry, stirring constantly, until fragrant, about 2 minutes. Add meat and fry 1 minute, then stir in potatoes, 200 milliliters water and coconut milk and bring to a boil. Reduce heat to medium and cook, stirring frequently until potatoes are tender and liquid has evaporated, 10 to 12 minutes. Season with salt to taste. Let cool completely.

3. Start heating oil for deep-frying. Working with half the dough at a time, roll it out 2 to 3 millimeters thick. Cut out 10-centimeter rounds. Place about a tablespoon of filling on one round, and fold pastry in half to form a semicircle. Press edges to seal, expelling as much air as possible so pastry lies flush against filling. Beginning at one end of sealed edge, fold it over in small, successively overlapping sections, pressing hard, to form a crimped edge. Lay finished puffs on a lightly floured plate, and freeze uncovered for 15 minutes to firm up pastry, while you tackle remaining half of dough. (Any leftover pastry or filling may be frozen.) Deep-fry puffs in small batches, turning them once or twice, until deep golden brown, 4 to 5 minutes per batch. Drain puffs on kitchen paper and serve slightly warm.

Chef's note:

If you can't buy a good meat curry powder, try a blend of these: 1 1/2 tablespoons ground coriander, 2 teaspoons ground cumin, 2 teaspoons ground fennel, 2 to 4 teaspoons chili powder, 3/4 teaspoon each of ground black pepper, ground turmeric, and ground cinnamon, and 1/4 teaspoon each of ground fenugreek and ground cloves.

Curry leaves (*murraya koenigii*) are small, diamond-shaped and grow in feathery sprays on thin stems. In Indian and Malay dishes they are typically fried in hot oil to release their warm, peppery, citrusy aroma.

To make a sardine filling, take 400 grams canned sardines in tomato sauce. Remove bones if desired and flake meat coarsely. Heat up 2 tablespoons oil, then fry 20 curry leaves, 1 tablespoon finely minced ginger, 4 chopped shallots, 2 sliced red chilies and 2 sliced green chilies for 1 to 2 minutes until fragrant, then stir in sardines. Let filling cool, then fold in 2 coarsely chopped hard-boiled eggs.

Serikaya

Egg and coconut jam

In the course of trading and settling their way around Asia, the Portuguese left a delicious legacy of hybrid dishes, Asian ingredients woven after European patterns. One of those is serikaya, or kaya — which means "rich" in Malay — for short, a jamlike egg custard that uses coconut milk where its distant ancestor, the Portuguese ovos moles, called for water.

As perfected by the Malays and Nyonyas, kaya made with white sugar and infused with the color and scent of green pandan leaves is traditionally daubed onto squares of glutinous (sticky) rice to make the dessert pulut taitai. Early in the last century it was adopted as a breakfast spread by Hainanese coffee shops, which slathered a sweeter, caramel-hued version on charcoal-toasted bread with pieces of cold butter, accompanying the sticky, sweet, smoky, sandwich with a cup of bracing coffee. A barely set soft-boiled egg with dark soy sauce and white pepper is the last member of what has become an iconic breakfast trio.

Over the past few years two of the oldest and most well-known Hainanese kopi tiams have spawned franchises across Singapore and elsewhere in Asia, with branded merchandise and canny advertising trumpeting the virtues of kopi and kaya toast. One uses thick, spongy white bread for its toast; while the other uses "brown" bread — brown from caramel, not bran — whose slices are toasted, then split into wafer-thin halves for the sandwich. Customers are fiercely loyal to each rendition!

Nowadays, even souvenir stands sell jars of kaya to tourists — although we must insist that home-made is by far and away the best. Do not expect a perfectly smooth custard texture. The large amount of eggs yields a dense mass of tiny curds with a faintly grainy mouthfeel — this is perfectly correct. When chilled, Nyonya serikaya should be firm enough to cut into neat slices.

Makes about 600 - 700 milliliters serikaya

250 milliliters thick coconut milk (see Chef's note on page 207)
10 pandan leaves, washed

6 duck eggs or 8 chicken eggs
275 grams caster sugar
1/4 teaspoon salt

1. Pour coconut milk into a pot. Knot pandan leaves together, crushing them with your hands to help their juices flow, and add to the pot. Bring coconut milk just to a boil over medium-low heat.

2. Meanwhile, combine eggs, sugar and salt in a large bowl. Stir — do not beat — with a whisk until sugar almost completely dissolves; this will take at least 5 minutes.

3. When coconut milk just reaches the boil, pour it, leaves and all, onto eggs, stirring constantly until blended. Strain mixture through a fine strainer back into the pot, reserving pandan knot, and cook over low heat for 10 to 12 minutes, stirring constantly and scraping the pot bottom, until mixture thickens slightly. Don't worry if a few coagulated bits form; they will disappear into the texture of the final *kaya*.

4. Pour custard into a heatproof bowl or loaf tin, then return pandan knot to the bowl. Bowl should be big enough so that *kaya* is not more than 5-centimeters deep. Cover bowl tightly with foil, leaving a crack for steam to escape.

5. Place bowl on a rack in a steamer. Steam over medium heat for 90 minutes to 2 hours, topping up boiling water at intervals as necessary. When properly done, *kaya* should be slightly grainy and quite firmly set. If any liquid has collected in the casserole, steam it uncovered for a few minutes so that the *kaya* can dry out.

6. Once *kaya* is completely cool, transfer it to a spotlessly clean container, and touch it only with clean utensils. It will keep, covered and stored in the coldest part of the refrigerator for at least a week. Serve it on hot, toasted bread with thin slices of cold butter.

Chef's note:
Pandan or screw pine leaves have a unique aroma that is equal parts new-mown grass and vanilla, with hints of jasmine. There is no exact substitute; however, some Indian groceries sell a bottled essence of *kewra* flower, a pandan relative that smells similar, but stronger. You can use 1 to 2 drops of this instead.

Duck eggs have large, orangey, rich yolks that make superbly suave *kaya*. However, *kampung,* or free-range chicken eggs, are just as good.

Whether you are using fresh, canned or frozen coconut milk, the procedure for getting thick coconut milk is the same — let it stand in a deep, narrow bowl for a while in a cool place, and the thickest portion of the milk (coconut cream) will rise to the top, from which it can be skimmed off along with some of the milk underneath.

Thailand

Introduction by Cora Cunanan Sukhyanga
Recipes by Mali Pimnart

The great variety of dishes and regional specialties that make up Thai cuisine has made it one of the most interesting in the world. It is renowned for its visual appeal and nutritive value, but it is the harmonious and subtle blend of the spicy, sweet, sour and salty that makes Thai cuisine truly unique.

Known for their gentle and hospitable nature, the Thais are a fun-loving people whose sense of *sanook* ("to enjoy, have fun") extends to mealtimes which are occasions to share with others — whether at a posh restaurant, at a roadside stall, at the office desk-cum-dining table or in the middle of a rice field. Individual dishes are served in platters or bowls and placed in the center of the table. Everyone is free to eat any and all of the dishes he chooses.

In ancient times, Thais ate with their hands. Spoons and forks are a foreign import introduced during the reign of Rama V at the turn of the twentieth century (King Chulalongkorn or Rama V reigned from 1869 to 1910). However, they do not use them in the same way as Europeans do. Knives are almost never used, since most ingredients are cut into small pieces before they are cooked. Chopsticks, introduced by Chinese traders, are also commonly used when noodle dishes are served. But when it comes to eating E-san (another name for the northeastern region) food, Thais still eat with their hands, kneading the glutinous (sticky) rice with their fingers to make it soft before consuming it.

The Thais have mastered the art of carving fruits and vegetables to resemble flowers, among many other things. The real flowers pale in comparison beside these beautiful hand-crafted creations.

THIS PAGE Food vendors prepare to sell khao kaeng (or rice and curry) the Thai equivalent of take-home TV dinners.

OPPOSITE A street vendor dishing up steaming noodles.

Nothing seems to spoil the Thais' sense of *sanook*. Not even the little things that people from other parts of the world may find problematic, such as eating food prepared out in the open at roadside stalls enveloped in the fumes of traffic-clogged Bangkok. Today these roadside stalls are generally deemed safe, not only because the food is prepared on the spot and heated sufficiently, but also because of new hygiene regulations recently imposed by the Thai government.

Similar to the rest of Southeast Asia, rice is the staple of the Thai meal. However, owing to the abundance of inexpensive street food, busy Thais living in urban areas seldom cook at home. Imagine spending just under 60 baht (about US$1.50) for a plate of rice served with a choice of two meat, fish or vegetable dishes and a glass of iced tea to boot!

The country's long coastline bounded by numerous rivers and canals has made seafood, especially fish, a key element of its cuisine. *Nahmpla* (fish sauce) and *kapi* (shrimp paste) are used in almost every Thai recipe. A typical Thai meal is eaten with rice and may include a clear soup, a steamed dish, a fried dish, a *yam* or hot salad and a variety of sauces into which food is dipped. This may be followed by sugar-laden desserts, but modern, health-conscious Thais prefer to have fresh fruits, which grow in abundance in Thailand.

Fresh herbs and spices are used not only to create a uniquely Thai taste but to enable diners to benefit from their medicinal and healthful properties. Herbs and spices such as basil, black pepper, chili, cilantro, garlic, blue ginger, ginger, spring onion, mint, lemongrass, shallot, tamarind and turmeric are considered to have healing qualities and are used by country folk to alleviate various health conditions. For example, *ma-krut* (kaffir lime) which is prized for its strong citrus aroma is believed to help cure indigestion and increase one's appetite. Its glossy leaves contain beta-carotene which helps to ward off cancer. *Horapha* (sweet basil) aids digestion, kills germs and clears phlegm. Ancient Thais used *horapha* leaves as a breath freshener by chewing on them. *Gaphrao* (holy basil), a common ingredient in Thai dishes, prevents cancer and blood disorders, and strengthens the bones. Lemongrass, another key ingredient, is considered a good cure for an upset stomach and indigestion. Lemongrass juice is a popular traditional Thai herbal drink. *Kha* (blue ginger) is said to soothe swollen tonsils, stimulate digestion and reduce flatulence.

Thais take great pride in being one of the few nations in the world that have never been colonized. Thus centuries-old traditions and ancient methods of food preparation have largely been retained as family "secrets" which have been passed down from one generation to the next. To better appreciate the diversity of Thai cuisine, we take you on a cultural and culinary journey through Thai history.

INSIDE THE THAI KITCHEN

The Thai kitchen is ideally located outside the house because the constant pounding of the pestle on the mortar, the quick-frying over intense heat, the smoky aroma of marinade spilled onto hot embers and the pungent combination of sautéed herbs and chili would be enough to literally bring tears to the eyes.

Nahmpla (fish sauce), palm sugar, lemon and vinegar are some of the most common ingredients found in Thai kitchens. *Si-u khao* (light soy sauce), *kapi* (shrimp paste), oyster sauce, chili sauce, coconut milk and a variety of *prik gaeng* (curry pastes) are also central to preparing Thai cuisine. The key curry pastes include *nahmprik gaeng ped* (red curry paste), *nahmprik paow* (roasted chili paste), *gaeng hung lay* (northern-style pork curry) and *massaman neua* (*massaman* beef curry).

Regular fish sauce (*nahmpla*) is made of salted and preserved anchovies, which are then filtered to make a clean sauce. It has a pungent aroma. Thai food always comes served with *nahmpla prik* (fish sauce with a few drops of lime juice and slices of chili).

ESSENTIAL COOKING TECHNIQUES

Boiling, simmering, blanching, frying, roasting and steaming are commonly used cooking techniques. Marinated meat or seafood is often grilled over a charcoal fire. The Chinese also introduced the quick-fry technique, which is often done in a wok placed over intensely high heat.

History

Official records show that the Thais migrated from the area now known as China over a thousand years ago around the time Kublai Khan conquered Nan-Chao in 1253. They followed rivers into northern Thailand and southward to the Chao Phya valley. With them they brought a culinary culture which would later become a part of Thai cuisine.

Being a nation of warriors, the Thais immediately made their presence felt, adapting the Indian culture prevalent in the area to correspond with their own traditions. They practiced Theravada Buddhism and adapted Brahman customs and traditions. Thailand's history can be divided into the four main periods outlined below.

Sukhothai Era (1238-1350) — The first Thai kingdom, stretching from Lampang in the north to Vientiane (located in present-day Lao PDR) and in the south to the Malay Peninsula, was founded in Sukhothai in 1238. This period is considered the golden age of Thai culture, when a distinctively Thai civilization, arts and architecture developed. The basic diet of the time comprised of rice, fish and vegetables flavored with garlic, black pepper and fish sauce.

Ayutthaya Era (1350-1767) — In 1350 the capital was moved to Ayutthaya because it offered superior geographic and economic advantages and was located at the confluence of three rivers: the Chao Phya, Pasak and Lopburi. Ayutthaya's proximity to the sea led to profitable maritime trade. During this period, Ayutthaya became the dominant power in the fertile Chao Phya basin and one of the most beautiful cities in the East.

The sixteenth century was marked by the arrival of European pioneers and by continual conflict with Myanmar. Among the first European settlers were the Portuguese, who introduced the use of eggs, which eventually became a key addition to the flour, sugar and coconut products already used in creating Thai desserts. These desserts — known as *thong yip*, *thong yod* and *foi thong* — continue to be served on special occasions and at ceremonies because *thong*, meaning gold, is considered auspicious.

The Portuguese are also credited with insinuating the fiery hot chili pepper from South America into the Thai diet along with the equally popular coriander, lime and tomato. Such external influences served to further develop the unique characteristics of Thai cuisine.

THIS PAGE and OPPOSITE Local delicacies, fresh fruits and vegetables are among the top attractions at the Floating Market, a highly popular tourist destination in the outskirts of Bangkok.

Thonburi Era (1767-1782) — Although it remained a large and prosperous capital for over four centuries, Sukhothai eventually fell into the hands of Myanmar in 1765. The new capital was relocated to Thonburi, on the banks of the Chao Phya River. Situated closer to the sea, the new site facilitated foreign trade. It also made defense and withdrawal easier in the event of another attack by Myanmar. As the Thais regained control of their country, many migrated to the northern and central parts of Thailand.

Rattanakosin Era (1782 to the present) — The Chakri Dynasty, from which the present and much-loved King Bhumibol Adulyadej (Rama IX) descends, began during the Rattanakosin period with the establishment of Bangkok as the capital.

During this era, King Mongkut, or Rama IV (1851-68), made many social and economic reforms. His son, King Chulalongkorn, or King Rama V (1869-1910), who presided over the country for close to 42 years, continued his father's work and transformed Siam into a modern twentieth-century kingdom. The most famous of his reforms was the abolition of slavery.

King Chulalongkorn is largely credited with introducing the use of the fork and spoon to the kingdom. He loved to cook. Early photographs show this revered monarch clad in a Thai *sarong* hunched over a cooking fire as he personally prepared an *alfresco* meal. He even wrote a recipe book featuring over 200 dishes. It was during the reign of King Prajadhipok (1925-35) that Thailand changed from an absolute monarchy to a constitutional monarchy. The country's name was changed from Siam to Thailand in 1939, a democratic government.

Geography

Thailand is a predominantly Buddhist country which covers a land area of 510,000 square kilometers (about the same size as France) and has a population of 64 million people. Located in the heart of mainland Southeast Asia, the kingdom shares its borders with Myanmar in the west and north, Lao PDR in the northeast, Cambodia in the east and Malaysia in the south. Its central and southern regions also border the Gulf of Thailand and the Andaman Sea. With China and Viet Nam within 100 kilometers of Thai territory, both countries have influenced many aspects of Thai society, cuisine and culture.

However, nothing has had a more profound impact on Thailand's history and culture than the Chao Phya River. From Ayutthaya to Bangkok, successive capitals have been built at various points along the river in the last thousand years. It has sustained Thailand's agricultural economy by supporting rice cultivation and providing waterways for the transport of goods and people.

THIS PAGE These dumplings consist of sago stuffed with minced pork. They are steamed over a traditional Thai steamer designed specifically for this purpose and are then eaten with fresh vegetables.

OPPOSITE (top right) Traditional kitchen implements that were more commonly used in the past. The ladles are made of coconut shells, as are the fork and spoon.

ESSENTIAL KITCHEN IMPLEMENTS

The *krok* (mortar and pestle) is used to pulverize and grind ingredients for pastes such as garlic seasoning paste; or to blend various ingredients, as in *som tam*. Thai mortar and pestles are usually carved out of solid wood or stone. While it may be tempting to replace them with a food processor or blender, the experienced Thai cook will tell you that using the mortar and pestle makes a huge difference in taste, texture and authenticity.

The versatile *kata* (wok) is used to stir-fry, deep-fry, roast or steam dishes. Woks are usually made of spun carbon steel, stainless steel or aluminum.

Gratha thong leung (brass pans) are preferred when making Thai desserts such as *foi thong* because the metal's low heat conductivity prevents sugar from burning. Brass knives are also used for peeling fruits such as mangoes because they prevent the outer surface of the peeled fruit from turning grey.

The *rang theung*, a special round, flat steamer made of steel or bamboo, is used for steaming delicate fish, shrimp, crabs, dumplings and desserts. Small cups are used to steam rice in a multilayered Thai steamer. The *huat* is a traditional Thai bamboo steamer used to steam glutinous (sticky) rice. Designed like a cone or inverted hat, it allows the rice to be steamed evenly without the cook having to turn the steamer around. A *kra tip* is made from reeds and is used to hold glutinous rice.

Landforms and waterways divide the country into four regions: the Bangkok and central, northern, northeastern and southern regions. Each has its own distinct food culture.

Northern region — Bordered by Myanmar and Lao PDR, northern Thailand encompasses part of the famous Golden Triangle. It boasts mountains, forests and fertile valleys where a series of rivers, including the Nan, Ping, Wang and Yom, unite in the lowlands to form the Chao Phya watershed.

The main staple in the north is glutinous (sticky) rice, which is softened before it is eaten by kneading it into small balls with the fingers. At traditional meals commonly referred to as *khantoke* dinners, diners sit on straw mats around a small, low teakwood table called a *khantoke* and help themselves to sticky rice and assorted northern dishes, such as spicy minced meat, curries, various sauces and condiments, and a choice of *nahmprik* — chili paste dips most commonly served with *kaeb moo* (fried pork rind). A great variety of *nahmprik* is available in the north. The most famous is *nahmprik noom* (young chili dip). Preserved meat called *moo yor and naem* (spicy pork sausages) are also unique to the region.

The Chinese influence is reflected in the widespread use of noodles. A popular noodle dish called *khanom jeen nam ngeow,* which consists of small spaghetti-like noodles (*khanom jeen*) served with fresh vegetables and a pork-tomato curry (*nam ngeow*), is the direct result of the influence of the Mon people in southern Myanmar during the sixteenth and eighteenth centuries when Myanmar occupied Chiang Mai, then the capital of the Lanna kingdom. The complex cultural diversity of the region is also evident in iconic dishes such as *khao soi*, a crispy rice or egg noodle dish served with a rich curry sauce cooked in coconut milk; *gaeng hung-lay*, a pork curry that relies on ginger, tamarind and turmeric for its flavor; and chili dips such as *gaeng aom* (pork curry with innards) and *nahmprik ong* (tomato chili dip with ground pork). Coconut milk is purportedly used in dishes to keep people warm in the cool mountain climate.

Northeastern region — Known to the Thais as E-san, this sprawling semi-arid northeast plateau is bordered by the Mekong River and Lao PDR in the north and east; and largely by Cambodia in the south. E-san experiences hot and long summers with very little rainfall. Although rice is cultivated here, life in this region is difficult due to the harsh weather and severe topography, both of which influence its people's eating habits.

Glutinous rice is a staple and the dishes, which are often fiery and hot, are simple and easy to prepare. Since meat is scarce, the principal sources of protein are

Thai-style rice pudding, or khanom tuay *(meaning sweets on a bowl) served in tiny bowls. Each contains a bottom layer of smooth, sweet, gelatinous starch, topped with a layer of thickened coconut cream.*

freshwater fish and shrimp. These are sometimes cooked with herbs and spices, and fermented so that they can be stored for a longer period of time. As a result, northeasterners have become experts at preserving fish by fermenting them.

Known to Thais as *pla ra* and in Lao PDR as *pla daek*, the fermented fish constitutes a main dish in almost every meal, eaten with sticky rice or added to other dishes. After *pla ra* is cooked, it is eaten with fresh or boiled vegetables. The strong-smelling fermented fish takes 6 to 12 months to ferment and is often added to dishes as a flavoring. *Pla som* (sour fermented fish) takes longer to make and contains rice which stimulates the fermenting process.

Nothing goes to waste. If meat is ever used, the accompanying innards are boiled, seasoned and served in *tom krueng nai*, a sour and spicy northeastern-style soup. Another famous product is the fermented E-san sausage. Leftover meat is sun-dried (*nuea daed diew*) and kept for later use.

The influence of neighboring Lao PDR is evident in highly seasoned regional dishes such as *larb* (made with spicy minced meat or chicken), *som tam* (green papaya salad), *gai yang* (barbecued chicken), *nahm tok*, *sup nor mai* (bamboo shoot soup) and the mouth-watering *jim jaew* or chili dip. Among the cuisine's wilder, more exotic dishes are *rot duan* (bamboo worms), *khai mot* (ant eggs) and *chingrit* (crickets) fried with garlic and pepper. They are major sources of protein. Fried ants, grasshoppers and frog curry are also not uncommon to the northeastern diet.

Prepared with very lean meat and served with green, leafy, raw vegetables, E-san dishes are considered some of the healthiest in Thai cuisine. As people from this region moved into the larger Thai city centers, they brought their spicy E-san cuisine with them. Initially, it was largely available at gas stations and meant to cater to the needs of traveling E-san truckers. Today it is also served at the most stylish restaurants and exclusive hotels.

Central region — The central region, affectionately known as Thailand's rice bowl, is the economic and cultural heartland of the Thai nation. It is also considered one of the world's most fertile rice and fruit-growing areas because of the mighty Chao Phya River, which sustains and supports a unique, waterborne way of life here.

The central region extends from the rugged mountains in the west bordering Myanmar to the northeast plateau to the east; northward to Nakhon Sawan where the Ping, Wang, Nan and Yom Rivers unite to form the Chao Phya River, which flows southward to dissect Bangkok before entering the Gulf of Thailand; and southward to Prachuap Khirikhan.

Most central Thai food is not too spicy. Central Thais favor plain rice which is usually steamed but sometimes fried or boiled. Seafood, harvested from the nearby gulf, is abundant while the wide range of fresh vegetables and fruits available is unlike any found anywhere else in the world.

No meal is complete without dessert and the Thais have turned the preparation of desserts into an art. Flour, coconut and sugar are the basic ingredients in traditional desserts such as *tabtim krob* (jelly-dipped chestnuts in sweet coconut milk), which literally means crisp rubies, *bualoy phuek* (boiled taro in sweet coconut milk) and *gluay khai chueam* (bananas in syrup). Fresh fruits are also a favorite. A popular and refreshing variation often enjoyed in summer is *graton loy kaew* (*santol* in light clear syrup) served with crushed ice.

Bangkok lies in the heart of the central plain. Its large and prosperous Chinese community, which has been assimilated into the Thai population, has introduced a variety of noodles to the region which are now very much part of local cuisine. Shops specializing in specific noodle dishes can be found almost everywhere.

The central region is also home to royal Thai cuisine, a more sophisticated version of the local regional cuisine. Influenced by the kitchens of the royal court, the dishes are elaborately put together, making them as much works of art as culinary masterpieces. One of the most interesting royal Thai dishes is *khao chae* (literally, rice soaked in water), which was reportedly invented during the reign of Rama II. It is prepared during the hot summer months and consists of scented cold rice soup eaten with side dishes of fried shrimp paste balls, stuffed pepper, pickled strips of Japanese turnip, sweetened pork and shredded beef. It is also garnished and eaten with cucumber, green mango and wild ginger.

A dessert that truly reflects the time, effort and attention to detail that go into preparing palace food is *look choop*, miniaturized replicas of Thai fruits which are actually hand-shaped out of sweet mung bean paste and then dipped in colored jelly so that they resemble actual fruit.

To scent princely desserts, jasmine and other aromatic flowers are first soaked in water. The scented water is then made into a syrup. Aromatic candles are also lit and placed in containers with cakes or cookies. Cookies are sometimes even decorated with slivers of gold leaf!

The ancient art of fruit and vegetable carving closely associated with Thai cuisine was originally an aristocratic art. It flourished throughout the Ayutthaya period, and reached its zenith during the Bangkok reign of King Rama II when court ladies created flowers, fish, vases, bowls and other decorative objects from watermelons, cucumbers, tomatoes, onions and other garden produce.

Southern Thailand — Southern Thailand is a narrow peninsula dotted with mountain ranges and dense jungle which extends through the Kra Isthmus from Chumphon, 460 kilometers south of Bangkok, to the Thai-Malaysian border. It is bordered in the east by the Gulf of Thailand, to the west by the Indian Ocean.

The cuisine of the south is hot and spicy. Locals believe that the heat from the food will protect them from fevers brought on by the humid climate. Unsurprisingly, coconut — which grows throughout the region — is very much a part of the southern diet. Coconut milk is said to temper the heat of chili-laced soups and curries, while coconut oil is used for frying. Grated coconut flesh is served as a condiment.

Cashew nuts, a local produce, are eaten as appetizers or stir-fried with chicken and dried chilies, while *sataw* (twisted cluster beans), which are valued for their medicinal qualities, add an exotic and somewhat bitter flavor to dishes. Regional fruits include finger-size bananas, mangosteens, durian and small, sweet pineapples.

THIS PAGE Fruits, like mango and guava, are often pickled while bael fruits or Indian quince (ma-toom) are coated in sugar to allow for a longer life span and storage period. Sugar-coated bael fruits are also boiled and made into thirst-quenching fruit juice.

OPPOSITE Thong yip, thong yod and foi thong are typically presented on a bed of desserts made to resemble flowers. These desserts, often scented, are served at Thai celebrations and ceremonies. Thus much effort is made to present them in a beautiful manner.

As can be expected, there is an abundance of fresh seafood here. Phuket rock lobsters, crabs, prawns, scallops, fish, squid, clams and mussels are common ingredients. One of the local specialties is an unusual and delicious jellyfish salad.

In the south, seafood is flavored with aromatic herbs and spices before it is grilled, boiled or roasted. Prawns are cooked with bamboo shoots in coconut soup (*goong ga-thi nor mai sod*) or fried with twisted cluster beans (*goong pad sataw*) and crabs are fried in yellow curry (*poo pad pong gari*).

Owing to its proximity to Malaysia, southern Thailand has a large Muslim community, and Islamic culture has naturally been incorporated into its dishes. This is evident in the extensive use of turmeric, which gives southern dishes such as *gaeng lueng* (spicy coconut shoot soup), *khao mok gai* (turmeric rice topped with chicken) and *gaeng som* (tamarind-flavored soup) their characteristic yellowish hue. Other famous southern dishes include *gaeng tai pla* (fish viscera curry), *gaeng massaman* (a mild Indian-style curry seasoned with cardamom, cloves and cinnamon) and *satay* (a skewered meat dish served with a spicy peanut sauce which has Indonesian origins). From this diversity of influences and contributions from other ethnic peoples, Thai cuisine has become internationally renowned for its unique and interesting blend of flavors and aromas.

THIS PAGE (left) The Marketing Organisation of Thailand's popular agricultural outlet, Or Tor Kor Market, offers fresh fruits and vegetables, rare delicacies as well as traditional fare; (right) Ripe lamud (sapodilla; ciku; chico) has an earthy, sweet flavor.

OPPOSITE A fishmonger at a downtown wet market, Bangkok.

Khao tang na tang

Rice patties with pork, chicken or shrimp topping

The literal meaning of "khao" in the Thai language is rice, but it can also connote food. To the Thais, every little grain of rice is precious and the careless dropping of rice onto the floor would necessitate asking Mae Phosop, the Goddess of Rice, for forgiveness.

As creative and enterprising as the Thais are, they are also frugal. Khao tang na tang, which can be enjoyed as a snack or appetizer, was born of the need to use up whatever leftover rice there was. In ancient times rice was cooked in red clay pots, which were later replaced by more durable metal pots. During the reign of Rama V, imaginative Thais in the central region found some use for the hard layer of rice that would always end up stuck to the bottom of the pot.

Rather than disposing of the rice that stuck to the bottom of the pot, they scraped it off and then left it to dry in the sun. They then deep-fried these dry rice patties and gave them the name khao tang. Over the years, a dip of shrimp, pork or chicken was introduced and served together with the khao tang, making it a delicious family snack. The dish became known as khao tang na tang. Another dish that features khao tang is khao tang mieng lao, which consists of a minced pork and ground peanut mixture wrapped in pickled lettuce and then eaten with khao tang. For khao tang na muyong, another variation, nahmprik paow (roasted chili paste), is spread over the khao tang before dried shredded sweet pork is layered over it

Since today's automatic rice cookers do not leave any rice residue, rice patties are made with glutinous (sticky) rice rather than regular rice because the grains of glutinous rice stick together and are puffier when fried. The Thais like to cook their glutinous rice in a Thai-style steamer called huat, an upturned hat made of reeds inside a 20-centimeter-tall aluminum steaming pan. The shape allows the rice to be steamed evenly from all sides.

Chef's note:
To make the garlic seasoning paste, you will need 2 tablespoons finely chopped garlic, 2 tablespoons finely chopped coriander root and 1 teaspoon ground white pepper. Mix the ingredients in a mortar and pound to a pastelike consistency. Set aside. Any leftover can be kept for later use.

You may choose to add more garlic seasoning paste if you wish. This simply depends on just how flavorful and aromatic you would like the dip to be.

Some Thais like to add roasted ground peanuts and a little tamarind juice to make the dip creamy, crunchy and sweet.

Ground chicken may be used in place of the ground pork and shrimp.

Serves 4

For rice patties
1 kilogram glutinous rice
1 liter cooking oil for deep-frying

For the dip
250 milliliters thick coconut milk
100 grams ground pork

100 grams ground shrimp
50 grams white onion, peeled and finely chopped
1 tablespoon garlic seasoning paste (see Chef's note on this page)
2 tablespoons white sugar
1 teaspoon salt

1. To make the rice patties, soak the glutinous rice in water overnight to make it soft and thus easier to steam. Drain the excess water. There are several ways to steam rice, depending on the cooking implements you have. The traditional *huat*, which is fashioned from reeds, is most commonly used in Thailand to steam glutinous rice. To do this, place the soaked rice in the *huat*, then put it over an aluminum steaming pot filled with hot water. Steam for about half an hour. If you are using an automatic rice cooker, line the steamer-insert that comes with most rice cookers with a piece of muslin. Place the soaked rice on the muslin. Use 1.2 liters of water to steam the rice. When cooked, keep the rice warm for another half hour before setting it aside to cool.

Alternatively, line a perforated, heatproof container with muslin. Add the soaked rice. In a pot large enough to accommodate the perforated, heatproof container, bring some water to a boil. Insert a metal trivet and place the container of rice on it. Make sure that the water does not come into contact with the rice. Cover and steam for 30 minutes, then allow to cool.

2. Spread a 5-millimeter layer of glutinous rice over a board, then, using a round cookie cutter, make 4-centimeter-round patties. Leave in the sun to dry completely before storing the patties in a sealed container. Deep-fry until puffy just before preparing the dip. (The uncooked rice patties can be stored in the refrigerator for 1 to 2 months. Once fried, they keep for 3 days to a week.)

3. To make the dip, pour the coconut milk into a pan placed over medium heat. When bubbles form at the edges, add the ground pork and shrimp. Stir until cooked but do not let the coconut milk break into oil. Add the onions and garlic seasoning paste. Next, add sugar and salt (add more or less to taste), aiming for a balance between the salty, sweet and sour flavors. Stir for another minute or until mixture becomes slightly creamy. Pour the dip into a small bowl and serve slightly warm to complement the rice patties. The rice patties should be placed on a separate dish and dipped into the mixture only before they are eaten to prevent them from turning soggy.

Tom yam goong

Spicy prawn soup with lemongrass

Tom yam goong is the most famous of all Thai soups. As a starter, this famous soup awakens the appetite because of its uniquely Thai combination of salty, sour and spicy flavor. Although the dish originated from Thailand's central region, it has become such a favorite that every region in the country has its own variation of it. In northern Thailand, for example, roasted chili paste (nahmprik paow) is added to the soup; in the south, evaporated milk is added to make a milky soup. Below is a simple and authentic version of tom yam goong *as prepared by Mali Pimnart, the head chef of the Four Seasons Hotel Bangkok's Spice Market.*

Note that not everything in a tom yam *dish is edible. Herbs like lemongrass and* galangal (blue ginger) *are used for their aroma and flavor, but are not meant to be eaten. The small bird's-eye chilies are known as "torpedoes" among the Thais because of their fiery potency. The smaller the chili, the more potent it is. For this dish, it is best to combine salty, sour and spicy tastes without one overpowering the other.*

This soup is best served hot. Ideally, it should be presented in a tom yam *hotpot which has a central chimney where a tray holds a source of heat, which is usually burning embers from a charcoal fire.*

Tom yam can also be made with fish, pork or chicken. To avoid the fishy smell of freshwater fish, do not stir the soup. Bird's-eye chilies are crushed to add subtle flavor and aroma to the soup. Avoid boiling them in the soup because this will make the dish very spicy. For vegetarian tom yam, *use tofu, shiitake or straw mushrooms, and vegetables such as broccoli (for color) and baby corn. Season with light soy sauce (si-u khao) instead of fish sauce.*

Kaffir lime leaves

Chef's note:
For a more potent taste, place some of the fish sauce, lime and chili mixture in each serving bowl then pour just enough prawn soup into each serving bowl to balance the salty, sour and spicy flavors.

In the absence of straw mushrooms, use fresh champignons (button mushrooms) or canned mushrooms as a substitute. Always squeeze out the water in canned mushrooms before use.

Serves 2

200 grams prawns
30 grams fresh straw mushrooms
1 1/2 tablespoons lime juice
1 1/2 tablespoon fish sauce
10 bird's-eye chilies, crushed
1 stalk lemongrass, thinly sliced

3-4 thin slices *galangal* (blue ginger)
   or 1-centimeter piece of *galangal*,
   thinly sliced
2 kaffir lime leaves, torn
3 coriander roots, crushed
8 coriander leaves (4 for each bowl)

1. Shell and devein the prawns, keeping the tail intact. Cut a slit down the length of the prawns, taking care not to cut them in half. Keep the prawn shells and heads for preparing the prawn stock.

2. Make prawn stock by covering the prawn heads and shells with water (you will need 400 milliliters

of stock). Simmer gently for 30 minutes or until the stock is flavorful and the shells are pink. Strain and set the liquid aside.

3. Rinse the straw mushrooms and discard the stems. Dry well, then cut in half lengthwise.

4. Combine the lime juice, fish sauce and crushed bird's-eye chilies. Set aside.

5. Bring 400 milliliters of prawn stock to a boil in a pot. Add the lemongrass, *galangal*, kaffir lime leaves, coriander root and straw mushrooms. Then add the prawns and allow to boil just until the prawns turn pink.

6. Garnish with coriander leaves before serving.

Hor mok talay

Steamed seafood soufflé with creamy coconut

The word hor *means "to wrap" in Thai.* Hor mok *is a traditional dish from central Thailand that contains a mixture of seafood, coconut milk and seasonings, which is then steamed in small cups fashioned out of banana leaves.*

Steaming food in banana leaves enhances the smell of the dish. This is a common practice in many Asian countries and Thailand is no exception. The banana leaf is shaped into a container held in place by slivers of wood or toothpicks. These days, many hawkers and restaurants use an office stapler, which may be convenient but definitely not recommended, because the metal staples may get mixed into the food. Also bear in mind that the steamed banana leaf gives food an aroma but it is definitely not to be eaten!

In the absence of banana leaves, crab shells or seashells may be used as substitutes. Alternatively, you can use small heatproof bowls. The Spice Market at the Four Seasons Hotel Bangkok serves medium-size prawns as containers for this dish.

The "hor mok" container made from banana leaves

Chef's note:
For a modern-day variation, use prawns as containers for this dish. You will need 300 grams of prawns. Cut the prawns in half, then devein, keeping the shell and the head intact. Stuff the filling into the prawns, then steam for 10 minutes. Remove the shrimp containers from the steamer and top with sliced chili and kaffir lime and steam for another minute. Serve one prawn to a plate.

Grachai (finger root) is sometimes mistaken for *kencur* (lesser *galangal)*. This rhizome looks like a bunch of pale-brown, almost beige baby carrots. It is widely used in Thailand and brings a subtle spiciness to dishes.

Makes 4 portions

For the container
8 banana leaves

For the topping
250 milliliters *hua kati* (coconut cream)
1 tablespoon cornflour (cornstarch)
a pinch of salt

For the filling
20 grams *nahmprik gaeng ped* (red curry paste)
1 teaspoon garlic seasoning paste (see Chef's note on page 222)
1 teaspoon sliced *grachai* (finger root)
1 egg

100 milliliters *hua kati* (coconut cream)
2 tablespoons fish sauce
1 teaspoon white sugar
75 grams prawns, diced (traditionally river prawns are used)
50 grams seabass fillet, cut into small pieces
50 grams featherback fish or mackerel, minced
2 tablespoons basil leaves
1 tablespoon julienned cabbage
1 teaspoon thinly sliced *prik chee fa* (fresh red chili)
3 kaffir lime leaves, shredded

1. To prepare four containers, cut eight banana leaf circles measuring 13-centimeters across. You may use a round coffee saucer as a template. Place one of the cutouts over another (total of two) in such a way that the grains of the two leaves are perpendicular to each other. Place the leaves back to back so that only the dark-green portions are visible when folded. This prevents the leaves from tearing when they are folded. Create four corners to form a bowl, using half a toothpick to secure each corner. The cups must be at least 4-centimeters tall.

2. To make the creamy coconut topping, combine the *hua kati*, cornflour and salt in a pot. Cook over a low heat, stirring slowly until the topping thickens. Set aside to cool.

3. For the filling, mix the *nahmprik gaeng ped*, garlic seasoning paste, *grachai*, egg, *hua kati*, fish sauce and sugar. Combine in an electric blender to achieve a creamy consistency. Add the diced prawns, seabass and minced featherback fish or mackerel. Stir just enough to mix.

4. Line the bottom of each banana leaf cup with basil leaves and cabbage. Spoon in the seafood mixture, but fill it up only about three quarters of the way. Leave some space for the topping. Steam for 10 minutes.

5. Remove the cups from the steamer. Garnish with the topping, sliced *prik chee fa* and kaffir lime leaves. Steam for another minute before serving.

Additional Chef's note:
In the past, most housewives made their own *nahmprik gaeng ped* (red curry paste) mixture using a mortar and pestle. Today an electric blender is a much more convenient substitute. However, traditionalists will tell you, and rightly so, that pounding the ingredients brings out flavors that a blender will never be able to. Ready-made curry paste (*nahmprik gaeng ped*) is available at local supermarkets in Bangkok and at Thai stores around the world.

Som tam

Spicy green papaya salad

Som tam is northeastern Thailand's best-known dish. It is also one of the most nutritious. A spicy salad made of raw papaya, it was once known as a poor man's dish, because it is cheap and easy to prepare. However, as the people of E-san (another name for the northeastern region) migrated and traveled, this healthy dish eaten with raw vegetables has become a favorite among health-conscious urbanites who, with good reason, believe it is one of the best diet foods around.

Dubbed papaya pok pok because it is primarily prepared with a mortar and pestle (the pounding creates a "pok pok" sound), som tam is prepared using unripe or green papaya as a base. This dish also highlights the blend of spicy, sweet, sour and salty tastes that makes Thai cuisine unique. The best som tam can be found at roadside food stalls. It is usually served as a side dish to glutinous (sticky) rice and taken with raw vegetables such as white cabbage, string beans and sprigs of Thai basil.

Dried shrimp, available in various sizes

Chef's note:
Alternatively, *som tam* may be served with *khao man* (long-grained rice cooked in coconut milk). Combine 600 milliliters light coconut milk with 2 tablespoons sugar and 2 teaspoons salt. Strain into a pot. Add 300 grams of pre-washed rice, then steam in a rice cooker for about 30 minutes.

To best savor the crunchy texture of the papaya, raw beans and nuts that are part of this dish, it is best to prepare *som tam* just before you want to serve it.

You may replace green papaya with carrots. You can also use dark-brown sugar in place of palm sugar.

Serves 2

3 bird's-eye chilies
2 cloves garlic, peeled
25 grams string beans, cut into
  2.5-centimeter lengths
1 tablespoon dried shrimp, crushed
2 tablespoons fish sauce
1 tablespoon lime juice
1/2 tablespoon *nahmtan peep*
  (palm sugar)

2 tablespoons tamarind juice
80 grams peeled and shredded
  green papaya
3 cherry tomatoes, halved
1 tablespoon peanuts or cashew
  nuts, crushed

1. Wash and clean the mortar and pestle to remove any residue from previous use. Put the bird's-eye chilies, garlic, string beans and dried shrimp into the mortar and pound until well mixed. Add fish sauce, lime juice, *nahmtan peep* and tamarind juice. Mix until the palm sugar dissolves. Add the shredded green papaya and cherry tomatoes. Pound once again to release the flavors. It should have a sour, salty, sweet and spicy taste.

2. When done, garnish with the crushed peanuts (or cashew nuts). Serve with a wedge of raw white cabbage and raw string beans. Glutinous rice completes a meal of *som tam*. Thais use the traditional conelike basket, called *huat*, to steam glutinous rice, which is served in a cylindrical basket, called *kratip*, to keep it warm.

Nahm tok

Grilled meat salad

Nahm tok *is from E-san, Thailand's northeastern region. Like* som tam, nahm tok *is also eaten with raw vegetables and glutinous (sticky) rice. Glutinous rice is preferred to regular rice because just a little of it fills the stomach, thus effectively assuaging hunger pangs for many hours when farmers and their families are out in the fields.*

The uniqueness of nahm tok *stems from the way the meat is grilled. Technically, it should be cooked just enough to allow the meat juices to flow when it is added to the other ingredients. Once the fat becomes oil, the meat is considered too overcooked. The Thais refer to these flowing meat juices as* nahm tok *which, when transliterated means "falling water." A similar cooking principle is applied to* suea rong hai *(crying tiger), another E-san dish which consists of grilled beef that is cooked until the oil from the fat starts to flow.*

E-san dishes take some getting used to because they are spicy and because they are eaten with raw vegetables. But once you develop a taste for them, you are likely to be a permanent convert. This dish is one of the first Thais miss when they leave Thailand to work or study overseas.

Serves 1

250 grams collarbone pork meat sliced to
   2.5-centimeter thickness
1 tablespoon soy sauce, preferably Thai
2 tablespoons fish sauce
2 tablespoons lime juice

1 tablespoon sugar
1 tablespoon toasted glutinous rice
2 tablespoons sliced shallots
2 tablespoons chili powder

1. Coat the collarbone with soy sauce. Grill whole until medium rare or medium well (if it is cooked any more than this, the meat will be too tough and will not absorb the flavors of the dish). Remove from heat to a clean cutting board.

2. Using a sharp knife, slice the grilled collarbone sideways into pieces 5-millimeters thick and

8-centimeters long. Add the fish sauce, lime juice, sugar, toasted glutinous rice, shallots and chili powder. Use a spoon to mix the ingredients well or until the juice from the meat is blended in.

3. Serve with glutinous rice and raw vegetables such as mint, sweet basil, cabbage and string beans.

Chef's note:
Toasted glutinous rice gives a crunchy and nutty flavor to this dish. It can be prepared ahead of time, and if stored in an airtight container can keep for weeks. It is essential to use only glutinous rice grains since regular rice gains are too small for toasting.

To toast the rice, put 2 to 3 tablespoons of glutinous rice grains in a frying pan. Toast over a low heat until brown. Constantly toss the grains to keep them from burning. Leave to cool. Then pound to a coarse powder using a mortar and pestle.

Khao soi kai

Curry noodle soup with chicken

Typically found in northern Thailand, khao soi kai *is a perfect reflection of the complex cultural diversity of the region. Unlike most other Thai noodle dishes,* khao soi kai *has a coconut milk base and is very similar to a dish from the neighboring Shan state in Myanmar, where it is called* ohn no khauk-hswe. *It may have been the Chinese-Muslim Haw traders who brought this dish to Thailand, where spices were then added to the recipe. The word* khauk-hswe *in Myanmar simply means "noodles."*

Flat egg noodles are used in khao soi. *A portion is deep-fried and used as a topping. This dish can be prepared using chicken, beef or pork. The acidic condiments that accompany* khao soi *— shallots, lime and pickled lettuce — help to reduce the general oiliness of the dish.*

Serves 2 - 3

40 grams *nahmprik gaeng ped*
  (red curry paste), see Additional
  Chef's note on page 227
1 teaspoon *hung-lay* powder (optional)
2 teaspoons curry powder
400 milliliters light coconut milk
2 tablespoons fish sauce
2 teaspoons sugar
200 grams chicken breast, cut into
  2-centimeter squares
90 grams *bamee* (flat egg noodles),
  blanched
10 grams sawtooth herb, sliced
10 grams shallots, peeled and sliced
200 milliliters chicken stock

For the condiments
30 grams pickled lettuce or mustard
  greens, diced
1 lime, cut into wedges
1 teaspoon deep-fried chili powder
10 grams coriander
10 grams shallots, peeled and diced

For the garnish
30 grams *bamee* (flat egg noodles)
10 grams coriander

Chef's note:
Pickled lettuce or mustard greens, pre-made red curry paste, Myanmar *hung-lay* powder and curry powders can be bought at supermarkets and at Asian stores around the world.

In place of flat egg noodles, use spaghetti or egg fettuccine.

1. Over a strong heat, prepare the noodle garnish by quickly deep-frying the 30 grams of *bamee* until crisp (yellow, not brown). Set aside.

2. Heat the wok or saucepan to medium heat, then add the red curry paste, *hung-lay* powder and curry powder. Stir vigorously until well blended. Be careful not to burn the paste. Add coconut milk and bring to a boil. Reduce heat, add fish sauce and sugar to balance the flavor. Add chicken and cook for a few more minutes. If soup proves too thick, add some chicken stock.

3. Divide the blanched noodles and sawtooth herb between 2 and 3 deep soup bowls. Pour the soup into the bowls. Garnish with crispy fried noodles and coriander. Serve with the condiments placed in separate, individual bowls.

Hoi lai phad nahmprik paow

Fried clams in roasted chili paste

Thailand's long coastline in the eastern region abounds in seafood. This dish, usually eaten in communal, family style, is one of the simplest to prepare. Most people eat this dish in the evening or at dinner time. The key lies in using the freshest ingredients. Clams are succulent and tasty, but they should always be rinsed. Be sure to separate the good clams from the bad ones. Hoi lai phad nahmprik paow is usually served with a bowl of steamed or boiled rice.

Serves 2

300 grams fresh clams
20 grams *bai horapa* (sweet basil)
30 milliliters cooking oil
50 grams *nahmprik paow* (roasted
   chili paste)
1 tablespoon fish sauce or to taste
2 teaspoons sugar or to taste
5-6 bird's-eye chilies, crushed

1. Rinse the clams well, gently scrubbing sand off the shells. Soak in cold salted water for about half an hour or until the shells open and any mud or sand is spewed out. Discard any open shells that do not close back together when pressed. Rinse and drain.

2. Deep-fry *bai horapa* until crisp. Set these aside for garnishing the dish.

3. Heat the wok over high heat. Fry the *nahmprik paow* for a few minutes, then slowly add the clams. Stir-fry until the clams open slightly. Taste the sauce to see if it is salty and sweet enough. Adjust by adding fish sauce and/or sugar to taste. Before removing the clams from the heat, sprinkle with *bai horapa* and crushed bird's-eye chili. Transfer to a serving dish and serve immediately.

Chef's note:
When the clams open, it means that they are cooked. Do not overcook them as they will shrink and become tough.

Ready-made roasted chili paste (*nahmprik paow*) is available at local supermarkets in Bangkok and at Thai stores around the world.

Foi thong

Sugar-coated egg yolk

In Thailand, gold is often associated with wealth. Foi thong, which literally means "golden threads," is usually served on auspicious occasions and at ceremonies together with thong yip (golden pinch), which are small, cup-shaped sweets pinched to look like flower petals, and thong yod (golden drops), which are formed to look like drops. They are all made of egg yolk.

Unfortunately, the time-honored secrets of making these beautifully presented desserts are in danger of disappearing because younger Thais find the intricate process complicated and time-consuming; and the sweets too rich for their taste and diet.

This traditional central Thai dessert, which dates from the Ayutthaya period, is made purely of egg yolk. In the old days a small amount of egg-sac, the light egg white remaining in the egg shells, was also added. Duck eggs are preferred because their deep orange yolks come closest to the golden hue that makers of foi thong would like to achieve. However, chicken eggs can also be used. To create these beautiful skeins of gold, the egg yolks are passed through a cone or funnel held over a vessel of hot syrup.

A plastic strainer is used in place of the brass implement traditionally used to make foi thong

Makes 8 - 10 rafts

**30 egg yolks (from either duck or
  chicken eggs)
1 kilogram sugar**

Chef's note:
Brass utensils are ideal for making sweets because the low conductivity of brass will not burn syrups or sweets.

You can replace the brass funnel with a disposable plastic piping bag or a narrow cone made of waxed paper.

1. In order to achieve the desired stringy texture, the yolk must not be beaten but stirred in a slow circular motion until it is smooth and looks well blended. It is important to avoid creating froth or bubbles. Set aside.

2. Put an equal amount of sugar and water in a brass wok. Using fairly low heat, allow the mixture to boil until you get a syrupy consistency. To prevent the syrup from caramelizing, pour a little water around the edges of the boiling syrup.

3. Pour the yolk into a traditional brass funnel. Allow a fine string of the yolk to flow from the small hole at the tip of the funnel held 30 centimeters above the wok of bubbling heavy syrup. Move the funnel in a slow circular motion. One skein should take about 2 minutes or 20 revolutions to create. Scoop up the glazed egg strings with a wooden stick or skewer, then fold over using another skewer, to make a raft 10-centimeters long. Remove and place on a platter. Repeat.

4. For a drier finish, allow the skeins to drain in a separate vessel. Once they are drained, fold each skein several times to make smaller, thicker skeins. Traditionally, *foi thong* is served on a bamboo tray lined with banana leaves.

Viet Nam

Innumerable eateries line the busy streets of Ho Chi Minh City.

Introduction by Cathy Hong-Praslick
Recipes by Trieu Thi Koppe

I ts coastline curves against the Pacific Ocean like a sinuous snake; this was how I used to find the country on a map: the country that looked like an 'S.' "For Saigon," my mother would say.

The first kingdom was founded nearly 4,000 years ago. Today, Viet Nam has an estimated population of 70 million. The Red River Delta and the Mekong Delta bisect the mountains and provide fertile soil for crops in the south, and wet paddies in the north to nourish the rice crops.

There are about 56 ethnic minorities who live in the mountainous central highlands and in the north, including the Tay and the Hmong. It is no surprise then that the country's cuisine is inspired by its diverse ethnic and rich cultural influences. Viet Nam's neighbors include Thailand, Lao PDR and Cambodia. It also shares its northern border with China, whose rule the Vietnamese people endured for a thousand years. The Chinese introduced stir-frying, noodles and Buddhism (which, in turn, inspired vegetarian cooking). The Mongols, the next to invade, entered Viet Nam in the thirteenth century with their legacy of beef and hotpots in tow. Another colonizing power, the French, came in 1858 and stayed for nearly a century. They shared their sautéing techniques, dairy products and baked sweets. Lao PDR, Cambodia and Thailand contributed spices, herbs (such as mint and lemongrass) and curries. Most notably, *nuoc mam* (fish sauce), which is an essential ingredient in Vietnamese cooking, has roots in Thailand. Thais call it *nahmpla*. It is a salty extract, pressed from tiny anchovies, and is used to season food, flavor soups and serve as a versatile dipping sauce.

Vietnamese cuisine is broadly divided into three geographic regions: north, south and central Viet Nam. Northern cooking leans toward simpler fare; the south, which enjoys the largess of land and ocean, features seafood and vegetables. It is in central Viet Nam — particularly in Hue, the former seat of the emperors — where the food is spicy, exotic and singular. Northern cooking features beef, a tradition inherited from the Mongols. Central Viet Nam has a greater emphasis on numerous small dishes which are served either simultaneously or in a succession of courses. The southern table, on the other hand, is laden with the vegetables and herbs so abundant in the Mekong Delta. You'll also find that curries are served in the south. They are a Cambodian influence, although Vietnamese curries taste sweeter.

Noodles and soups

As in most Asian countries, rice is a staple, but the Vietnamese adore noodles. Noodle soups (noodles served in soup) are usually presented in individual bowls and not shared. Every region has its own specialty. The famous beef noodle soup, *pho*, comes from the north and the spicy *bun bo Hue* from the central region. The south has a myriad selection of *mi* and *hu tieu*. Soup stalls are ubiquitous on the streets of major cities and they serve just about every variety of noodle: flat white rice noodles for *pho*, crisp egg noodles for *mi*, chewy transparent glass noodles for *hu tieu* and rice noodles for *bun*. Noodles are eaten wet (served in a soup), dry or stir-fried. Meat or seafood is usually added to the dishes. Several variations of a noodle dish often exist because only the accompanying ingredients are changed. The most popular ones are *xa xieu* (spiced pork), *vit* (duck), *thap cam* (seafood) and *thit nuong* (grilled pork). Most Vietnamese start the day with a bowlful of *bun* served either in soup or dry with meat and vegetables. It is common for people to stop at a stall for a bowl of noodles on their way to work. All noodle soups will include a meat of some sort and a variety of vegetables and herbs — usually bean sprouts, green (spring) onions, chilies, lime, basil, coriander and mint.

Pho is the most well known of Vietnamese noodle soups. It is available in many countries around the world. However, the beef noodle version is specific to northern Viet Nam. The broth is made using beef-stock bones, cinnamon, star anise and ginger. Flat, wide rice noodles are cooked separately and flank steak is sliced wafer-thin. The bowl is first filled with cooked noodles, flank steak and other cuts of meat (tripe is also often included). Hot broth is then poured into the bowl, cooking the flank steak to medium rare. Onions, basil, bean sprouts, coriander, *hoisin* sauce and red chili sauce are also added to the bowl. The southern Vietnamese version is called *pho ga*. It is essentially a chicken noodle soup. In place of beef broth, a chicken stock flavored with ginger and coriander is used. Cooked chicken accompanies the *pho*.

THIS PAGE Pho has become so closely associated with Vietnamese cuisine that it is now considered the country's national noodle dish.

OPPOSITE Traveling street vendors provide conveniently quick and tasty meals.

INSIDE THE VIETNAMESE KITCHEN

Nuoc mam (fish sauce) is a key flavoring used in most Vietnamese dishes. Dried and fresh noodles such as *mi* (crisp egg noodles), *hu tieu* (glass noodles), *pho* (flat white rice noodles) and *bun* (rice noodles) are always on hand, as are cloud ear fungus, dried mushrooms (including shiitake and straw mushrooms), mung beans, lemongrass, peanuts and fresh herbs including basil, mint, *rau ram* (Vietnamese mint or polygonum), coriander and spring onions. Other essentials include fresh ginger, garlic, shallots, onion, star anise, cinnamon, jasmine rice, glutinous (sticky) rice, rice paper, rice flour, glutinous rice flour, tapioca starch, turmeric, Vietnamese five spice and tamarind. Other handy ingredients include *hoisin* sauce, red chili sauce and paste, oyster sauce, rice vinegar, rock sugar, sesame seeds, soy sauce, curry paste, coconut milk and sesame oil. Banana leaves are used to wrap foods for steaming. Dried shrimp are used to flavor some soups and stir-fries.

ESSENTIAL COOKING TECHNIQUES

Preparing Vietnamese dishes requires the use of many cooking techniques. These include braising and simmering (so that meats are tender and succulent), stir-frying, steaming, poaching, grilling, pan-frying and deep-frying.

ESSENTIAL KITCHEN IMPLEMENTS

A mortar and pestle are necessary for grinding spices and making marinades. Alternatively, a food processor or blender can also be used. A wok or large frying pan is useful for stir-frying and quickly heating ingredients. And a rice cooker is useful for cooking rice. Bamboo or metal steamers are handy for steaming rice cakes, vegetables and some meat dishes.

THIS PAGE (left) Essential condiments most commonly served with Vietnamese dishes; (right) This lady is making banh cuon wrappers made of rice flour which are traditionally filled with meat before they are rolled and served.

OPPOSITE (bottom right) Banh xeo is a popular coconut and rice flour crepe filled with vegetables, pork and shrimp.

The Vietnamese are so enamored with their soups that it would be remiss not to include what my family refers to as "drinking food." *Lau*, a broth version of fondue, is a family favorite. It's a potluck broth in which meats or seafood or vegetables are stirred into hotpots. *Lau* may include fresh cuts of fish, shrimp and vegetables. These are added into the pot and eaten with noodles or rice. For *bo nhung giam*, a beef version of this dish, a broth usually consisting of water and vinegar (although more esoteric versions include vinegar and beer, or vinegar and coconut soda — a carbonated coconut-flavored drink) is brought to a boil in a communal hotpot. Thin slices of flank steak are added and cooked according to personal preference. The cooked meat is most commonly eaten with rice. My family prefers to roll it up in rice paper with pickled carrots and radish, and dip it in an anchovy-pineapple sauce (my American husband nearly passed out when he smelled the sauce).

Appetizers

Almost every Vietnamese menu features spring rolls. *Cha gio* are crispy, fried rolls filled with pork, shrimp, glass noodles, onions and mushrooms. They are sometimes referred to as Imperial rolls and are best enjoyed with a sweet *nuoc mam* dipping sauce. *Goi cuon* (also known as summer rolls or fresh spring rolls) are packed with mint, basil, rice vermicelli, pork and shrimp, and served with a peanut-*hoisin* sauce. Vietnamese rolls are wrapped in rice paper that has been dipped in water. This makes the wrappers soft and pliable, making the rolling process easier. Other popular rolls include *bi cuon*, a mixture of shredded pork and pork skin, and jicama; and *bo bia*, which features fried daikon and carrots, sausage, and shredded omelet.

Steamed rice flour dishes such as *banh beo* (steamed rice cakes with ground shrimp and mung beans, served with *nuoc mam* flavored with shrimp broth) and *banh cuon* (steamed rice flour rolls filled with spiced ground meat and mushrooms) are also popular appetizers.

Banh xeo (sizzling rice crepe) is Viet Nam's elegant answer to the omelet. Its brilliant yellow hue comes from the turmeric that is mixed with the rice flour. The batter is made with coconut milk and spring onions which make for a delightfully rich crepe. It is often filled with pork, shrimp, mung beans and bean sprouts. Sometimes, fresh herbs are also added. It is traditionally served with *nuoc mam*.

Salads

Salads are very much part of the Vietnamese table, but they do not resemble European-style salads. Referred to as *goi*, these are distinct and singular regional dishes. The main ingredient of *goi* can be anything from fresh herbs to lotus flowers or shredded papaya. Usually accompanied by shredded meat (as in *goi ga*, chicken salad with mint), fruit or other vegetables. *Goi* are typically dressed with vinegar and sometimes flavored with sugar and *nuoc mam*.

Meat

Meat is never served in large pieces. A filet would never be placed on a Vietnamese table. Meat is usually cut into small, bite-size pieces and flavored with a blend of spices, sauces and marinades, then braised, simmered, grilled over hot charcoal embers or stir-fried. Although exotic meats such as snake are eaten, the average Vietnamese family is more likely to eat fish, fowl and beef.

Bo bay mon is one of the more famous Vietnamese specialties. It consists of seven courses of beef flavored in different ways and cooked using a variety of techniques. *Bo tay chanh* is a beef ceviche which is served with shrimp chips (puffy, shrimp-flavored crisps). The acidity in the lime juice pickles or "cooks" the thin slices of beef.

Pork is most commonly boiled or grilled. *Thit heo quay* (barbecued pork), for example, is often served at weddings. In terms of fowl, chicken and duck are most popular. They are usually marinated before they're stir-fried or roasted and served with rice.

THIS PAGE (above) Grilled shrimp paste wrapped around sugarcane skewers; (left) Pickling is a matter of national preference and taste, but it also preserves food over long periods of time in situations when refrigeration may not always be an option.

OPPOSITE A market vendor prepares Banh xeo. The batter gets its distinctive yellow coloring from the addition of turmeric.

The Pacific Ocean provides seafood that finds its way to kitchens in the south. Shrimp is frequently used in many different dishes. The most notable one is *chao tom*, which consists of finely minced shrimp that has been wrapped around sugar cane and grilled. Fish are steamed whole, stuffed and broiled, or simmered in aromatic sauces. *Ca kho to* is a popular dish of fish (usually catfish) simmered in an earthenware pot with caramel chili sauce. *Cua rang muoi* are crabs fried with salt and pepper, served with lime juice and salt. It is also not uncommon to be served frog's legs, eel, squid, cuttlefish and octopus.

Special occasions

Some dishes are prepared only for special occasions such as Tet (the celebration of the lunar new year) and weddings. *Banh chung* is a specialty made for Tet. The square block of glutinous (sticky) rice filled with mung beans, fatty pork and sesame seeds is wrapped in banana leaves. It also tastes delicious when served fried. Legend has it that the youngest son of King Hung Vuong made two rice cakes to celebrate the lunar new year — a round one signified the sky and a square one symbolized the earth. He offered these humble dishes to his father, explaining that because rice was the most valuable and precious food in their kingdom, the simple cakes represented his love for his people and for his country. Since then, the square-shaped *banh chung* has been a staple of Tet. A pyramid-shaped version, popular in the south, is called *banh u*.

Dinner together

Dinner is considered an important meal among Vietnamese families. It is common for families to sit together at mealtime and share their day as well as their food with one another. Often, extended family members join in as well. To the Vietnamese, food should be eaten communally and large gatherings of friends and family are normal. Dishes are brought to the table all at once. They usually include rice, a meat or meat substitute, and several plates of vegetables. Rice is served in small individual bowls (adults are always served first), and the main course platters are shared. Sometimes, a savory or sour soup, such as *canh*, is served to cleanse the palate. Alternatively, small bowls of broth called *sup* (a corruption of the French word for soup) are served individually or as an appetizer.

Sweets

For dessert, *che* is most frequently served. *Che* refers to a variety of sweet jellies and dessert soups usually filled with fruits, lotus seeds, mung beans and black beans. *Che dau xanh*, for example, is a syrupy rice pudding with green mung beans. Often, sweet coconut is spooned over *che*. Another classic dessert is *dau hu gung*, a sweet, warm beancurd served with a syrup of dark caramel and fresh ginger. *Khoai mi* (yucca cake) is a round, sticky wafer cake made of yucca, mung bean, sugar and coconut milk.

THIS PAGE A variety of che or bean and jelly desserts.

OPPOSITE (above) A vendor displays her wares — smoked fish and fresh herbs.

Fresh fruit is almost always served. Whatever is in season will inevitably find its way to the table. Litchis and longans, tropical fruits with white, tender sweet flesh, are served in their own syrup with ice. Jackfruit, star fruit and other tropical fruits are peeled and eaten at the table after dinner.

Drinks

Café sua da (iced sweet coffee) and nong (warm sweet coffee) are widely enjoyed. Vietnamese coffee is extremely strong and is usually combined with sweetened condensed milk. It can be served hot or poured over a glass of ice before it is drunk. Other than this sweet concoction, the Vietnamese also enjoy black and green teas, and ruou. Ruou refers to alcohol such as wine, beer and hard liquor.

Cha gio

Spring rolls

Vietnamese rice paper is a miracle of adaptation. It comes in many sizes, textures and shapes. Rice paper is most commonly made plain, but it can also be flavored with many different ingredients including coconut, sesame, dried prawn and tapioca. There are numerous ways to use rice paper. When toasted over a charcoal fire, it can be eaten like crackers. It can be moistened and used as a soft wrap. However, my husband and children all agree that it's best used as the skin for cha gio, *a Vietnamese specialty! Our family is now spread across the world. Whenever we gather,* cha gio *is always the first dish everyone asks me to prepare.*

Makes 100 pieces

5 grams dried cloud ear fungus,
    approximately 5 pieces
90 grams glass noodles
400 grams lean pork, minced
200 grams shrimp, shelled and minced
100 grams crabmeat
1 small carrot, peeled and coarsely grated
2 teaspoons garlic, minced
30 grams coriander, chopped
1 small onion, peeled and minced
1/2 teaspoon ground pepper
1/2 teaspoon salt
1 tablespoon fish sauce
1 egg, lightly beaten
100 round sheets of rice paper
    (approximately 15 centimeters
    in diameter)
oil for deep-frying

*For the nuoc mam ot
    (Vietnamese chili sauce)*
2 cloves garlic, peeled and minced
1 bird's-eye chili, minced
2 tablespoons white sugar
2 tablespoons fish sauce
2 tablespoons water
1/2 tablespoon lime juice

For the accompaniments
lettuce leaves
cucumber, sliced into semi circles
bean sprouts, raw
mint leaves
basil leaves

1. Place cloud ear fungus and glass noodles in separate cups of warm water. Once they are reconstituted, drain. Chop them roughly and mix in a bowl with minced pork, shrimp, crabmeat, carrots, garlic, coriander, onion, pepper, salt and fish sauce. Add egg and mix well.

2. To roll the *cha gio*, place a piece of rice paper on a clean, wet kitchen towel. Dip your fingers in a bowl of water and run them over the entire rice paper to soften it. Place approximately 1 tablespoon of filling on the moist rice paper, near the edge closest to you, fold the rice paper over the filling, tuck in the sides, then roll to form a cylinder about 6-centimeters long.

3. Next, fry the *cha gio*. Heat oil over low heat in a wok or large frying pan. Gently put in a few *cha gio* at a time (crowding the pan causes the rolls to stick together). Fry them slowly until golden brown (note that high heat causes the skin to bubble, break and burn).

4. To make *nuoc mam ot* (Vietnamese chili sauce), mix all the ingredients together.

5. Serve the fried *cha gio* in a plate. Place the accompaniments and dipping sauce in separate dishes around it.

6. To eat this dish, take a piece of lettuce, put a piece of *cha gio* on top of the lettuce, add cucumber, bean sprouts and mint. Roll up the leaf and dip in sauce.

Thit heo bam khoai nang, xuc banh trang mi nuoc dua

Minced pork with water chestnuts and toasted coconut tapioca paper

Binh Dinh is a Vietnamese province famous for its opera (Hat Boi Binh Dinh), martial arts, tapioca and coconuts. One of its specialties is coconut tapioca paper. When I was growing up, most families in our village made their own. It involves grating the tapioca and coconut; turning the two ingredients into a paste; steaming the paper over a special outdoor, wood-fired stove; and then drying it in the sun. My elder sister was always in charge of making the paper in our family. It was my job to keep the fire stoked, a job that invariably left me smelling of smoke and with tears in my eyes! It is toasted before it is eaten and still remains one of my favorite snacks.

Coconut tapioca paper

Serves 4 - 6

3 grams dried cloud ear fungus,
 approximately 3 pieces
30 grams glass noodles
30 milliliters cooking oil
2 cloves garlic, peeled and finely
 chopped
1 onion, peeled and chopped
400 grams lean pork, minced
250 grams water chestnuts, peeled
 and coarsely diced
200 milliliters coconut milk
2 tablespoons fish sauce
1/2 teaspoon salt

1/2 teaspoon ground black pepper
4 small red chilies, chopped
4 stalks spring onions, cut into
 1-centimeter lengths
30 grams coriander, chopped
 into 1-centimeter lengths

For the accompaniments
banh trang mi nuoc dua (coconut
 tapioca paper)
nuoc cot dua (coconut milk)
nuoc mam ot (Vietnamese chili sauce,
 see *cha gio* recipe on page 244)

Chef's note:
If coconut tapioca paper is not available, you may use prawn crackers as a substitute.

1. Place cloud ear fungus and glass noodles in separate cups of warm water. Once reconstituted, drain and chop cloud ear fungus roughly. Set aside. Drain water from glass noodles, cut into 3-centimeter lengths and set aside.

2. In a pan, stir-fry garlic and onion in cooking oil until onions are translucent. Add minced pork and stir-fry, breaking up the lumps of meat. When the juices drawn out from the meat during stir-frying evaporate, add water chestnuts and cloud ear

fungus. Stir for about 2 minutes before adding 3 tablespoons of coconut milk, fish sauce, salt and pepper. Turn off heat. Stir in chilies, spring onions, coriander and glass noodles. Toss all ingredients to mix evenly.

3. To prepare coconut tapioca paper, roast it over a charcoal fire until it blisters and puffs up a little. It should be crunchy, like a cracker. Alternatively, microwave it at the machine's highest setting for 1 minute on each side.

4. Place meat mixture on a plate. Serve it with toasted coconut tapioca paper, coconut milk and *nuoc mam ot*.

5. To eat this dish, break off a piece of the coconut tapioca paper and top it with some meat mixture, then drizzle with coconut milk and *nuoc mam ot*.

Bun bo Hue

Hue pork and beef noodle soup

Bun bo Hue is a famous dish which has origins in the old imperial capital of Hue. It is a favorite of Vietnamese around the world. In 1971, during the Viet Nam War, I left my village to live with my aunt in the city of Quy Nhon. A woman named Miss Lan had a small shop next door from which she sold bun bo Hue. Each day, before dawn, she would prepare enough soup for the day. If the breeze blew from just the right direction, the delicious smells from her kitchen would float into my room. That smell was irresistible and I had to have a bowl of her bun bo Hue every day. Each time I did, Miss Lan made sure to give me an extra piece of meat. I often sat and talked with her, watching her as she worked her magic in the tiny kitchen. Hers was the best bun bo Hue I have ever eaten. Sadly, when I returned to Viet Nam after the war, in 1992, I discovered that Miss Lan had passed on.

Serves 6 - 8

For the soup base
1 tablespoon vegetable oil
5 stalks lemongrass, bruised
2 cloves garlic with skin on
1 small red onion, peeled
500 grams shin beef
1 kilogram pork leg, cut into
   3-centimeter cubes
1/2 tablespoon shrimp paste
salt and pepper to taste

For the soup flavoring
1 tablespoon annatto (*achiote* or
   achuete) seeds
2 tablespoons vegetable oil
10-12 shallots, peeled and thinly sliced
1 stalk lemongrass, finely chopped
2 bird's-eye chilies, finely chopped
2 tablespoons finely chopped *ngo gai*
   (sawtooth herb)

For the accompaniments
1 kilogram fresh, thick rice noodles or
   500 grams thick dried rice noodle
   sticks, boiled and drained
2 stalks spring onions, chopped
10 leaves *ngo gai* (sawtooth herb), cut
   into 5-centimeter-long pieces
30 grams basil
200 grams banana blossom, thinly
   shaved or sliced
200 grams bean sprouts, cleaned
2 limes cut into wedges
3-4 tablespoons fish sauce
1 red chili, sliced

Chef's note:
Annatto seeds are primarily used to give dishes an orangey-red hue.

1. Heat a tablespoon of vegetable oil in a large soup pot. Add bruised lemongrass, garlic and onion. Stir-fry until aromatic (1 to 2 minutes). Add 5 liters of water, bring to a boil. Carefully drop in the whole piece of shin beef and pieces of pork leg. Reduce heat and simmer until meat is tender (about 90 minutes). Remove and discard the lemongrass, onion and garlic. Remove beef from broth and let cool. Cut beef into thin slices (5-millimeter thickness) and set aside. Add shrimp paste to the stock and season with salt and pepper to taste.

2. In a small pan, sauté the annatto seeds in vegetable oil over low heat until the oil becomes reddish-yellow. Strain and discard the seeds. Return the oil to the pan and add sliced shallots, chopped lemongrass, chilies and chopped *ngo gai*. Sauté for a few more minutes, then pour this into the broth. Keep simmering over low heat until ready to serve.

3. To serve, warm the rice noodles by blanching them in hot water for 10 minutes. Place rice noodles in a large soup bowl. Arrange pork and sliced beef on top of the noodles. Pour in hot broth. Garnish with chopped spring onions. Serve with a plate of *ngo gai*, basil, shaved banana blossom, bean sprouts and lime wedges, as well as a small bowl of fish sauce and sliced chilies on the side.

Ga xao sa ot voi nuoc mau

Lemongrass chicken with caramel sauce

Each time I breathe in the delicate aroma of lemongrass in my cooking, I remember a very angry father. As a young girl, I enjoyed tagging along with my brothers whenever they got up to their various exploits. It seemed that they were always doing something much more exciting than I was. Of course, they weren't usually happy with me being there and tried many ways to discourage me from trailing them. One evening, they decided to cook a chicken with their friends. Of course, I made sure I was there as they started the fire. They lined an empty 20 liter tin with rock salt. Then they wrapped a chicken with whole stalks of lemongrass and placed it on the salt. They covered the tin with a conical hat and placed it on the fire to cook. Soon, the rock salt began to pop like popcorn. They knew that when the popping stopped, the chicken was ready to eat. The smell of the chicken was delicious!

But, there was more to this little party than just chicken. The boys produced a bottle of rice wine to enjoy with the meal. They gave me my first taste of alcohol. In our small village, girls were not supposed to drink alcohol. That evening, my father caught me drinking and I was in real trouble! But I still remember the lovely aroma of that meal and never forgot how wonderful the combination of chicken with lemongrass is, as well as how angry my father was!

Serves 4 - 6

2 shallots, peeled and finely chopped
1/4 teaspoon freshly ground black pepper
1/4 teaspoon salt
1 tablespoon fish sauce
4 skinless, boneless chicken legs, cubed
2 teaspoons cornflour (cornstarch)
1 medium white onion, peeled and cut into
  1-centimeter-wide wedges
1 tablespoon white vinegar

6 tablespoons vegetable oil
2 stalks lemongrass, thinly sliced and
  finely chopped (white part only)
3 cloves garlic, peeled and finely
  chopped
1 red chili, chopped
2 tablespoons white sugar
2 teaspoons roasted white sesame seeds

1. Mix chopped shallots, black pepper, salt and fish sauce together. Add this marinade to the chicken and stir to mix. Sprinkle cornflour over the chicken and stir to coat evenly. Set aside to marinate for 30 minutes.

2. In the meantime mix onion wedges and vinegar in a bowl and set aside.

3. Heat 4 tablespoons vegetable oil in a wok over high heat. To ensure that the chicken pieces are evenly browned, sear the marinated chicken in the hot vegetable oil in four separate batches. They should only be lightly browned. Set aside.

4. Heat the remaining 2 tablespoons of vegetable oil in a clean wok. Add chopped lemongrass, chopped garlic and chili. Stir-fry until aromatic (1 to 2 minutes). Add the browned chicken and continue to stir-fry until all the juice evaporates.

5. When ready to serve, heat a frying pan. Add sugar and a teaspoon of water. Let the sugar caramelize, taking great care not to let it burn. It should turn dark brown. Remove from heat, add the cooked chicken and stir to mix well. Drain the vinegar from the onion wedges and add to the chicken. Stir to mix well. Transfer to a serving plate, sprinkle with roasted sesame seeds. If you wish, garnish with fresh red chili strips and chopped coriander leaves. Serve immediately.

Suong heo nau nuoc dua

Pork stew in young coconut water

Oddly, pork played a large part in my life. Indeed, were it not for pork, I may not have been born! My mother was always doing business and before my parents were married, the only way my father could find an excuse to spend time with my mother was to tempt her with the prospect of a profitable business proposition. One day, he approached her with the idea of selling pork. He began to buy pigs, butcher them, then bring the meat to my mother, always ensuring that she got the bigger portion to sell. This was how their courtship began! Ever since then, our family has always had the choicest cuts of pork to cook with and it is always served on special occasions. This is a tradition I continue to subscribe to today.

Serves 12

1 kilogram pork loin (bone in), cut into
  2 pieces
4 cloves garlic, peeled and finely
  chopped
1/4 teaspoon salt
1/4 teaspoon ground pepper
1 tablespoon palm sugar
4 tablespoons fish sauce

2 liters young coconut water
  (2-3 coconuts)
2 carrots, peeled and cut into
  thick batons
2 potatoes, peeled and cut into
  thick batons (like thick-cut fries)
fresh coriander leaves for garnish

Chef's note:
Coconut water is the liquid found inside the coconut. Do not use coconut milk.

Choose a cut of pork loin that is well suited to braising. It should be closer to the sirloin or hind-loin end.

1. Wash pork and pat dry. Mix chopped garlic, salt, pepper, palm sugar and fish sauce. Rub this mixture onto the pork and marinate for 1 hour. Sear the marinated pork in a wok with a little oil.

2. Put coconut water into a large pot and bring to a boil. Add seared pork. Skim off any scum that rises to the top. Reduce heat and simmer until tender (about 5 hours). Add carrots and potatoes 30 minutes before the dish is done. Season with salt and pepper to taste.

3. To serve, carefully place each piece of pork into a large bowl. Divide the carrots and potatoes equally between them. Garnish with coriander leaves. This stew is usually served with baguettes.

Chao ga and goi ga cap cai

Chicken rice porridge and chicken cabbage salad

My home province, Binh Dinh, can be cold and wet during the winter months. When we were young, we often came down with colds in the winter. My mother's remedy for colds was always a bittersweet affair. She would sit us on the bed, place a pot of herbal concoction in front of us, drop a hot stone into the pot to produce steam, cover us with a blanket and instruct us to inhale the vapors. It was definitely not my favorite thing! After this ordeal, we would be presented with a bowl of steaming hot, delicious chicken rice porridge. I don't know if it was the herbal vapors, the rice porridge or the combination of both that did the trick. But the next day, we'd always be out playing as usual. I still love to eat chicken rice porridge, regardless of whether I'm sick or not!

Serves 6 - 8

For the rice porridge
1 large chicken, thoroughly cleaned
4-centimeter piece ginger
100 grams rice
2 teaspoons fish sauce
salt and ground white pepper to taste
30 grams Vietnamese mint (polygonum)
  leaves, chopped

For the salad dressing
1 tablespoon minced chilies
3 cloves garlic, minced
2 tablespoons white sugar
3 tablespoons sesame oil
1 lime
2 tablespoons fish sauce
1 tablespoon light soy sauce

For the salad
1 package instant noodles, about 80
  grams (use the noodles only, discard
  the seasoning)
2 tablespoons sesame oil
200 grams cabbage, shredded
1 small carrot, peeled and shredded
1 medium tomato, deseeded and
  julienned
1 small onion, peeled and thinly sliced
20 grams Vietnamese mint (polygonum)
  leaves, chopped
30 grams coriander, chopped into
  1-centimeter lengths
20 grams roasted peanuts, crushed
nuoc mam ot (Vietnamese chili sauce,
  see *cha gio* recipe on page 244)
roasted rice paper (optional)

1. To make the rice porridge, rub salt over the outside of the chicken and insert ginger in the cavity. Put chicken in 3 liters of water and bring to a boil. Skim off the scum, reduce heat and simmer for 45 minutes to make broth. Remove chicken from broth. Set aside to cool.

2. Wash the rice and add to the chicken broth along with fish sauce. Cook over medium heat for 50 minutes or until the rice is soft and the broth thickens. Season with salt and white pepper

to taste. Before serving, add in the chopped Vietnamese mint leaves.

3. Remove the breast meat from the chicken, and tear it into strips. Set aside.

4. Heat sesame oil in a small pan and toast the dry instant noodles over low heat until lightly browned. Break the noodles into bite-size pieces. Set aside.

5. In a large bowl, prepare the salad by mixing the cabbage, carrots, tomatoes, onions, Vietnamese mint leaves, coriander and chicken strips. Mix all the salad dressing ingredients in a separate bowl and pour into the salad. Toss in toasted noodle pieces and sprinkle with crushed peanuts.

6. Serve chicken rice porridge hot with the salad, some *nuoc mam ot* and roasted rice paper on the side.

Banh it nhung dua

Little steamed glutinous rice cakes with coconut filling

Banh it means "little cake." Traditionally, it is given to someone to convey a little "thank you." It is also presented as an offering at family altars. My sister's father-in-law was my father's best friend. They had been childhood buddies. For as long as I can remember, banh it *played a small part in their friendship.*

Whenever one of them attended a function without the other, they would return with a banh it *for the person who missed the event. This went on throughout their entire lives. After my father's best friend passed away, my father continued to return with a* banh it*, which he would place at his friend's family altar. Now that they have both passed on, I am sure that they are still sharing* banh it *in heaven.*

Makes 8 pieces

For the coconut filling
200 grams shredded coconut,
  white part only
100 grams light-brown sugar
1 teaspoon grated ginger
a pinch of salt

8 banana leaves
200 grams glutinous rice flour
a pinch of salt
60 milliliters vegetable oil

1. In a medium saucepan, combine coconut, brown sugar, ginger and salt. Cook slowly over medium heat until jam like. Stir frequently. Remove from heat and let cool. Divide into 8 equal portions. Set aside.

2. Wipe the banana leaves clean. Dip them in a basin of hot water for a short while to soften. Wipe off water and cut into circles measuring 20 centimeters across. Fold the circles in half, keeping the grain of the leaves perpendicular to the fold and the dark-green side of the leaf on the outside. Fold one corner toward the center of the semicircle (forming a small pie-wedge shape). Flip it over and fold the other corner toward the center. You should end up with one fold in front and one fold behind, creating a wide pie wedge.

3. Mix the glutinous rice flour and salt. Create a well in the center and add 150 milliliters of very warm water (but not boiling). Gather all the flour into a ball and knead until it forms a smooth

dough. Divide into 8 equal portions. Form each portion into a ball. To keep them moist, cover with a damp cloth.

4. Working as fast as possible, flatten each dough ball into a thin disc. Place one-eighth of the filling in it. Seal completely, forming a ball. Dip the whole ball in oil. Open the mouth of a banana leaf cone and place the filled dough ball in it. To seal, first fold one of the sides where the leaf overlaps (and where it is thickest) over the ball. Repeat by folding the opposite side down over the ball. Fold over the remaining sides. It should end up looking like a pyramid. Repeat until all the banana leaf cones are filled.

5. Place the *banh it* (with the top of the pyramid pointing upward, do not lay them on their sides to prevent them from opening) in a steamer. Steam for 1 hour. Remove from the steamer, shake off excess water and set aside to cool. Serve *banh it* at room temperature.

Muc dua

Candied coconut

The Lunar New Year is known as Tet in Viet Nam. It is a time for visiting family and friends. Traditionally, the Vietnamese do not celebrate individual birthdays. They celebrate everyone's birthdays at Tet. I remember it as a time of great excitement. This was when as a child I could wear my new clothes, receive gifts of new money and eat lots of delicious candy! It remains a time for family reunions. Families gather to share a meal on New Year's Eve. This is followed by continued cooking throughout the night in preparation for the big day. Muc dua is one of the traditional dishes that is never omitted. The word dua, which means coconut, sounds like the Vietnamese word for enough. Thus muc dua is served in the hope that we will enjoy a plentiful year ahead.

Coconut with outer husk removed

Makes 500 grams

1 coconut
1 tablespoon lemon juice
1 kilogram white sugar

1. Shell and skin the coconut. Using a vegetable peeler, thinly slice the coconut.

2. Place 2 liters of water in a pot, add lemon juice and bring to a boil. Add coconut slices and blanch for 2 minutes. Drain and dry off excess water using paper towels. Add sugar and coat the coconut slices thoroughly. Marinate overnight.

3. Put marinated coconut in a big wok over very low heat. Cook slowly, stirring frequently until any residual moisture is absorbed and the sugar becomes dry and powdery. Remove from heat and cool. Shake off the excess sugar before transferring the candied coconut to a container. Store in a cool place.

ABOUT THE COUNTRY CONTRIBUTORS

Reda Jasmine Abdul Rahman Taib
(Brunei Darussalam)
Jasmine was born, raised and educated in Brunei Darussalam. Her early days in the kitchen were heavily influenced by her mother Datin Edah and late grandmother Datin Nafsiah. Now a mother of three, Jasmine continues to add to her knowledge of local cuisine by consulting her mother-in-law Hjh Sharifah Sajartudor.

Jasmine has a Master's degree in Southeast Asian Studies from the School of Oriental and African Studies, University of London. Her first job was as a Research Officer at the Ministry of Foreign Affairs, Brunei Darussalam. Currently, apart from caring for her children, she also manages Aranda Café, a restaurant located in the boutique hotel her family runs, and owns a floral, landscaping and maintenance business. She enjoys hosting dinner parties, and cooking for friends and family. Jasmine intends to write her own cookbook about traditional Bruneian cuisine some time in the future.

Her Royal Highness Princess Marie Ranariddh Norodom
(Cambodia)
HRH Princess Marie Ranariddh Norodom is the wife of HRH Samdech Krom Preah Norodom Ranariddh, former president of the National Assembly and prime minister of Cambodia from 1993 to 1997. During two decades of conflict in Cambodia, Her Royal Highness Princess Marie dedicated herself to assisting refugees and improving the lives of Cambodian women and children.

In 1985, Princess Marie established the Samdech Rasmi Women's Foundation at the Site B Refugee Camp on the Cambodian-Thai border. In 1992 the association moved its base to Phnom Penh and changed its name to the Sobbhana Women's Foundation, in commemoration of HRH Samdech Rasmi Sobbhana, His Majesty King Norodom Sihanouk's aunt, who devoted her life to promoting the role of Khmer women in society, for the betterment of their own lives.

Today, through the work of the Women's Foundation, Princess Marie is reviving the ancient tradition of silk weaving and simultaneously creating job opportunities for women in Cambodia. The exquisite handmade silk products produced by these female weavers are then sold by the Sobbhana Boutique. As a result, the Boutique's proceeds fund the Sobbhana Foundation's social initiatives. In addition to the skills training program, the Sobbhana Foundation is focused on providing access to critical health care and funding educational opportunities for Cambodian girls.

Through her efforts, HRH Princess Marie is addressing some of the greatest challenges facing Cambodia today by giving people the hope and skills necessary to build a better future.

Sri Owen
(Indonesia)
Sri Owen was born in Sumatra, where, as a child in her grandmother's kitchen, she first acquired a love of good food. She was still a small girl when her family moved to Java. During the next seven years they endured Japanese occupation and the struggle which led to Indonesia's independence. Ten years later, she was a lecturer in English Literature at the new nation's oldest university, and it was here that she met and married an English colleague. Together, they went to London, and Sri made a successful career with the BBC Overseas Service while, at many dinner parties, introducing her friends to Indonesian cooking. Her first cookbook was published in 1976. Ten more followed: *The Rice Book* and *Indonesian Regional Food and Cookery* are still in print. She and her husband now live in London, travel widely together, and are working on *The Oxford Companion to Southeast Asian Food*.

Somsanouk Mixay
(Lao PDR)
Somsanouk Mixay was born in Vientiane, Lao PDR. He earned his baccalaureate degree in France, studied ethnology and history of religions at the Sorbonne and graduated from the National School of Oriental Languages in Paris.

After returning to Lao PDR, he became editor of the English weekly *Vientiane News* while starting an English news service on Lao National Radio, where he held the post of Deputy Director General. He then started *Vientiane Times*, an English-language weekly, where he was Director General and Chief Editor. Later, he started *Le Renovateur*, a French-language weekly, and became Director General of the Lao Press in Foreign Languages. More recently, he started news services in English and French on Lao National Television.

Somsanouk has written a number of articles and features in English and French, and has published *Treasures of Lao Literature,* Vol. 1 and 2 (in English) and *Thank You for Looking* (in Laotian) with photos by Hans Berger.

Julie Wong
(Malaysia)
An Arts graduate from the National University of Singapore, Julie Wong was editor of several lifestyle magazines in Singapore, including a motoring and women's magazine, before she headed back to Kuala Lumpur to join *The Star* daily newspaper in 1991. She worked at various desks including city, features and the main subbing desk before she became the editor of the media group's food and wine lifestyle magazine, *Flavours*, in 1999. Wong has been with the magazine since. Passionate about food and the promotion of local cuisines, she collaborated with the State Chinese Association of Penang to produce the cookbook, *Nyonya Flavours — A Complete Guide to Penang Straits Chinese Cuisine*, which was on the bestsellers' list for several months after its release in December 2003. Wong has been a judge at various national and international cooking and wine competitions, the most recent being the Chaine de Rotisserie's Best Commis Rotisseur (2005), MLA's Butchers Challenge (2005), Classic Fine Food's Culinary Grand Prix (2004) and the Vinitaly International Wine Competition (2005).

Redzuawan "Chef Wan" Ismail
(Malaysia)
Redzuawan Ismail, better known as Chef Wan, is an actor, talk-show host, comedian, lecturer and food ambassador all rolled into one. He gave up his career in accountancy to earn an associate degree in Professional Chef Training and Hotel Management from the California Culinary Academy, San Francisco, and a degree at the Ritz Hotel's Ritz Escoffier Ecole de Gastronomie Francaise, Paris. Over the past twenty years Chef Wan has hosted cooking shows all over the world and published dozens of cookbooks. Some of the books he has written include *Chef Wan Around the World*, *Chef Wan's Sweet Treats* and *Simply Sedap*. He is now a household name in Malaysia and is one of Malaysia's best-loved icons. On top of all this, he has found time to star on the stage and act in films.

Ma Thanegi
(Myanmar)

Ma Thanegi grew up in Yangon and was educated at the Methodist English High School, the Yangon State School of Fine Arts, the Foreign Language Institute (French and German), and the Institute of Economics. She first began her career as a painter and has had seven solo shows. At present, Thanegi is a freelance writer who contributes articles on culture, arts and history to numerous publications.

She has written numerous books including *The Illusion of Life: Burmese Marionettes, The Native Tourist: In Search of Turtle Eggs, Paw Oo Thett: His Life and Creativity, An Introduction to Myanmar Cuisine, Inle: Blue Sea in the Shan Hills* and *Myanmar Architecture: Cities of Gold*. Thanegi lives in Yangon, Myanmar.

Michaela Fenix
(Philippines)

Michaela Fenix is a food writer and researcher. She writes a weekly column, "Country Cooking," for the *Philippine Daily Inquirer*, and contributes to magazines specializing in food. She was previously food editor at *Today*, a daily newspaper, for more than a decade. She is a founding member of the Manila Ladies Branch of the International Wine and Food Society and serves as editor of the Society's *Asia Pacific Zone* newsletter. She has also served as chairman of a national food writing competition for the past five years. She has authored *Philippine Cuisine: A Country's Heritage* and *Cooking with Filipino Chefs*. She has edited several cookbooks and has contributed essays to books and pamphlets on Filipino food such as *Slow Food: Filipino Culinary Traditions* and *Comforting Cuisine*. She is currently editing a book for Project Kulinarya, a group that aims to standardize Filipino recipes.

Christopher Tan
(Singapore)

Christopher Tan is a writer, editor, food consultant and cookbook author. Raised partly in Singapore, partly in London, and mostly in the kitchen, he often gets asked how his psychology honors degree squares with his current food-related work, to which he replies that he's in digestive therapy. Currently based in Singapore, he contributes articles, photographs, and recipes to international publications, including Singapore's *Straits Times*, *TODAY* newspaper, *Gourmet* (US), *The Edge Singapore*, *Silver Kris* (Singapore Airlines' inflight magazine), and the Singapore, Thailand, Malaysia and Indonesia editions of *Her World* magazine. In his previous tenure as food editor at *Wine & Dine* magazine, Chris and his team won the Best F & B Article trophy at the World Gourmet Summit Awards of Excellence. Besides this he also does food styling, recipe development, collateral editing and other consultancy work for food and publishing companies. Chris is the co-author of three cookbooks: *Shiok!*, a celebration of Singaporean food, *Cooking with Asian Leaves* and *Cooking with Asian Roots*. More books are in the works: you can find out more on Chris's website, www.foodfella.com.

Cora Cunanan Sukhyanga
(Thailand)

Cora Cunanan Sukhyanga's love affair with Thai food began over three decades ago when she settled in Thailand with her Thai husband. She remembers missing the dishes of her native Philippines, but it was her husband's discerning taste for good food and his love of cooking that would awaken her to the rudiments of home-cooked Thai cuisine.

Self-taught and fluent in the Thai language, she found a career in the fields of marketing, advertising and eventually in journalism. It was her Thai colleagues who would eventually introduce her to Thai street food and she soon acquired a taste for spicy E-san cuisine.

As editor of *Thailand Tatler*, and *Femme* weekly magazine, and later, as social columnist for *The Nation* newspaper, she had the chance to meet and interview the world's most famous chefs, and to attend (and review) wine-tasting and culinary events in Thailand and overseas.

Mali Pimnart
(Thailand)

Chef Mali has been with Four Seasons Hotel Bangkok for the past 23 years. She has spent 18 of those years as the head chef of The Spice Market, which was voted the "Most Delicious Thai Restaurant in Bangkok" by local diners. Before her Spice Market tenure, she was the chef in-charge of the employee cafeteria, Tamnaknai. Heading the cafeteria may not sound impressive but the hotel's 600-plus employees loved her Thai dishes and often complain that they can't enjoy the same delicious cuisine she has become famous for (unless they pay to go to The Spice Market). Over the years, The Spice Market has earned a reputation for being one of the best Thai restaurants located in a hotel in Thailand and has been touted by Lord Lichfield's *Courvoisier's Book of the Best* as the "most delicious Thai restaurant." Chef Mali and the team at the Four Seasons Hotel Bangkok created the recipes which appear in our chapter on Thailand.

Cathy Hong-Praslick
(Viet Nam)

Cathy Hong-Praslick was born in Viet Nam and emigrated to the United States in 1975. A food writer and strategy executive, she has worked as a freelance consultant on several food-related projects. Having spent her formative years in her mother's and grandmother's kitchens, she has a deep affinity for classic and traditional Vietnamese home cooking. Her family has a long tradition in food service, having owned restaurants in Viet Nam, France and the United States. The family owns the luxury Sea Horse Resort in Phan Thiet, Viet Nam, and a chain of gelato restaurants throughout the country.

Trieu Thi Koppe
(Viet Nam)

Trieu Thi Koppe was born and raised in Binh Dinh Province, Viet Nam, during the "French War" and grew up during what the Vietnamese call the "American War." She left Viet Nam just before the fall of Saigon at the end of the latter and traveled to America and to Singapore, where she met her husband. They have since lived in Indonesia and the United Arab Emirates where they now reside. They have three children, two in America and one in Singapore, and five grandchildren. Trieu Thi is currently the coordinator for the largest ladies' group in Abu Dhabi. Previously, she served as the Hospitality Chairman for the group and put her interest in food to work organizing functions. She continues to visit Viet Nam at least once a year.

GLOSSARY

Agar-agar Agar-Agar is a unique vegetable substitute for gelatin which is derived from a red seaweed (of the genus *Eucheuma*) or red algae (of the genus *Gelidium*). Agar-agar is typically sold as packaged strips of washed and dried white, semi-translucent seaweed, or in powdered form.

Annatto seed Annatto seeds are a derivative of *achiote* or lipstick trees. They are used as a red food coloring. Annatto seeds are brick red, triangular in shape, and are 3 to 5 millimeters long. The seeds are available whole, but can often be purchased in a block or paste form.
Scientific name: *Bixa orellana*

Bamboo shoot Bamboo shoots are the tender young growth of bamboo, a huge tropical grass that can grow several meters tall. The shoots are harvested before they reach 30 centimeters in height, generally before they are two weeks old. The young shoots are crisp and tender like asparagus and are widely used in Asian cooking. Bamboo shoots are available canned, though fresh bamboo shoots are far superior in taste and texture.
Scientific name: *Dendrocalamus latif lorus, Munro*

Banana blossom Also known as banana heart or banana flower. It is deep purplish-crimson in color and tear drop shaped. The heart of the blossom contains small flowers that, if left undisturbed, will grow into bananas.
Scientific name: *Syconycteris australis*

Banana leaf Banana leaves are large, flexible, and waterproof. They are used to line cooking pits and to wrap everything from whole pigs to rice before they are cooked. The leaves impart a subtle anise fragrance to food and protect it while it is cooking. Frozen leaves, once thawed, work just fine. Boil the leaves before using them to keep them from tearing.

Banana stem Only the inner stem of the banana tree is used. The layers curve tightly around each other and the tough outer layers are discarded. The cylindrical inner stem should not be sliced too thinly. It is usually added to soups and vegetable stews. Banana stem has no taste, but has a crunchy texture.

Basil Basil is an aromatic herb native to Southeast Asia. Many varieties exist. Some of the ones mentioned in this book are:

Sweet basil Also known as Thai sweet basil, this tender herb is cultivated all year round in warm, tropical climates. Fresh sweet basil has a subtle anise scent and strong licorice flavor.
Scientific name: *Ocimum basilicum*

Basil continued...

Wild basil Also known as tea bush, clove basil, tree basil, East Indian or African basil, it is tall and an extremely fragrant shrub. Its leaves are lemon-scented.
Scientific name: *Ocimum gratissimum*

Bay leaf Strong and spicy, the whole glossy leaves of the bay laurel tree are indispensable in savory preparations. The leaves are almost always sold dried and should be removed from a dish before serving.
Scientific name: *Laurus nobilis*

Bean sprout The tender, edible seedlings of certain bean plants, especially those of the mung bean. It usually has a slender and crisp white body, 3 to 5 centimeters long, and a small mung bean head.

Blue ginger An aromatic and fibrous rhizome from the ginger family which has pale pink young shoots. It is aromatic, pungent and spicy. Used to flavor soups, stews and curries, it is often pounded with other herbs and spices to make a spice paste.
Scientific name: *Alpinia galanga*

Calabash gourd The calabash (not to be confused with the *calabaza*) is a vine grown for its fruit, which can either be harvested young and used as a vegetable or harvested mature, dried, and used as a bottle, utensil, or pipe. For this reason, one of the calabash subspecies is known as the bottle gourd. The fresh fruit has light green smooth skin and white flesh.
Scientific name: *Lagenaria siceraria*

Candlenut A round, cream-colored waxy nut, 4 to 6 centimeters in diameter. It has an oily consistency and is used to add texture to a dish and serve as a thickening agent. They are also used to make candles, thus the name candle-nut.
Scientific name: *Aleurites moluccana*

Cardamom Oval pods which are usually used whole. They contain 15 to 20 black seeds and have a sweetly fragrant, almost peppery flavor.
Scientific name: *Elettaria cardamomum*

Chameleon leaf A low-growing plant that is sometimes considered a substitute for cilantro. It has heart shaped green, yellow and pink leaves.
Scientific name: *Brookesia spectrum*

Chili Chilies are integral to Southeast Asian cuisine. A variety of them are used in the region. Even though they look similar and have similar names, they are not always identical. Bird's-eye chilies from Thailand, for example, do not taste exactly the same as their counterparts from Indonesia. While it may not be possible for you to find the exact same species of

chilies, when a recipe simply calls for fresh chilies, it is generally referring to long, skinny, fingerlike red chilies measuring between 10 to 15 centimeters long. Look for finger, Dutch or Holland chilies. Occasionally, green chilies are specified in recipes. Use green finger chilies.

Bird's-eye chili A small chili no more than 4-centimeters long. Its size is deceptive because it is one of the fieriest of chilies.
Scientific name: *Capsicum frutescens*

Dried chili This really means dried red chilies. Look for them in Asian gourmet stores or supermarkets. They should look like dried red finger chilies.

Chinese cabbage Also known as napa cabbage. The most cabbage-shaped of the Chinese green vegetables, the heads of Chinese cabbage are large and barrel shaped. The tightly packed leaves are crinkly and lighter green than ordinary cabbage leaves.
Scientific name: *Brassica pekinensis*

Cinnamon The cinnamon commonly used in most Southeast Asian dishes is actually cassia (*Cinnamomum aromaticum*), the deep reddish-brown bark of a tree cultivated in most parts of the region, not true cinnamon (*Cinnamomum verum*). Sold in the form of thick, tubular quills or sticks (true cinnamon is paper thin) or powdered; cassia has a sweet, peppery flavor. True cinnamon sticks are light brown or tan.

Clarified butter Also known as ghee. It has a nutty, caramel-like flavor and does not leave a residue.

Cloud ear fungus Also known as black fungus, wood ear, or black jelly mushroom. It is usually sold dried, but is also available fresh. When dried, this dark brown, almost black fungus looks like small crumbled pieces of black paper. When soaked before use or reconstituted in water, they swell up and look like ears. Although cloud ear fungus has no taste of its own, it takes on the flavors of other ingredients and is prized for its slippery texture.
Scientific name: *Auricularia auricular-judae or Auricularia polytricha*

Clove Whole cloves are actually the sun-dried, unopened flower buds of clove trees. They add a sweetly spicy flavor to dishes and can be used either whole or ground. As they have an extremely strong flavor, they should be used sparingly.
Scientific name: *Syzygium aromaticum*

Coconut The coconut is the fruit of the coconut palm. You will find that all parts of the coconut palm (even its leaves) are widely utilized in kitchens across

Coconut continued...

Southeast Asia. Coconut milk or cream, in particular, is used in everything from curries to desserts. It is usually extracted by mixing freshly grated mature coconut flesh with tepid water. As a very rough guide, combine 500 grams grated coconut with about 200 milliliters water. Adjusting this ratio alters the thickness or richness of the resulting coconut milk. The mixture is passed through a sieve or piece of muslin and the remaining coconut is kneaded and squeezed (over the same sieve or piece of muslin) so that only pure coconut milk is collected.

However, different cooks have different preferred methods of extracting coconut milk and there is a confusing list of terms used to define the richness or thickness of the coconut milk that is required for a particular dish. You will notice that throughout this book, the terms coconut cream, thick coconut milk, coconut milk and thin or light coconut milk have been used. While we have tried our best to be as clear as possible in our definitions of these terms below, you should also feel comfortable with simply picking the kind of coconut milk you prefer to use in a recipe. As you grow to understand how each different kind of coconut milk influences your finished dish, you will be better able to decide which type of milk works best for you in each situation.
Scientific name: *Cocos nucifera*

Coconut cream By definition, this is the richest of all extractions. Some cooks define coconut cream as the liquid that is squeezed from grated coconut flesh with only a little or no warm water added. Alternatively, you can skim off the cream that rises to the top when the first pressing of coconut milk is left to stand in a deep, narrow receptacle for awhile in a cool place (this method works with fresh, canned and frozen coconut milk, but not diluted homogenized coconut cream).

Coconut milk This is a blend of the first and subsequent pressings which should result in coconut milk of average richness.

Coconut water or juice Not to be confused with coconut milk, this is the translucent, subtly sweet liquid found inside coconuts. If you intend to drink coconut water, it is best to pick young and green fresh coconuts.

Thick coconut milk This is generally defined as the milk derived from the first pressing. Ideally, it would be a combination of coconut cream and a bit of the residual milk from the first pressing.

Thin or light coconut milk This is the milk derived from subsequent pressings.

Coriander Also known as cilantro. The fresh leaves and roots of the coriander plant are essential ingredients in many Southeast Asian dishes. Coriander leaves are small and round with jagged edges. Since heat diminishes their flavor quickly, the leaves are often used raw or added to the dish right before serving.
Scientific name: *Coriandrum sativum*

Coriander seed The fruit of the coriander plant contains two seeds which, when dried, are the portions used as the dried spice. When ripe, the seeds are yellowish-brown in color. Coriander seeds are available whole or ground. It has a fragrant flavor that is reminiscent of both citrus peel and sage.

Cornflour Also known as cornstarch, cornflour is the finely powdered white starch extracted from maize kernels. It is virtually tasteless and is used as a thickening agent. It cuts down the need for fat as, unlike other flours, it blends to a smooth cream when it is combined with a liquid.

Cotton beancurd Firm tofu cakes, made by compressing beancurd in order to remove most of the water in them. Cotton beancurd are sold in squares or larger blocks.

Cumin The dried seed of the herb *Cuminum cyminum*, a member of the parsley family. It has an earthy, pungent, slightly bitter flavor and is a critical ingredient in annatto seed blends, *adobos*, *garam masala*, and curry powder.

Curry leaf The leaf of the deciduous curry tree which originates from the Indian subcontinent. They are small, diamond-shaped and grow in feathery sprays on thin stems. In Indian and Malay dishes they are typically fried in hot oil to release their warm, peppery, citrusy aroma. Used fresh or deep-fried, it has an unusual scent of curry powder. Dried leaves lose their flavor.
Scientific name: *Murraya koenigii*

Daikon Though most widely known as daikon, it is also known as Japanese or Chinese radish, white radish or winter radish. It resembles the carrot, but is usually white in color (although there are purple and green varieties). Daikons can be between 12 to 40 centimeters long.
Scientific name: *Raphanus sativus*

Dried lily flower Also known as golden needle. The long stems and petals of delicate lily flowers are dried in the sun where they turn a dark yellow. They sometimes have a strong smell and some cooks like to soak them in water for half an hour before use.
Scientific name: *Hemerocallis*

Eggplant Also called aubergine or brinjal. The raw fruit can have a somewhat bitter taste but, when cooked, becomes tender and develops a rich, complex flavor. There are many varieties of eggplant.
Scientific name: *Solanum melongena*

The following have been mentioned in this book:

Mark uek These are sour and hairy orange or yellow eggplants that are slightly smaller than a golf ball. Scientific name: *Solanum ferox*

Pea eggplant A type of eggplant that grows in clusters. They are tiny green spheres which, in spite of being tough-skinned and somewhat bitter, are used whole in curries or eaten raw.
Scientific name: *Solanum torvum*

Round eggplant Also known as Thai eggplant or kermit eggplant, they are round and white or green. Round eggplants are about the size of a golf ball.
Scientific name: *Solanum xanthocarpum*

Fennel seed The seed of the fennel plant. They look like larger, paler versions of the cumin seed, but have a distinct anise seed flavor.
Scientific name: *Foeniculum vulgare*

Fish sauce Fish sauce is made by packing small fish (often anchovies) with salt and water, which is left to ferment. It is often used in moderation because it is intensely flavored.

Glass noodle Also known as mung bean vermicelli, cellophane noodle or bean thread noodle. They are translucent noodles made from mung bean starch and are generally sold dried. Reconstitute by soaking briefly in hot water.

Glutinous rice Also known as sticky rice or sweet rice. Long-grained glutinous rice is most widely used in Lao PDR, Cambodia, northern Thailand and parts of Viet Nam. Short-grained varieties are used in Chinese and Japanese cuisine. Glutinous rice may be white or black.

Hoisin sauce A thick, almost pasty deep brown or black-colored sweet and salty bean sauce most commonly used in Chinese cuisine. *Hoisin* sauce is sold in jars or cans and can easily be purchased at Asian specialty stores.

Jicama See Yam bean.

Kaffir lime leaf The leaves of kaffir lime trees have a strong, distinctive fragrance and flavor (a combination of lemongrass and lime). They are about 8-centimeters long and have two lobes. The tree itself produces ping-pong-ball size, knobbly limes with little juice.
Scientific name: *Citrus hystrix*

Kalamansi Also known as kasturi limes or calamondin. Across Southeast Asia, the juice of this tiny, round, usually dark green lime originating from the Philippines is used to make a sweet, yet refreshingly tart cold drink most commonly referred to as lime juice. Kalamansi juice is also used to introduce a sour, counterbalancing flavor to grilled, fried or greasy dishes, as well as salad dressings, marinades and spicy dishes or condiments. Its zest is also used in desserts.
Scientific name: *Citrofortunella microcarpa*

Lady's finger Also known as okra, the lady's finger is a green, tapering pod 5 to 20 centimeters long which contains numerous round white seeds embedded in a gelatinous substance. Only use tender, young lady's fingers as they grow woody as they mature.
Scientific name: *Abelmoschus esculentus*

Lemongrass Tall lemon-scented grass used to flavor curries and soups. Use the lower 5 to 6 centimeters only. The plant looks like an untidy clump of tall grass except that it gives off an intensely lemony fragrance. Cut off the roots and peel off the hard outer leaves to use the tender white portion found at the base of the stalk.
Scientific name: *Cymbopogon citrates*

Lup cheong Firm, dry-cured Chinese sausages made from pork, sometimes enriched with pork liver or duck liver. They are fine-textured but studded with bits of fat, and have a concentrated sweet-salty flavor. Lup cheong is usually steamed or fried before it is eaten.

Mustard greens, preserved Whole pickled mustard greens are usually displayed in large tubs or sold packaged in bags. They usually taste salty and mildly sour, but a salty-sweet version is also used in Thailand.

Palm sugar Also called jaggery, or palm honey. It is a sugar produced from the sap of the palmyra and sugar palms (*Arenga pinnata*), and varies from almost white to dark brown in color. The dark brown varieties have deep, complex flavors akin to that of muscovado sugar.

Pandan leaf A fragrant, flat and green leaf. It is used to color and add fragrance to desserts, rice, curries, and other savory dishes. Knot the pandan leaf before adding it to your dish to release its fragrance. The leaves can also be used to wrap food or are made into containers for sweets.
Scientific name: *Pandanus odoratissimus*

Polygonum Also known as *laksa* leaves, Vietnamese mint or scented Solomon's seal. There is no substitute for this herb, which has a distinctive lemony scent which some liken to coriander.
Scientific name: *Polygonum odoratum*

Pomelo A large citrus fruit that is slightly pear-shaped, with a thick rind that can easily be peeled away. The fruit flesh can be light yellow to coral pink and taste tart to sweet.
Scientific name: *Citrus maxima*

Pumpkin leaf shoot The shoot of a pumpkin plant. Shoots can sometimes reach up to 3 meters.

Rice flour Rice flour is gluten-free and should not be substituted with all-purpose flour. It is used to make rice noodles and serves as a binding or thickening agent. Glutinous or sticky rice flour is mainly used in desserts and dumplings where chewy, sticky doughs are desired.

Rice noodle Also known as rice vermicelli or rice sticks. These tender, white noodles made of rice flour are cut into varying widths and sold fresh or dried. Reconstitute dried noodles by soaking them in water until they are soft.

Sago pearls Made from an edible starch extracted from the pithlike center of a mature sago palm. The starch is processed to form small granules. When cooked, they look like small translucent balls with a bouncy-chewy consistency.

Salam leaf Also referred to as Indonesian bay leaf. This green leaf is palm-size and has been likened to curry leaves, but does not have a distinctly powerful scent or flavor.
Scientific name: *Eugenia polyantha*

Sawtooth herb Also known as sawtooth coriander, or eryngo. This herb has long, flat, green leaves with serrated edges like the teeth of a saw. It is most often used as a garnish and tastes very much like coriander.
Scientific name: *Eryngium foetidum*

Shallot The shallots most widely used in Southeast Asia are small and grow in clusters. They taste more pungent and intense than onions. The outer, papery skin should be reddish-brown or coppery, and the flesh should be purplish pink.
Scientific name: *Allium oschaninii*

Shrimp paste A common ingredient used in Southeast Asian cuisine. It is either sold dried or as a thick paste that can be spooned (the latter is usually referred to as shrimp sauce) and consists of fermented and salted shrimp. Its pungent aroma can be off-putting to the uninitiated.

Star anise These small, dried, star-shaped seed pods are the key ingredient in Chinese five-spice powder. Each point of the star-shaped seed pod contains a seed. They are small and taste like anise seed or licorice.
Scientific name: *Illicium verum*

Star fruit The mild, sweet and sub-acid flavor of the star fruit complements many juice drinks. When sliced, cross sections of the fruit are star-shaped. It is often eaten on its own or served in salads and other dishes.
Scientific name: *Averrhoa carambola*

Tamarind These are the seed pods of the tamarind tree. They are also called Indian date. Juice from green or unripe tamarind (the pods look greenish brown) is used in the preparation of *sinigang* in the Philippines. When ripe, the pod turns reddish-brown and has a thin brittle shell. It is a key souring ingredient in many Asian dishes.
Scientific name: *Tamarindus indica*

Dried ripe tamarind The seeds and shells are removed from the ripe tamarind seed pod and the pulp is dried in the sun so that it is no longer damp but remains somewhat soft. These are often sold in blocks. Sometimes, only the shell is removed. To use, it is soaked in water and the softened paste is sieved before use to get rid of stray bits of shell or seeds.

Tamarind pulp or paste This is purely the pulp of the tamarind seed pod. It is often sold in a jar.

Tamarind slices These are actually not from the tamarind tree. They are from a sour-tasting fruit which is sold sliced and dried (it looks like small, shriveled cross-sections of apple). Tamarind slices are also used as a souring agent, but they have a more subtle flavor.

Torch ginger flower The flower bud of the torch ginger, also known as phaeomaria. The bud emerges directly from the ground among the leaf stems and opens into a flower, like a many-layered lotus blossom.
Scientific name: *Etlingera eliator*

Turmeric A member of the ginger family, fresh turmeric root has a brilliant orange-yellow flesh. Turmeric is pungent and can make food bitter if too much is used. It is most commonly available as a powder and is sometimes referred to as the poor man's saffron.
Scientific name: *Curcuma longa*

Twisted cluster beans As its common English name suggests, twisted cluster beans grow in twisted clusters. However, they are also widely known as stink beans. Each bean or seed is close to the size of a fava and tastes slightly bitter. Outside Southeast Asia, only canned beans are usually available.

Water chestnut Also called the Chinese water chestnut or the water caltrop, it is a tuber vegetable that resembles a chestnut in color and shape.

Water chestnut continued...

Originating in Southeast Asia, water chestnuts are the roots of an aquatic plant that grows in freshwater ponds, marshes and lakes, and in slow-moving rivers and streams. The nut is slightly sweet and crisp to the tooth.
Scientific name: *Trapa natans*

Water convolvulus Also known as morning glory and swamp cabbage. This aquatic and semi-aquatic plant has trailing vine-like stems. The stems are hollow which allows it to float in water. It has arrow or heart-shaped leaves which are 12 to 26 centimeters long.
Scientific name: *Ipomoea aquatica*

Winter melon This large melon, with its characteristic frosty tint, can weigh up to 15 kilograms. Its snowy white porous flesh becomes translucent when cooked.
Scientific name: *Benincasa hispida*

Yam bean Also known as jicama. A sweet turnip-shaped tuber root of a twining plant. It has sand-colored skin and white crisp flesh.
Scientific name: *Pachyrhizus erosus*

Yanang leaf This comes from a climbing plant with deep green leaves and yellowish flowers native to mainland Southeast Asia and used particularly in the cuisines of northeast Thailand and Lao PDR. It is used to flavor stews and soups or add a green color to dishes.
Scientific name: *Tiliacora triandra*

SOURCES:
DK Smithsonian Handbooks on Herbs by Lesley Bremness, Dorling Kindersley Limited, London, 2002; asiafood.org; austmus.gov.au; britannica.com; ces.ncsu.edu; coconutresearchcenter.org; invasivespeciesinfo.gov; plantnames.unimelb.edu.au; postharvest.ucdavis.edu.

WEIGHTS AND MEASURES

The weights and measures listed here have been rounded off. We have refrained from using cup measurements as they vary across the region. To be as accurate as possible, we have used standard US measuring spoons, and metric and imperial measurements.

LEGEND: ml = milliliters; fl oz = fluid ounce; g = grams; kg = kilograms; oz = ounce; lb = pound

LIQUID MEASURES

METRIC	IMPERIAL	TABLESPOON	TEASPOON
30 ml	1 fl oz	2	6
60 ml	2 fl oz	4	12
90 ml	3 fl oz	6	18
125 ml	4 fl oz (1/4 US pint)	8	25
150 ml	5 fl oz	10	30
180 ml	6 fl oz		
240 ml (0.24 liter)	8 fl oz (1/2 US pint)		
300 ml	10 fl oz		

WEIGHTS

METRIC	IMPERIAL
30 g	1 oz
90 g	3 oz
125 g	4 oz (0.3 lb)
250 g	8 oz (0.5 lb)
500 g (0.5 kg)	17 oz (1 lb)
1000 g (1 kg)	35 oz (2 lb)

TEMPERATURES

FAHRENHEIT	CELSIUS	GAS MARK
225	105	1/4
250	120	1/2
275	135	1
300	150	2
325	165	3
350	175	4

LENGTHS

MILLIMETER	CENTIMETER	INCH
25.4	2.54	1
10	1	0.4

Tita Mendoza prepares pinakbet, a popular Ilocano vegetable dish in the home of Bonito Singson, Vigan, Ilocos Sur, Philippines. The kitchen in this old home has been remodelled for modern living and a narrow vent lining the perimeter of its ceiling encourages small birds to enter, sit and sing while the family has breakfast.

INDEX

A

Acar mentah See Salads, Raw
Adobo, 156, 162
    Baboy at manok See Pork, And chicken *adobo*
Agar-agar, 148, 260
Appetizers, 17, *145*, *147*, 192, *222*, 219,
    239-240, 242
Asinan Jakarta See Salads, Jakarta fruit
    and vegetable
Ayam mBok Berek See Chicken, Original fried
    of Kalasan

B

Baked rice flour and coconut milk cake, *41*
Bamboo, 28, 68, *70*, 113, 135, 215
    Basket, 68, 88
    Chicken in, 113
    Groves, 99
    Huts, *102*
    Ornamental, 187
    Pavilion, 136
    Shoot, *35*, *99*, 115, 131, *146*, *194-195*, 260
        Soup See Soup, Bamboo shoot
    Sieve, 46
    Skewers, 68, *77-78*, 180
    Steamer, 215, 238
    Sticks, 180
    Tray, *232*
    Utensils, 84, 86, 93
    Worms, 217
Banana, 29, *41*, *94*, *100*, 165, 219
    Blossom, *96*, *248-249*, 260
    Fritters, 29
    In syrup, 218
    Leaf, *36*, *38*, 68, *80*, 88, 91, *98*, *104*, *126*, 131,
        141, 156, *166*, *171*, *177*, *226-227*, *232*, 238,
        242, *256*
            rice, 112
    Stem, *150*, 260
Banh it nhung dua See Little steamed glutinous rice
    cake with coconut filling
Bangkwang See Yam bean
Basil, 49, 66, *78*, 211, *226-228*, 237-239,
    244, *248-249*, 260
    Asian, 49
    Holy, 211
    Sweet, *102*, 211, *229*, *231*, 260
    Thai, *228*
    Wild, *102*, 260
Beans, 62, 130-131, *166*, *228*
    Black, 242
    Boiled, 131, 135
    Butter, *147*
    Green, 29, *168*, *194*
    Long, *35*, 119
    Mung, *138*, 161, 238, 240, 242

    Soy, 183, 187, *194*, *199*
    Split, 29
    String, *146*, *228*
    Sweetened, 163
    Twisted cluster, 26, 219, 221, 262
    Winged, 25
    Yard-long, *94*, *96*, *102*, 114, *172*
Bebek betutu See Traditional long-cooked
    Balinese duck
Beef, 28, 66, *95*, 136
    Bouillon, *118*
    Cambodian stew, 59
    Curry
        Spicy braised, *32*
        Paste, *119*
    Liver, *34*
    Long-cooked in coconut milk with spices,
        66, *70*
    Noodle soup, 237
    Putri manis, *116*
    Soup, 237
    Wrapped in lettuce leaf, 100
Belacan See Shrimp paste
Bibingka, 161
Biko See Rice, Sweet cake
Bingka dadak See Baked rice flour and coconut
    milk cake
Boiled taro in sweet coconut milk, 218
Boo thee kyaw See Calabash gourd fritters
Bringhe See Rice, Glutinous, with chicken
Brunei Darussalam
    Chinese influence, 22
    Description, 22
    Festivals, 31
    Manners and customs, 22
Bualoy phuek See Boiled taro in sweet coconut milk
Buddhism, 110, 234
    Rituals, 135
    Theravada, 212
Buffalo, 26, 28, *32*, *70*, *102*, 108, 115, 131
    Skin, 93, 102
Bun bo Hue See Hue pork and beef noodle soup
Bunga Kantan See Torch ginger flower
Burmese, 131-132

C

Calabash gourd fritters, *151*
Cambodia
    Chinese influence, 42
    Cuisine, 42, 50
    Food habits, 50
    Geography, 47
    History, 42
    Manners and customs, 42
    Meals, 42, 45-47, 49
    Religion, 45
    Rice varieties, 45

    Royalty, 50
    Social life and customs, 49
Cambodian beef stew, *59*
Cha gio See Spring roll, Fried
Chao ga and *goi ga cap cai* See Chicken, Rice
    porridge and cabbage salad
Chao Phya River, 214, 217
Chhouchi fragrant shrimp, *56*
Chi sang hom See Mint, Cambodian
Chicken, 26, 28, 66, 69, 86, *96*, 108, 113, 136, 156,
    162-163, 217, 241
    And jackfruit, long-cooked Yogya-style, 69, *74*
    Barbecued, 217
    Boiled with papaya and chili leaves, 162
    Curry
        country-style, 112, *144*
        noodle soup with, *230*
    Eggs, 206, *232*
    Noodle soup, 237
    Original fried of Kalasan, *76*
    Rice, Hainanese, *200*
    Rice porridge and cabbage salad, *254*
    Steamed in banana leaf, *98*
    Stew with squash, 162
    With caramel sauce and lemongrass, *250*
Chickpea powder, 132, *140*, *150*
Chili, 24-26, 42, 63, 65-66, 68-69, *76*, *78*, *94*, *96*,
    108, 111, 113, 115, 130-131, 136, 181, *204*, 211,
    219, *224*, *226*, 237, 260
    Bird's-eye, 24-25, 27, 106, *200*, *224-225*, *228*,
        231, *244*, *248*, 260
    Dip, 216-217
    Dried, 24, 92, *120*, *126*, 187, 219, 260
    Dried paste, *32*

Green, 93, 128, *147*, 183, *205*
Green finger, 157, 162, *172*
Grilled dried, 93
Hot pepper, 212
Leaves, 162
Padi See Chili, Bird's-eye
Powder, *95-96*, *205*, *230-231*
   roasted dried, *138*
Prawns, 38
Paste, *32*, *36*, *80*, *116*, *120*, 185, *194-195*,
   216, 238
   fried clams in, *231*
   roasted, 211, *222*, *224*, *231*
Red, *56*, 59, 108, 128, *150*, 183, *192*, *194*, *199*,
   205, *226*, *246*, *248-251*
Sauce, 200-201, 211, 237-238, 242-244
Chinese
   Malaysia, 112
   Philippines, 154, 157-158, 160
   Singapore, 187
   New Year, 110, 187
   New Year raw fish salad, *192*
Christmas, 161
   Philippines, 158, 161
   Singapore, 187
Chuchi pra kong See Chhouchi fragrant shrimp
Cloud ear fungus, *99*, 161, 238, *244*, *246*, 260
Coconut, *76*, *166*, 183, 185, 213, 218-219,
   244, *246*, *257*, 260-261
   Candied, *257*
   Cream, 108, *148*, *177*, 261
     pumpkin leaf shoots cooked in, *35*
   Curry, toasted, 185
   Custard steamed in pumpkin, *104*
   Egg jam, 178
   Filling, little steamed glutinous rice cakes
     with, *256*
   Flavored drink, carbonated, 239
   Flower, *80*
   Juice See Coconut, Water
   Glutinous rice with chicken, *166*
   Grated, 111, 183, 219
   Grater, 46, 111
   Gravy, 114, 187
     spicy noodles in, *96*
   Jam, egg and, *206*
   Milk, 26, 29, *38*, *41*, 65, 69-70, 88, 111-112, 114,
     158, *174*, 183, *206*-207, 211, 216, 218-219,
     226, 230, 238, 241-243, 261
     cake, baked rice flour and, *41*
     with spices, long-cooked beef in, *70*
   Oil, 68-69, 219
   Rice dish, 106
   Sago cookies, 180
   Sauce, beef in, 69
   Shell, 25, 68, 88
   Shoot soup, spicy, 221
   Soda, 239
   Soup, 221

Steamed in pumpkin, *104*
Steamed seafood soufflé with creamy, *226*
Sticky rice cake, 29
Sweet, 242
Tapioca paper, *246*
Water, 69, *76*, *252*, 261
Stir-fries, 185
Coffee
   Brunei, 40
   Indonesia, 62-63
   Shops, Singapore, 206
   Viet Nam, 243
Cookies, 15, 115, 162-163, 180, 219
   Butter, 168
   Coconut-sago, 180
   Hojaldres, 162
   Machacao, 162
   Saint Nicholas, 163, *174*
Crab, 215, 221
   Chili, 180-181
   Fried with salt and pepper, 242
   Mangrove, 156
   Meat, *244*
   Shells, *226*
Crème caramel, 163, *176*
Curry, 28, 66
   Beef, 211
     spicy braised, *32, 34, 38*
   Chicken, 112
   Country-style chicken, *144*
   Dal, 112
   Debal, 187
   Dishes, 50, 130
   Fish, 36, 221
     head, 112, 185
   Frog, 217
   Indian-style, 221
   Korma, 112
   Laksa, 108
   Leaf, 49, 106, 111, 183, *205*, 261
   Mee, 114
   Noodle soup with chicken, *230*
   Paste, 108, 211, *230*, 238
   Powder, *32, 34*, 47, 130, 183, *205*, 230
   Pork, 211, 216
   Puffs, *204*
   Sauce cooked in coconut milk, 216
   Yellow, 221

D

Daging dinding See Spicy braised beef curry
Dalca kambing See Mutton *dalca*
Daun nyirek, *38*
Desserts, 17
   Brunei Darussalam, 24, 29, 31, *41*
   Cambodia, 45
   Malaysia, 114, *116*

Myanmar, 128, 132, *148*
Philippines, 163, *176*
Singapore, 183, 187, 206
Thailand, 211-212, 215, 218-219, *232*
Viet Nam, 242
Dumplings, 214-215

E

Egg and coconut jam, *206*
Ethnic groups
   Brunei Darussalam, 22
   Lao PDR, 86
   Malaysia, 112-113, 115
   Myanmar, 131
   Viet Nam, 234
Exotic foods, 217, 241

F

Family, 15, 17-18
   Brunei Darussalam, 31
   Cambodia, 50, *54*
   Indonesia, 62-63, 69-*70*
   Lao PDR, 84, 86, 89, 91, 93, *96*, *100*
   Malaysia, 113
   Myanmar, 132, 135, 137, *142*, *144*, *146*
   Philippines, 158
   Singapore, 178, 180, 188
   Thailand, 211, *222*
   Viet Nam, 239, 241-242, *257*
Farmers
   Cambodia, 45
   Myanmar, 136-137
   Thailand, *229*
Fermentation, 217
Fern, 113, 115
   Shoot, 26, 66
Fiddlehead, 26, *35*, 66
Fish, 108, *120*
   Cake salad, *138*, *140*
   Fermented, 43, 47, 49, 87, 89, 217
   Freshwater, 28, 47, 131, 217
   Grilled, 50
     or boiled spicy, *36*
   Hot and sour, *120*
     from Ujung Pandang, *72*
   Milkfish in sour broth, *172*
   Paste, 87
   Preservation, 47
   Raw, *192*
   Salad, *55*
   Salted, 131
   Sauce, 43, 65, 87, 130, 211, 234, 238, 261
   Soup and rice noodles, *150*
Flavoring sauces, 217
Foi thong See Sugar-coated egg yolk

Food
    Folklore, 132
    Portugese-Eurasian, 114
    Preservation, 165
    Religious aspects
        Buddhism, 136
        Islam, 132
        Stalls, 69, 180
Food habits
    Bruneians, 26
    Burmese, 132
    Indonesian, 63
    Malaysians, 114
    Muslims, 156
    Singaporean, 180, 187
    Vietnamese, 242
Fragrant stuffed frogs, *58*
French baguette, 42, 45
Fried clams in roasted chili paste, *231*
Fritters See Calabash gourd fritters
Fruits
    Brunei, 26, 29, 31, *41*
    Cambodia, 49, *54*
    Indonesia, 60, 65, 69, *74*, 82
    Lao PDR, *100*
    Malaysia, 110, 113-114
    Myanmar, 131, 136
    Philippines, 162-163, 165
    Singapore, *202-203*
    Thailand, 206, 211-212, 218-219, 221
    Viet Nam, 240, 242-243

G

Ga xao sa ot voi nuoc mau See Lemongrass,
    Chicken with caramel sauce
Gai yang See Chicken, Barbecued
Galangal See Ginger, Blue

Ginger, 24, *32*, *34*, 46, 50, *52*, 66, 100, 106, 108,
    110-111, 115-*116*,*118-119*, *126*, 128, 130, *138*,
    141-142, *144-145*, *150-151*, 154, 157-158, 187,
    192, *198*, *200-201*, *204-205*, 216, 219, 237-238,
    242, *254*, *256*
    Blue, 24, 46, 49, 65, 69, *74*, *99-100*, 106, 111,
        118, 183, 211, *224*, 261
    Juice, 151
    Tea, 161
Glass noodle soup, 132, *138*, *140*
Glossy red pork, 135, *142*
Gluay khai chueam See Banana, In syrup
Goi See Salads
Golden heart cooler, *148*
Goong ga-thi nor mai sod See Soups, Bamboo
    shoot, in coconut
Graton loy kaew See *Santol* in light clear syrup
Grilled meat salad, *229*
Grilled shrimp paste relish, *145*
Gudeg Yogya See Chicken, And jackfruit, long-
    cooked Yogya-style
Gulai asam pedas See Fish, Hot and sour

H

Hainanese chicken rice, *200*
Hawker centers, 188-189
Herbs, 25, 47, 49, 88, *95*, 106, 108, 112,183, 217,
    234, 237-238, 240, 243
    Therapeutic use, 211
Hoi lai phad nahmprik paow See Fried clams in
    roasted chili paste
Hojaldres See Cookies
Hor mok talay See Steamed seafood soufflé with
    creamy coconut
Hotpot, 108, *224*, 234, 239
Hta ma nai See Rice, Glutinous, with sesame
Hue pork and beef noodle soup, *248*
Hygiene, 31
    Regulations, 211

I - J

Ikan masak ampap See Fish, Grilled, or boiled spicy
Indonesia
    Description, 60
    American influence, 63
    Arab influence, 62
    Chinese influence, 60
    European influence, 63
    Festivals, 62
    Indian influence, 62
    Manners and customs, 63
    Migration, 66
    Portuguese influence, 66
    Islamic culture, 221
Jelly-dipped chestnuts in sweet coconut milk, 218
Jicama See Yam bean
Jim jaew See Chili dip

K

Kaffir lime, 211
    leaf, 46, 49, *58*, *96*, *98*, 111, *122*, 183,
        192, *224-227*, 261
    zest, 49
Kalamansi, 25, 106, *168-169*, *172*, *177*, 185,
    192-193, 262
    Juice, 26, *36*, *78*, 108
Kang-kep baob See Fragrant stuffed frogs
Kangkong See Water convolvulus
K'tieu Phnom Penh See Noodle, Khmer
Kaeng nor mai See Soup, Bamboo shoot
Kalia hati See Beef, Liver
Karla thar chet See Chicken, Curry, county-style
Kayan chin thee nga pi chet See Tomato and shrimp
    paste relish
Kelupis See Steamed glutinous rice parcels
Kerabu udang dan soohoon See Prawn and glass
    noodle *kerabu*
Khai chae See Rice, Soaked in water
Khao soi kai See Curry, Noodle soup with chicken
Khao tang na tang See Rice, Patties with pork,
    chicken or shrimp topping
Khaow poun nam kathih See Spicy rice noodles in
    coconut gravy
Kitchen utensils, implements
    Brunei Darussalam, 24
    Cambodia, 46
    Indonesia, 68
    Lao PDR, 84, 88, 93
    Malaysia, 112-113
    Myanmar, 130
    Philippines, 158, *168*
    Singapore, 184
    Thailand, 215, *232*
    Viet Nam, 238
Kitchens, 18
    Brunei Darussalam, 24, *41*
    Cambodia, 46
    Indonesia, 65
    Lao PDR, 88-89, 93
    Malaysia, 111
    Myanmar, 130, 141
    Philippines, 157, 162-163
    Singapore, 183
    Thailand, 211
    Viet Nam, 238
Kuih, 180, 183
    Tart, *232*
    Tu tu, 180
Kyan zan chet See Glass noodle soup

L

Lahpet See Pickled, Tea leaf
Lao PDR
    Description, 84

Festivals, 86, 89, 91
Manners and customs, 84, 86-87, 89, 93
Religion, 84
Laotian stew, 102
Laksa, 106, 108, 115, 187
    Asam, 114
    Johor, 114
    Laksam, 114
    Noodle soup, 106, 108, 187
    Salad, 106
Larb See Spicy minced meat in chicken
Larp, 95
Leche flan See Crème caramel
Lechon See Roasted pig
Leftover, *119-120*, 131, 165, *177*, 217, 222
Lemak pucuk labu See Pumpkin leaf shoots cooked
    in coconut cream
Lemongrass, 24-26, 32, 39, 49, *55-56*, 58, 68,
    70, *72*, *80*, *96*, *98-99*, *100*, 102, 106, 111, *118*,
    144, *150-151*, 183, *200*, 211, *224-225*, 234,
    238, *248-249*, 262
    Chicken with caramel sauce, *250*
    Spicy prawn soup with, 162, *224*
Lent, 91, 163
Little steamed glutinous rice cake with
    coconut filling, *256*
Lotus, 42, 50
    Flower, 240
    Leaf, 49
    Seed, 242
Lumpia See Spring roll

M

Machacao See Cookies
Malaysia
    Chinese influence, 108, 110
    Cuisine, 110, 114
    Dutch influence, 114
    Folklore, 108
    Indian influence, 112
    Manners and customs, 115
    Portuguese influence, 114
    Religion, 110
    Thai influence, 114
Mawk kai See Chicken, Steamed in banana leaf
Menudo See Pork, Stew, with liver
Milkfish in sour broth, *172*
Mingalar (Auspiciousness), 132, 135
Mint, 46, 49, *55*, 66, *95-96*, *100*, 211, *229*, 234,
    237-240, *244-245*
    Cambodian, 49
    Spearmint, 49
    Vietnamese, 49, 238, *254-255*, 262
Monhinga See Fish, Soup and rice noodles
Monks
    Burmese, 132, 135
    Lao PDR, 84, 89
    Philosophy, 135
Mortar and pestle, 18, 24-25, 46, 49, 84, 88, 108,
    112, 136, 158, 184, 211, 215, 222, 227-229, 238
Muc dua See Coconut, Candied
Muslims, 60, 112, 156, 221
Myanmar
    Description, 128
    Ethnic groups, 131
    Festivals, 132, 135-136
    Meals, 128, 131
    Religion, 131
    Snacks, 128, 132
    Social life and customs, 135-136

N

Nasi kapau See Rice, steamed with meat, fish
    and vegetables
Nasi lemak See Rice, Cooked in coconut milk
Nasi minyak See Rice, Saffron
Nahm tok See Grilled meat salad
Nga hpai thoke See Fish, Cake salad
Nga pi daung See Grilled shrimp paste relish
Nga pyaw oo See Banana, Stem
Nhoam krauch th'long See Salads, Pomelo
Noodle, *97*, 108, 112, 114, 128, 132, 136, 161, *168*,
    183, 188, *199*, 208, 210, 218, 234, 237, 239, *248*
    Curry, *230*
    Egg, 180, 216, *230*, 237-238
    Fried, 108, 110, 112, 185
    Glass, 122, 132, *138*, *140*, 161, *168*, 237-239
    Hakka, 114
    Khmer, *52*
    Laksa, See *Laksa*

Pancit, 161, 165, *168*
    Rice, *96*, 110, 114, *150*, 180, 187, 216, 237-238
    Soup, 42, 132, 138, 140, 150, 161, 168, 180, *230*,
    237, *246*, *248*
    Nyonya birthday mee
        See Nyonya birthday noodles
Nyonya birthday noodles, *199*

O - P

Oh larm See Laotian stew
Or chor ter kar See Pig's trotters braised with black
    vinegar and ginger
Pagoda festival, 136
Pallu mara ikan See Fish, Hot and sour, from
    Ujung Pandang
Palm sugar pancakes, *40*
Pamapa itum See Spices, Muslim spice mix
Pan San Nicolas See Cookies, Saint Nicholas
Pancit sotanghon See Noodles, Pancit
Pandan leaf, 29, 108, 180, 183, *206-207*, 262
Pastries, 66, 204-205
Penyaram See Palm sugar pancakes
Phan sin choun See Beef, Wrapped in lettuce leaf
Philippines
    Chinese influence, 154, 161
    Franciscans in the, 162
    History, 154, 165
    Manners and customs, 161, 163
    Religion, 156
    Spanish influence, 154, 163, 165
Pickled
    Foods, 217
    Tea leaf, 130, 137, *147*
Pig's trotters braised with black vinegar and
    ginger, *198*
Pineapple tarts, *202*
Plastic bags, 210
Pleah trey See Salad, Fish
Popiah See Spring roll, Fresh
Pork, *142*, *198*, 241
    And chicken *adobo*, *171*
    Braised with black vinegar and ginger, *198*
    Minced with water chestnuts and toasted tapioca
        paper, *246*
    Satay, 66
        Menado-style, *78*
        minced with Balinese spice-mixture, *77*
    Stew
        in young coconut water, *252*
        with liver, 165, *170*
Prawn See Shrimp
Prawn and glass noodle *kerabu*, *122*
Pumpkin leaf shoots cooked in coconut cream, *35*

R

Rendang See Beef, Long-cooked in coconut milk
    with spices
Restaurants, 61-66

Rice, 25, *39*, 45, 66, *141*, 157-158, 183, *222*, *231*, 240
    Cooked in coconut milk, *126*
    Crepe, 240
    Flour, 238, 240, 262
    Glutinous, 8, 29, 68, *70*, 84, 86, 91, 93, *104*, 108,
        116, 136, *148*, 183, *198*, *206*, 208, 215-216,
        222, 228-229, 238, 242, 261
        cakes with coconut filling, little steamed, *256*
        flour, 183, 187, 238
        khaow buer, 102
        nasi dagang, 114
        parcels, steamed, *38*
        with chicken, 158, *166*
        with sesame, *141*
        toasted, *229*
    Leftovers, 131, *222*
    Noodles, 96, 237-238, 262
    Paper, 238, *244*
    Patties with pork, chicken or shrimp topping, *222*
    Saffron rice, *39*
    Sizzling crepe, 240
    Soaked in water, 219
    Steamed with meat, fish and vegetables, 66
    Steamed flour, 240
    Sweet cake, 161, *171*
    Varieties, 43, 45
Roasted pig, 155-156
Roscas See Cookies, butter

S

Sago, 60, 115
    Cookies, 180
    Flour, 26, 29
    Pearls, 29, 131, *148*, 183, 262
Salad, 49, *82*, 128, 132, *140*, 240
    Chicken cabbage, *252*
    Fiddlehead, 26
    Fish, *55*
    Fish cake, *138*, *140*
    Gado-gado, 69
    Goi, 240
    Grilled meat, *229*
    Hot, 211
    Jakarta fruit and vegetable, 69, *82*
    Jellyfish, 221
    Kerabu, 106, 108
    Mumbai *chaats*, 185
    Pomelo, *54*
    Pounded sour, 89, *94*
    Raw, *124*
        fish or prawn, 113
    Rojak, 112, 114
    Rujak, *82*
    Spicy green papaya, 217, *228*
    Ulam, 25
    Viet Nam, 240
    Yu sheng See Chinese, New Year raw fish salad
Salon Culinaire Mondial, 191
Sambal belacan See Shrimp paste, dried
Sambal sotong See Spicy squid
Sangkhanya mak ueh See Coconut, Custard
    steamed in pumpkin

Satay, 62, 68, 106, 108, 113, 154, 188, 221
    Goat, 60
    Pork See Pork, *Satay*
Saté babi Menado See Pork, *Satay* Menado-style, 78
Saté pentul See Pork, *Satay*, minced with Balinese
    spice-mixture, 77
Sautéed mung bean vermicelli, *168*
Seafood
    Brunei, 25, *36*
    Crab See Crab
    Dried, 184
    Fish See Fish
    Hor mok talay See Steamed seafood soufflé with
        creamy coconut
    Indonesia, 68
    Malaysia, 114-115
    Myanmar, 131
    Philippines, 157
    Prawns See Shrimp
    Shrimp See Shrimp
    Singapore, 183-185, 187
    Thailand, 211, 218, 221, *231*
    Viet Nam, 237, 239, 242
Serikaya See Egg and coconut jam
Shrimp, 50, *56*, 130, 158, 162, *172*, 215, 217,
    222, *226*, 239-240, 242
    Broth, 240
    Chips, 241
    Chhouchi fragrant, *56*
    Dried, 69, 108, 131, *146*, 183, *228*, 238
    Paste, 24, 25-26, 31, *35-36*, 46-47, 63, 65, 93,
        106, 111, 130, *145*, 183, 211, 219, 241, 262
        dried, 106, 108
        fermented, 49, 68-69, 183
        relish
            grilled, *145*
            tomato and, *146*
    Prawn, 25-26, 28, 112-113, 115, 131, *172*,
        221, *224*, *226*
        and glass noodle *kerabu*, 122
        chili, 38
        crackers, 246
        dried, 244
        mee, 110
        noodle, 114
        soup with lemongrass, spicy, 162, *224*
        spicy, *126*
        stock, 26
Shwe yin aye See Golden heart cooler
Singapore
    Culinary National Team, 191
    Eurasian cuisine, 185
    Food culture, 180, 183, 185
    History, 178
    Immigrants, 178, 183
    Indian influence, 185
    Peranakans, 187
    Social life and customs, 188-189
Sinigang, 154, 162
    Bangus See Milkfish in sour broth
Som tam See Spicy green papaya salad
Sotanghon See Noodles, Glass

Soup, 42, 46, 48, 86, 88, 112, 128, 136-137, 158,
    211, 219, 234
    Bamboo shoot, 99, 217
        in coconut, 221
    Cantonese, 183
    Coconut, 221
        shoot, 221
    Foochows, 183
    Laksa See *Laksa*
    Milkfish in sour broth, *172*
    Myanmar, 146
    Noodle, 42, 180, 237, *246*, *248*
        curry, with chicken, *230*
        glass, 132, *138*, *140*, 161, *168*
        Hue pork and beef, *248*
        rice with fish, *150*
    Oxtail, *118*
    Samla, 50
    Soto, 66
    Spicy prawn, with lemongrass, *224*
    Tahai masak api, 26
    Tamarind, 221
    Tom krueng nai, 217
    Vietnamese, 237-239, 242
Spices, 31, 159, 211
    Candlenut, *32*, *34*, 69, 74, *80*, 183, 260
    Cardamom, 24, 31, *39*, 112, 183, 221, 260
        green, *80*
        pods, *118-119*, 204-205
        seeds, 77
    Cinnamon, 183, 187, 193, 221, 238, 260
        bark, 24
        ground, *192*, *205*
        sticks, *39*, *77*, *80*, *118-119*, *202*
    Cloves, 39, 77, 112, *118-119*, 134, 183, *202*,
        221, 260
        ground, 187, *205*
    Coriander, 24, 31-32, 46, 49, *95*, *100*, 110-112,
        116, *138-140*, *144-146*, *150-151*, 212, *230*,
        237-238, *244*, *246*, *254-255*, 261
        ground, 74, *205*
        leaf, *56*, *122*, 130, 183, *192*,*199-201*,
            224-225, *251-252*
            sprigs, *192*, *194*
        root, 222, *224-225*
        seeds, *56*, 77, *80*, *116*, *118*, 183, 261
        stems, 49, *52*
    Cumin, 24, 31-32, 111-112, 183, 261
        ground, *116*, 118, *205*
        seeds, 77, *80*
    Fennel, *32*, 111-112, *118*, 183, 261
        ground, *205*
    Fenugreek, 24, 112
        ground, *205*
    Five-spice, *192*
        powder, 183
    Muslim spice mix, 159
    Nutmeg, 31
        grated, ground, 77, *80*
    Star anise, 24, 31, *39*, 59, *118-119*, 183, *202*,
        237-238, 262
    Turmeric, 31, 49, 77, 106, 108, *120*, 128, 130,
        138-139, *144-146*, *150-151*, 158, *166*, 183,
        221, 238, 240-241, 262

Spicy braised beef curry, *32*
Spicy green papaya salad, *228*
Spicy minced meat in chicken, 217
Spicy rice noodles in coconut gravy, *96*
Spicy squid, *123*
Spirits, 135-136
Spring roll, 160, 190, *194*
    Fresh, 110, *194-197*, 239
    Fried, *244*
    Lumpia, 160
Steamed glutinous rice parcels, *38*
Steamed seafood soufflé with creamy coconut, *226*
Sugar-coated egg yolk, *232*
Suong heo nau nuoc dua See Pork, Stew, in young
    coconut water
Sup ekor See Soup, Oxtail

T

Tablewares, 228
Tabtim krob See Jelly-dipped chestnuts in sweet
    coconut milk
Tam mak som See Salad, Pounded sour
Tamarind, 25, 62, 65, 68, 112, 130, 187, 211,
    216, 238, 262
    Curries, 183
    Gravy, 187
    Green, *172*
    Juice, 26, *32*, *222*
    Paste, 25, 132, *140*, 262
    Powdered, *172*
    Pulp, 24, *32*, *72*, 183, 262
    Slices, *asam gelugor*, 24, 262
    Soup, 221
    Water, 68, *72*
Tam mak
Taro, 218
Tarts, 202-203
Tea, 128-129, 147
Technique, 67, 112, 130, 157, 184
Tengang daga See Cloud ear fungus
Thailand
    Chinese influence, 216
    Cuisine, 208
    Folklore, 219
    Food culture, 208, 211-212
    Lao PDR influence, 217
    Geography, 214, 216
    History, 212, 214
    Kings and rulers, 217
    Manners and customs, 211
    Regions, 216-219, 221
    Religion, 212, 214
*Thit heo bam khoai nang, xuc banh trang mi nuoc
    dua* See Pork, Minced with water chestnuts and
    roasted coconut tapioca paper
Tinola See Chicken, Boiled with green papaya and
    chili leaves
Tom yam goong See Lemongrass, Spicy prawn
    soup with
Tomato and shrimp paste relish, *146*
Tomatoes, 134
Tonle Sap Great Lake, 47
Torch ginger flower, 106-107, 111, 262
Traditional long-cooked Balinese duck, *80*

V - W - Y

Viet Nam
    Appetizers, 239
    Cuisine, 237
    Description, 234
    History, 234
    Influences, 234
    Manners and customs, 237, 242
Water convolvulus, *94*, *96*, 156, *172*,*199*, 263
Whet thani chet See Glossy red pork
Yam bean, *52*, 82, 112, *194-195*, 239, 261, 263
Yu sheng See Chinese, New Year raw fish salad

ACKNOWLEDGMENTS

Inside the Southeast Asian Kitchen is a regional endeavor that has brought together a formidable team of food writers and experts from the ten countries that belong to the Association of Southeast Asian Nations (ASEAN) — Brunei Darussalam, Cambodia, Indonesia, Lao PDR, Malaysia, Myanmar, Philippines, Singapore, Thailand, and Viet Nam. We thank Reda Jasmine Abdul Rahman Taib, Her Royal Highness Princess Marie Ranariddh Norodom, Sri Owen, Somsanouk Mixay, Julie Wong, Redzuawan "Chef Wan" Ismail, Ma Thanegi, Michaela Fenix, Christopher Tan, Cora Cunanan Sukhyanga, Mali Pimnart, Cathy Hong-Praslick and Trieu Thi Koppe. We feel fortunate to have worked with all of them. We were equally fortunate to have a thorough and skilled editor in Tan Su-Lyn.

Much gratitude is owed to the vision and leadership of H.E. Ong Keng Yong, Secretary-General of ASEAN. Without his guiding hand and support for this project, this publication would not have seen production. We cannot thank Pratap Parameswaran, Assistant Director of the ASEAN Secretariat enough for breathing life into a project that will offer new perspectives of the culinary traditions of Southeast Asia. We also thank the coordinating team at ASEAN, which was led by Serena Wong, Erie Vitria Trisanty and Susiana Rusanti.

All 80 recipes in this book were tested and prepared by Christopher Tan, and photographed by Neal Oshima at the Miele Active Kitchen in Singapore. Indeed, Miele helped us prove that many of the traditional Southeast Asian dishes featured in this book can easily be prepared in any contemporary kitchen today. We thank Mario Miranda — Managing Director, Miele Pte Ltd (Singapore) and Bing Blokbergen-Leow — General Sales & Marketing Manager, Miele Pte Ltd (Singapore), for allowing us the use of a great working kitchen, and introducing us to the wonders of the steam oven which made preparing many of the dishes featured in this book all the more effortless.

All throughout Southeast Asia, there were many other countless kind people who extended their hospitality, facilitated meetings and arrangements, and helped us in one way or another. To them we extend our endless thanks.

Our photographer would like to sincerely thank the hundreds of market vendors, cooks, housewives, waiters and waitresses, who, in the midst of trying to eke out a living, took time from their work to allow him to photograph them and their food. They are the soul of Southeast Asian cuisine and the basis of this book.

In particular, he wishes to thank the following people who made his experience in their home countries all the richer and more interesting: Reda Jasmine Abdul Rahman Taib, Hajah Zainah (Brunei Darussalam); Dr. Lai Ky and family (Cambodia); William Wongso and his family, Bondan Winaro (Indonesia); Somsanouk Mixay, Hansana Sisane, Bouasonkham Sisane, Bouavanh Phouminh, Khamkhong Kongvongsa (Lao PDR); Teresa and Leslie Hayward, Veronica Pedrosa and family (Malaysia); Ma Thanegi, Phone Kyaw (Myanmar); Mark Medina and family, Claude and Maryann Tayag, Ugu Bigyan, Paul and Nina Poblador (Philippines); Russel Wong, Carrie and Paloma Brooks (Singapore); Cora Cunanan Sukhyanga and Annabelle Daokaew of Four Seasons Hotel Bangkok (Thailand); and Tran Huu Van (Viet Nam).

In addition, we thank the following individuals and organizations:

Brunei Darussalam
Ambassador V. P. Hirubalan
Sheikh Jamaluddin Sheikh Mohamed, Director-General, Brunei Tourism
Jean Christophe Robles Espinosa, Director of Marketing, Brunei Tourism
Jeffrey Sunnylai, Brunei Tourism
Tony Chieng, Managing Director, Sunshine Borneo Tours &Travel Sdn Bhd
Sandra Tan, Sunshine Borneo Tours & Travel Sdn Bhd
Brunei Tourism
Sunshine Borneo Tours & Travel Sdn Bhd
The Empire Hotel & Country Club

Cambodia
Ambassador Roland Eng
Ambassador Lawrence Anderson

Indonesia
Upiek H. Sadkar, Director, STP Bandung
Anang Sutono
Suseno Kardigantarar
Jemy Yacub
Riva Pandu
Yanti Korompis
Derry Mansur
STP Bandung
Bandung Institute of Tourism - Indonesia
Bandung Tourism Academy

Lao PDR
Ambassador Karen Tan

Myanmar
Ambassador T. Jasudasen

Philippines
Al Caronan

Singapore
Kathy de Guzman
Matin Tran
Elaine Hollmann
Diana Jean Reyes
Cheryl Yuen, Marketing Manager, Miele Pte Ltd (Singapore)
Mr. and Mrs. Lim Choon Ngee, Roland's Restaurant
Roland Lim, Managing Director, Roland's Restaurant
Lily Lim, Banquet Sales Manager, Roland's Restaurant
Chef Yong Bing Ngen, Majestic Restaurant
Kway Guan Huat

Thailand
Four Seasons Hotel Bangkok

Viet Nam
Ambassador Tan Seng Chye